Your Daughters Will Prophesy

MOVEMENT RHETORIC/RHETORIC'S MOVEMENTS
Victoria J. Gallagher

Also of Interest

Activist Literacies: Transnational Feminisms and Social Media Rhetorics, Jennifer Nish

The Democratic Ethos: Authenticity and Instrumentalism in US Movement Rhetoric after Occupy, A. Freya Thimsen

Liturgy of Change: Rhetorics of the Civil Rights Meeting, Elizabeth Ellis Miller

Peace by Peace: Risking Public Action, Creating Social Change, Lisa Ellen Silvestri

YOUR DAUGHTERS WILL PROPHESY

Religion and Rhetoric in
the Nineteenth-Century
Woman's Movement

LISA MARIE GRING-PEMBLE AND MARTHA WATSON

© 2025 University of South Carolina

Published by the University of South Carolina Press
Columbia, South Carolina 29208

uscpress.com

Printed in the United States of America

Library of Congress Cataloging-in-Publication Data can be found at
http://catalog.loc.gov/.

ISBN: 978-1-64336-567-1 (hardcover
ISBN: 978-1-64336-568-8 (paperback)
ISBN: 978-1-64336-569-5 (ebook)

To our historic foremothers
Jarena Lee
Sarah Moore Grimké
Lucretia Coffin Mott
Frances Elizabeth Caroline Willard

To the women in our families of origin who encouraged and shaped us
Martha's beloved sister: Alys McLaughlin Frazier
Lisa's beloved mother: Susan Dietrich Gring

To those who follow us
Martha's children: Dr. Karrin Solomon Lukacs and Dr. Martha Trenna Valado
Martha's grandchildren: Matilda Caroline Lukacs, Michael Bellamy Lukacs,
Celsa Meredith Valado, and Rosa Elaine Valado
Lisa's children: William David Pemble and Austin Charles Pemble

I will pour out my spirit on all flesh;
your sons and your daughters shall prophesy.

—JOEL 2:28

CONTENTS

List of Illustrations : viii
Series Editor's Preface : ix
Preface : xi
Acknowledgments : xix

ONE
Wellspring of Argument: The Reformation and
the Opening of Discursive Space : 1

TWO
Jarena Lee's *Religious Experience and Journal*:
A Nascent Feminist Hermeneutic : 19

THREE
Sarah Moore Grimké's *Letters on the Equality of the Sexes*:
The Bible through a Woman's Eyes : 49

FOUR
Lucretia Coffin Mott's "Discourse on Woman":
Woman as God Meant Her to Be : 83

FIVE
Frances Willard's *Woman in the Pulpit:* Awakening Women
to the Possibilities of True Womanhood : 109

Conclusion : 141

Appendix A. Brief Overview of Scholarship on
Women and Rhetoric : 157
Appendix B. Contested Passages in Scripture : 161
Notes : 163
Bibliography : 197
Index : 219

LIST OF ILLUSTRATIONS

TABLE 5.1. Contrasting Passages : 130

SERIES EDITOR'S PREFACE

The University of South Carolina series "Movement Rhetoric/Rhetoric's Movements" builds on the Press's long-standing reputation in the field of rhetoric and communication and its cross-disciplinary commitment to studies of civil rights and civil justice. Books in the series address two central questions: In historical and contemporary eras characterized by political, social, and economic movements enacted through rhetorical means, how—and with what consequences—are individuals, collectives, and institutions changed and transformed? How and to what extent can analyses of rhetoric's movements in relation to circulation and uptake help point the way to a more equal and equitable world?

Drs. Lisa Marie Gring-Pemble and Martha Watson make a significant contribution to contemporary scholarship on social movements, feminist theory, and rhetorical history by illuminating the key traits of a distinctive feminist hermeneutic that emerged in the nineteenth century. Through their examination of four case studies, the authors deftly reveal the following discursive traits: recovery of previously overlooked stories about women in the Bible, reconstruals or refutations of other passages traditionally used to circumscribe women's activities, and contestations of translations and interpretations that diminish or misconstrue women's roles. Gring-Pemble and Watson show how working with and through this feminist hermeneutic, the women featured in the book empowered themselves to assume traditionally circumscribed or prohibited roles because they were, indeed, responsible moral agents. Each of the featured women claimed moral and rhetorical agency, ultimately changing the discursive rules of their society, and setting the stage for public advocacy and rhetoric's movement into the twentieth and twenty-first centuries.

PREFACE

Then afterward I will pour out my spirit on all flesh; your sons
and your daughters shall prophesy.

—JOEL 2:28

It is not good for man to stand alone.

—ANNA HOWARD SHAW, "THE FUNDAMENTAL PRINCIPLE OF A REPUBLIC"

In her review of three exhibits at the Library of Congress celebrating the
centenary of the passage of the 19th Amendment, Jennifer Schuessler observed: "Together, these shows—all curated by women—make up one of
the richest explorations of women's history yet assembled in the capital,
or anywhere else. But they also offer a lesson in the messiness, complexi-
ties, and compromises involved in any movement for social change—and
the fraught politics of historical memory itself."[1] As Schuessler suggests, in
constructing a historical narrative, each author or curator's decision to tell a
particular story or highlight a specific element necessarily leaves other stories untold or other elements unexamined; some may almost disappear from
view. So, for example, in her book *The Myth of Seneca Falls,* Lisa Tetrault
demonstrates how some early leaders, in editing the multivolumed *History
of Woman Suffrage,* shaped that narrative in ways that ignored other women's
contributions to and perspectives about that history.[2]

Although no single account can capture the complexity of the nineteenth century American woman's movement, scholars agree that one significant obstacle to women's public participation in religious and civic life
was a series of biblical passages carefully selected and reiterated by an almost entirely male church leadership that dictated women's submission to
men and their silence in church. Male leaders first pointed to Genesis 3:16
that described God's punishment of Eve: "Your desire will be for your husband, and he will rule over you." To that they added Ephesians 5:22–24:
"Wives, submit yourselves unto your own husbands, as unto the Lord. For

the husband is the head of the wife, even as Christ is the head of the church: and he is the savior of the body. Therefore as the church is subject unto Christ, so let the wives be to their own husbands in everything." Church leaders further insisted that 1st Corinthians 14:34–35 determined women's proper role in churches: "Let your women keep silence in the churches: for it is not permitted unto them to speak; but they are commanded to be under obedience as also saith the law. And if they will learn anything, let them ask their husbands at home: for it is a shame for women to speak in the church."[3] 1st Timothy 2:11–12 affirmed: "Let the woman learn in silence with all subjection. But I suffer not a woman to teach, nor to usurp authority over the man, but to be in silence." Taken together, these passages offered, in the male view, a divine mandate for woman's consignment to the domestic sphere in subservience to her husband and her silence in any church gathering.

As both Catherine Brekus and Michael Casey point out, there were exceptions to this rule, most notably the Quakers and other evangelical groups. Brekus estimates that between the beginning of the First Great Awakening in 1740 and 1845, more than 100 women were active as preachers in the United States.[4] Casey suggests that "When the first important American female secular speakers emerged, they were stepping into an almost two-hundred-year-old tradition of female oratory."[5] These women were, however, as Brekus notes, outliers who saw themselves as "strangers in a strange land" and as "strangers and pilgrims on earth."[6]

For most women in nineteenth century America, a code of social rules, grounded in biblical passages, circumscribed the proper realm of activity for the White middle-class women who would comprise a significant part of what became the effort for woman's suffrage. As Linda M. Perkins explains: "Throughout the antebellum years, White women were deluged with sermons and speeches which stressed the 'duty' of a 'true woman.' These speeches and sermons were reinforced by a proliferation of magazines, journals and other printed materials that focused upon instructing women of their proper sphere."[7] Near the end of her long life, Elizabeth Cady Stanton complained: "From the inauguration of the movement for woman's emancipation the Bible has been used to hold her in the 'divinely ordained sphere,' prescribed in the Old and New Testaments."[8]

Barbara Welter referred to these social constraints as the "Cult of True Womanhood."[9] Simply stated, "The attributes of True Womanhood, by which a woman judged herself and was judged by her husband, her neighbors and society could be divided into four cardinal virtues—piety, purity, submissiveness and domesticity. Put them all together and they spelled mother, daughter, sister, wife—woman. Without them, no matter whether there was fame, achievement or wealth, all was ashes. With them she was promised happiness and power."[10] These virtues defined femininity, narrowly circumscribed women's roles, and became the "centerpiece of nineteenth-century female identity" for many women who eventually joined the movement.[11] Women who defied expectations about their appropriate roles and duties were described as "unseemly" or "unsexed."[12] Those who stepped outside of the home were often soundly rebuked and disparaged. As Mary Louise Roberts points out, the Cult of True Womanhood "justified women's exclusion from participatory democracy."[13]

Many women could not adhere to these middle-class standards. Economic necessity drove many women into the workforce, compelling them to leave the snug safety of home and hearth. For African American women, many of whom worked outside the home, "the restrictions of woman's sphere held contradictory implications." Still, some more affluent African Americans endorsed the idea of domesticity with its attendant virtues not only as a way to challenge negative racial stereotypes, but also "as evidence of achieving middle-class status."[14] Perkins suggests that for free Black women, the trappings of True Womanhood became linked to "racial uplift," the process of helping advance their race.[15]

However, in the early days of the nineteenth century, the Second Great Awakening and the emergence of controversies over Indian removal and abolition began to erode the boundaries of True Womanhood.[16] As it encouraged greater earnestness in Christian living and regular attendance at religious services, the evangelical zeal that swept the country also "ushered in a period of extraordinary religious freedom for women" and produced "unprecedented" opportunities for them as denominations sought effective evangelists of either sex to spread the Gospel.[17]

As the public controversy over the plight of Indians and slaves became salient, other women, caught between their sense of themselves as Christians and the social norms that silenced them in the public arena, gradually began to challenge the discursive rules in their society so that they could fulfill what they saw as their responsibilities as moral beings. In grappling with that conflict, these women necessarily turned to scripture to discern their path forward. Drawing on the hermeneutical power opened up by the Reformation and reflecting changes in American Christianity in the aftermath of the American Revolution, some women evolved a distinctive exegetical approach to combat discursive rules that prohibited their participation in the public arena and to warrant their public involvement.[18] Drawing on what Jane Donawerth describes as "conservative strategies of biblical close reading," they developed and employed what scholars today would label a feminist hermeneutic.[19] That hermeneutic entailed reinterpreting familiar biblical passages, recovering and highlighting previously overlooked stories about women, and contesting passages traditionally used to circumscribe their activities. Although not the first women to use a feminist hermeneutic, these women used it adroitly to address and critique their political and social status in American society. Through their efforts, the Bible, so often deployed to circumscribe their activities, became a powerful, invaluable tool for women in their struggle to gain a voice in the pressing affairs of their day.

To explore how women employed a feminist hermeneutic in biblical exegesis to secure their own empowerment, we will consider four texts that played distinctive roles in women's struggle for voice and vote. These texts are important parts of a larger conversation about woman's rights, a conversation that included and is reflective of many diverse voices. However, each of these texts entered that conversation at a critical juncture and helped develop and disseminate a feminist hermeneutic that profoundly shaped the early woman's movement over the course of several decades. Although we will examine each text separately, our primary focus is on the strand of argument based on scripture that runs through each of them. We will argue that with and through a feminist hermeneutic, women: (1) argued for their status as moral agents, gradually progressing to claim their place as political activists; (2) adopted a posture of dissent[20] that grounded their calls for reform in widely accepted social ideals, making their appeals more palatable to many women; and (3) became prophetic voices, envisioning a future that more fully reflected God's divine plan, if Americans heeded their calls for change.

Building on and extending scholarship on the nineteenth-century woman's movement, our project explores a stream of argument that permeated the early woman's rights movement from its inception and was crucial to the movement's success. Two things make this study unique. First, we trace a strand of argument rather than focusing on an individual or event. We are interested both in how an idea, an argumentative strategy, makes its way into the movement and the rhetorical impact it has. Second, we identify a feminist hermeneutic which produced and grounded that argument. Through and with that feminist hermeneutic, women developed and deployed a cache of arguments, grounded in the Bible, that was essential in claiming their rightful place in public life. On a theoretical level, our analysis will also demonstrate how a posture of dissent and a prophetic persona are inextricably linked in this movement and the part they played in the movement's emergence and survival. Further, we will contend that dissent and prophecy are integral to all reform movements in large part because they are crucial to attracting and empowering followers.

That these texts emerge within the Protestant tradition is significant. The Reformation was not only a theological and ecclesial upheaval but also, and perhaps equally important, a hermeneutical shift of cataclysmic proportion. Reformation ecclesiology and theology dramatically shifted the rules controlling biblical interpretation on two fronts. First, Protestant groups made scripture widely available in the vernacular for all people to read for themselves. Second, leaders like Luther encouraged lay people to test practices and traditions within and outside religious circles in light of their own readings of scripture. Lay men and women rose to the challenge. The phrase "sola scriptura"—"only scripture"—became a cornerstone of Protestant thinking. Later in the United States, the Revolutionary War prompted changes in American Protestantism that further emphasized individual engagement with scripture. Empowered by what they discerned in the Bible as they studied it for themselves, in and through the texts we profile in this volume, women gradually began to dismantle many social constraints they confronted.

Four Texts That Shaped the Debate about Women's Roles

Jarena Lee's *Religious Experience and Journal,* Sarah Grimké's *Letters on the Equality of the Sexes*, Lucretia Mott's "Discourse on Woman," and Frances Willard's *Woman in the Pulpit* all challenged biblical passages used to constrain women's full participation in church and civic life. And all catalyzed and participated in a larger cultural conversation about women's proper roles.

In making our selections, we are sensitive to the warning of Carole Spitzack and Kathryn Carter that certain influential women often get significant attention, while "women who are not famous, exceptional, or great by male standards remain invisible."[21] We recognize that some other women within the movement articulated these arguments. Arguably, in tracing the trajectory of an argument through the early woman's rights movement, influential leaders of that movement merit attention since their works often set the tone and tenor of group efforts. However, our choice of texts reflects the importance of the texts themselves, not primarily the status of the women. Responding to persistent issues around women's activism, each text in this volume played a distinctive, important role in the struggle for women's rights; emerging at critical junctures, each spoke to a particular controversy, asserting women's responsibility to fulfill their moral obligations as Christians.

Lee's autobiography, the first written by an African American woman, offered a compelling argument for a woman's right to preach if God called her to that role. Her narrative reveals a nascent feminist hermeneutic, not fully articulated, that would echo through the abolitionist and woman's rights movements enabling both to attract and empower women as advocates. Lee's *Religious Experience and Journal,* for example, ignites a conversation about women's roles within the African Methodist Episcopal Church that will continue throughout the century and influence later women in this tradition to claim their right to ordination.

Frustrated by objections to her work as an abolitionist activist, Sarah Grimké's *Letters on the Equality of the Sexes* deployed a fully formed feminist hermeneutic to argue that women had a moral responsibility, grounded in their identity as Christians, to engage in reform efforts in American society. This "feminist manifesto" inspired later leaders like Lucretia Mott, Lucy Stone, and Elizabeth Cady Stanton. In some senses, her text laid some of the theological groundwork for the Declaration of Sentiments from the 1848 Seneca Falls meeting.

Mott, an experienced Quaker minister and leader in women's antislavery, was a key figure in organizing that first meeting to discuss woman's rights. Her "Discourse on Woman" not only skillfully refuted popular arguments for limiting women to traditional roles, but also emphasized the contributions of women who moved beyond the domestic sphere without sacrificing their femininity. Reflecting the feminist hermeneutic that Grimké had so effectively articulated, Mott's speech, together with her appealing public persona and considerable ethos, moved this scriptural approach to the forefront of the woman's movement.

Later in the century, as leader of the largest women's organization in the United States at the time, Willard brought thousands of women into support for suffrage under the call for "home protection." By her era, women had made significant strides in the civic arena, for example, in gaining access to higher education, securing some property rights, and engaging in public advocacy. However, with the exception of the Quakers and a few other small groups, church leadership and preaching remained almost exclusively male bastions. Because her own denomination, Methodism, and other groups were grappling with the issue of women's preaching, she focused on arguing for women's right to preach. Her argument in *Woman in the Pulpit* relied on the feminist hermeneutic her predecessors had evolved and refined. Her text provided a firm rationale for women's preaching, which informed discussions within Methodism and in the larger social context about proper roles for women. Willard's arguments moved many conservative women, who saw themselves as moral agents, into being political activists. Taken together, these four texts reveal how women artfully grappled with and refuted the biblically grounded prohibitions on their role in the public arena. These texts were key in attracting and empowering women in significant reform efforts.

Further, these texts reveal how women, through scriptural exegesis, claimed their roles as preachers (Lee's *Religious Experience and Journal*), as moral agents empowered to advocate for change (Grimké's *Letters on the Equality of the Sexes*), as full participants in the affairs of their day (Mott's "Discourse on Woman") and, ultimately as engaged political activists working to perfect American culture (Willard's *Woman in the Pulpit*). Drawing on a feminist hermeneutic, these texts shaped the ongoing debate about women's proper roles as Christian women in American society. Indeed, in our view, the arguments these texts articulated were critical in the final success of the movement and are an important strand in the story of the diverse, complicated struggle for women's rights.

A further note. This work is a book about the social movement that is called variously "the woman's rights movement," "the women's rights movement," and "the suffrage movement." Honoring the usage of the women engaged in these efforts, we will refer to it as the "woman's movement."[22] Our work will delineate one significant dimension of the broad call for women's rights in the nineteenth century: the right to speak in the public arena. Rather than examining an individual or an event, our focus will be on a thread of argument that we believe was crucial to the success of the movement.

Organization of the Book

After providing historical context on the Reformation and the woman's movement, the balance of the book focuses on four case studies of texts that, employing various media, slowly attracted, inspired, and empowered women to advocate for their own rights. Significantly, the authors of these texts were involved in the life of their families, as wives, mothers, daughters, and/or sisters; they were not, as their Roman sisters in religious communities had been, devoted exclusively to life in the church.[23] Rather they managed, around the demands of hearth and home, not only to be interested in unfolding events around them, but also to participate in ways that shaped those events. Our women did not always win the battles they enjoined; sometimes they were silenced; sometimes they were ignored. But ultimately, they contributed significantly to women's achieving greater gender equality.

In each case study, we will provide substantial historical context to situate the texts and women in the milieu they confronted and to make clear the challenges within their social and religious contexts. Although the situations they faced were different, these texts enabled women to dissent decorously; drawing on scripture they evinced their devotion to Christianity and to God's divine plan even as they challenged entrenched male interpretations of scripture that they were convinced erroneously circumscribed their roles. By grounding arguments in scripture, their texts positioned each woman as a prophetic voice, urging others to live into their role as moral agents and later political activists working to perfect their society.

Our conclusion will draw together our case studies, suggesting how collectively they enhance our understanding of the larger movement for woman's rights. Because we are scholars of communication, we pay close attention to both the rhetorical features of the works of these women and how their efforts responded to the situations they confronted. As we look across these women and their works, we consider situational conditions that seem to produce fertile opportunities for their efforts. Moreover, in adding a strand to the complex history of women's involvement in public life, we also hope to discern how marginalized groups can challenge and ultimately change the discursive rules of their communities, which often discount or even silence their voices.

Finally, the book provides two appendices. In recent years, the scholarship on women and rhetoric has burgeoned. Although sometimes connected only tangentially to this project, that research provides a rich background for our work. Appendix A offers a brief overview of that research. Moreover, throughout their struggles for their rights, women in different situations repeatedly reinterpreted and challenged particular biblical passages. Appendix B identifies those passages.

ACKNOWLEDGMENTS

Any work of this sort depends on many people to bring it to fruition.

Martha—
I thank Dr. Beverly Mitchell of Wesley Theological Seminary, who introduced me to Jarena Lee and Argula Von Grumbach and helped me understand the power of the Reformation; Rev. Dr. Lucy Lind Hogan, who, as my first PhD student, introduced me to the idea of women's preaching and later, as my homilectics professor at Wesley, helped me learn to preach and who continues to support my ministry, my preaching, and this book; the librarians of the University of Nevada Las Vegas, especially the Interlibrary Loan Staff who produced needed documents, even very obscure ones, quickly, and Professor Suzie Sklar, who tracked seemingly impossible tidbits; and the good people of St. Mary's Episcopal Church, Woodlawn, Maryland, whose preacher and minister talked far more about Jarena Lee, Sarah Grimké and the nineteenth-century woman's movement than they anticipated.

Finally, I am, as always indebted to my two daughters, Thing One and Thing Two, for their unfailing love, support, and encouragement.

Lisa—
I thank Maoria Kirker, a senior librarian and the Lead of the Teaching and Learning Team at George Mason University; Janet Olson, Archivist at the Frances Willard House and Museum and Woman's Christian Temperance Union archives; Tess Goodman, head of Special Collections at Wesleyan University; Andy Klenklen, director of the Library at Wesley Theological Seminary; Elizabeth Novara, American Women's History Specialist at the Library of Congress; and Shir Bach, a junior fellow at the Library of Congress, all of whom were incredibly helpful in quickly locating seemingly impossible to find historical documents that were essential to this work. I am also grateful to Dr. John Woolsey and the George Mason University Honors College for encouraging my development of an undergraduate course on the early woman's movement, which grew directly out of this project.

Most of all, I am indebted to my family for their steadfast love, faith, and encouragement. A heartfelt thanks to my sons Will and Austin; my parents, Susan and David; and to the love of my life, Geoffrey.

Lisa and Martha—
We thank Dr. Karlyn Kohrs Campbell, who introduced us and so many, many others to the nineteenth-century woman's movement and to three of the women in this book. In addition, we are grateful to Victoria J. Gallagher, series editor of Movement Rhetoric/Rhetoric's Movement and Aurora Bell, acquisitions editor, both of the University of South Carolina Press. Without their advice, encouragement, and patience, this project would not have been possible.

ONE

Wellspring of Argument

The Reformation and the Opening of Discursive Space

October 31, 1517: Martin Luther posts his 95 Theses on the door of the church in Wittenberg, Germany, sparking the beginning of the Protestant Reformation.

August 18, 1920: By a single vote, the state of Tennessee became the 36th state to ratify the 19th Amendment to the United States Constitution that granted women the right to vote.

Separated by just over four centuries and thousands of miles, these two events have no obvious connection. However, an intriguing thread connects what might be considered the *first social movement in Western European history* and what is the *longest social movement in United States history.* The theological developments and ramifications of Luther's reforming efforts that began in 1517 opened a cache of rhetorical resources that were vital to nineteenth century women's arguments for their own empowerment in the United States. In this volume, we hope to elucidate that connection and trace how American women used these resources in their struggle to become public advocates and preachers.[1] Elucidating the connection between the sixteenth century Germany religious controversy and the twentieth century US political landscape requires understanding both the implications of the Reformation and the challenges facing American women at the beginning of the nineteenth century.

The Reformation and the Disruption of Discursive Rules

When nineteenth century American women like Jarena Lee, Sarah Grimké, Lucretia Mott, and Frances Willard (whose texts will be the focus of this volume) turned to scripture to claim the right to preach and to advocate for themselves and others, they were drawing on rhetorical resources that had been largely closed to women as well as the majority of men for most of Christian history. Immediately prior to the Reformation, clergy defined and articulated biblical truth for lay people; women were, of course, excluded from any clerical position. But in the nascent days of Christianity, women played important roles. So, for example, although the Gospels differ in many details, they all agree that women were the first to discover the Resurrection. Indeed, in John's account Jesus specifically charges Mary Magdalene to report the resurrection to the male disciples.[2] Paul also lists several women as his co-workers and helpers during his missionary journeys. In particular, Paul labels Phoebe, one of his helpers, as a *diakonon,* or minister.[3]

However, as the Church became institutionalized, particularly after Christianity became the official religion of the Roman Empire in the early fourth century, males assumed complete control of its operations. Theologian Francine Cardman observes: "[A]s Christianity made its way through the Greco-Roman world, women's leadership and ministry were increasingly pushed to the side of evolving church structures. The process of institutionalization of the churches was already under way by the end of the first century CE [Common Era]; by the end of the fourth, it was essentially complete."[4]

Moreover, the entirely male church leadership selected and emphasized particular biblical passages that seemingly supported women's submission to men and their silence in church.[5] For example, Ephesians 5:22 asserted: "Wives, submit yourselves unto your own husbands, as unto the Lord. For the husband is the head of the wife." 1st Corinthians 14 stressed: "Let your women keep silence in the churches: for it is not permitted unto them to speak." The reiteration of and emphasis on these snippets obscured other passages and examples that supported a different view. Male-controlled exegesis largely silenced and disempowered women within the church.

This interpretative control had profound implications, not only for women, but for everyone under the church's sway. Pointing to Jesus's empowerment of Peter as leader of the Christian community, the institutionalized church claimed temporal jurisdiction over human souls.[6] Because of that authority, by the time of the Reformation, the Church in Rome exercised extensive control over many dimensions of individual lives. Every aspect of religious life, every moral issue, every ethical issue, all standards of personal behavior were subject to evaluation and, if necessary, correction through appeal to and application of appropriate scripture or traditional resources. The adjudicator of such discussions was always and only the Church.

Disrupting the Church's firm control over biblical interpretation was a substantial challenge. However, a bold, ambitious Augustinian friar, speaking from a position within the Church's hierarchy, significantly shifted the rules around interpreting Christian scripture.

Empowering Believers

When Martin Luther posted his invitation to a debate at Wittenberg University on All Saints Eve 1517, he had no intention of starting a revolution, theological or discursive. Posting such announcements or invitations on the door was commonplace; indeed, his posting them in Latin indicated his desire for an academic rather than public debate. As Peter Marshall characterizes it: "Because of its handy location, the door of the Castle Church served as the University's bulletin board, and Luther's gesture has been seen as no more dramatic than pinning up a lecture list in a modern college."[7] Still, with this mundane act, Luther became, as Alister McGrath notes, "the accidental revolutionary."[8]

Despite Luther's intentions, events, as they were to do repeatedly throughout the Reformation, took a path of their own. Translating Luther's theses from Latin into German, printers circulated them widely. Although the paucity of presses made copies in the vernacular less common in England, by the time Luther completed his translation of the New Testament from Greek into German, there had been eighteen separate editions of translations of the entire Vulgate into that language.[9] Soon people all over Germany were discussing Luther's theses with their direct challenge to the selling of indulgences and their implicit undercutting of ecclesial authority in biblical interpretation. But even if many people now had access to the Bible in their own language, the Church still claimed the right to determine which interpretations and applications of scripture were valid.

Such prohibitions on the production of and participation in discourse are ubiquitous in human society. To assure social order and preserve stability, every society has rules that permit some and exclude others from participating in various spheres of discourse. In his "Discourse on Language," French philosopher and social critic Michel Foucault explains:

> in every society the production of discourse is at once controlled, selected, organised and redistributed according to a certain number of procedures, whose role it is to avert its powers and its dangers, to cope

with chance events, to evade its ponderous, awesome materiality. In a society such as our own we all know the rules of *exclusion.* The most obvious and familiar of these concerns is what is *prohibited.* We know perfectly well that we are not free to say just anything, that we cannot simply speak of anything, when we like or where we like; not just anyone, finally, may speak of just anything.[10]

However, such discursive rules are not impenetrable. Indeed, as rhetorical scholar Kendall Phillips argues, a discursive formation "is not an 'ideal, continuous, smooth text . . . rather it is rife with points of disjuncture and contradiction.'"[11] At certain times, historical forces interact and coalesce to expose tensions and inconsistencies within these discursive rules. Phillips suggests that, when individuals notice those gaps, inconsistencies, and even contradictions in the taken-for-granted rules of discourse, questioning and contestation become possible.[12]

Indeed, the Reformation opened a hermeneutical space where such contestation was possible. The reverberations of Luther's work dramatically changed the relationship between human beings and the institutions and individuals who held authority, particularly religious authority, over them. As Derek Wilson points out: "When Luther gave men the open Bible, he gave them permission—by the application of reason to the plain text—to challenge centuries of official Church teaching. Well, if the pope and his minions were wrong, who was to say that other ancient authorities might not be doubted? Without intending to do so Luther encouraged men to use their God-given intellect to question *everything.*"[13]

The ecclesiastical consequences of Luther's benign invitation to academic debate are clear in the development and proliferation of Protestant denominations then and now. Indeed, "Reformation" is often almost synonymous with the founding of Protestantism. Wilson's observation about the impact of Luther's action—encouraging people to use their intellect to question the status quo in many arenas—directs attention to the sociological and political consequences of what began as an ecclesiological and theological discussion.

As Luther's controversy with the ecclesial authorities in Rome intensified, he challenged more explicitly its claims to the Church's exclusive right to interpret scripture. In fact, he specifically extended hermeneutical agency and power to lay people. The keys given to Peter through which the Church claimed all interpretive and sacramental powers were given, he insists, to the whole community, not solely to Peter.[14] He supports his view by turning to 1st Corinthians 12:12–14:27: "For just as the body is one and has many members, and all the members of the body, though many, are one body, so it is with Christ. For in the one Spirit we were all baptized into one body—Jews or Greeks, slaves or free—and we were all made to drink of one Spirit. Indeed, the body does not consist of one member but of many. . . . Now you are the body of Christ and individually members of it."[15] Citing Paul, Luther disagrees that the clergy constitutes a separate "spiritual" authority. In Christian teaching, he avers, all are one body.[16] Thus, interpretive power belongs not to the ordained few but to all believers.

Developing that line of argument, Luther articulates what came to be known as the "priesthood of all believers": "Thus we are all consecrated as priests by baptism, as St. Peter says: 'You are a royal priesthood, a holy nation.'"[17] The only real difference between "laymen and priests, princes and bishops, or as they call it, between spiritual and temporal persons . . . is one of office and function, and not of estate."[18] After that bold assertion of the power of lay people, he declares: "By these and many other texts we should gain courage and freedom and should not let the spirit of liberty (as St. Paul has it) be frightened away by the inventions of the Popes; we should boldly judge what they do and what they leave undone, by our own understanding of the Scriptures."[19]

With this argument, Luther laid a firm foundation for lay people's interpreting scripture for themselves and using it as they saw fit. For good or for ill, the ecclesiastical establishment was displaced as the sole arbiter of meaning in that text. The Bible, with all its rich diversity, was open for lay persons to explore and use. Thus, Luther opened a hermeneutical space for lay Christians by inviting and empowering them to engage in discussions and debates about the meaning of Biblical passages through, for example, juxtaposing seemingly contradictory verses.[20] In essence, Luther's revolution was not so much in giving people open Bibles, for many already had those. Rather the shift was, as Wilson observed, an invitation to use their own skills and abilities to interpret the text and, if appropriate, challenge established teachings and question any application of those teachings to their lives.[21] Calling the Reformation Christianity's "Dangerous Idea," McGrath highlights its implications: "The dangerous new idea, firmly embodied in the heart of the Protestant revolution, was that all Christians have the right to interpret the Bible for themselves. However, it ultimately proved uncontrollable, spawning developments that few at the time could have envisaged or predicted. . . . Protestantism took its stand on the right of individuals to interpret the Bible for themselves rather than be forced to submit to 'official' interpretations handed down by popes or other religious centralized authorities."[22]

The seismic hermeneutical shift emerging from the Reformation dramatically undercut the Church's control over biblical interpretations and empowered nonclerical people to offer their own, often creative and divergent, interpretations.[23] Although he is speaking specifically of translations, Richard Duerden's observations about the relationship of power to discursive practices are relevant here. He writes:

> The Reformation debate over Scripture in English included a subtext: the question of power. Power was won or exercised—in part—through textual and rhetorical strategies manipulating the authority attributed to scripture: claiming scriptural authority, denying the Church's or the reformers' claims to it, symbolically offering it to rulers or ministers. "Discourses are objects of appropriation," Foucault observes, and the Bible was a discourse many sought to appropriate. Such discursive forms of power "can be bent to any purpose. The successes of history belong to those who are capable of seizing these rules, to replace those who had used them . . . and redirect them against those who had initially imposed them; controlling this complex mechanism, they will make it function so as to overcome the rulers with their own rules."[24]

In some senses, much of post-Reformation Christian history is about the struggle of various individuals and groups to appropriate the power of scripture to advance their own interests. Nineteenth-century American women did just that.

The Woman's Rights Movement in the United States

These things are too much lost sight of.

—LUCRETIA MOTT, "DISCOURSE ON WOMAN"

Almost immediately, some women recognized and seized the power to interpret scripture in support of a cause. So, for example, Argula von Grumbach, a contemporary and great admirer of Luther, defended a young man disciplined for spreading Luther's views. Grounding her defense entirely in scripture, von Grumbach challenged the actions of religious authorities.[25] Almost a century and a half later, during the nascent days of Quakerism, Margaret Fell Fox provided a compelling and thorough theological argument for women's empowerment within religious circles by reinterpreting familiar biblical passages, highlighting overlooked passages, and noting examples of women's leadership in both Hebrew and Christian scriptures. In effect, she articulated a fully developed feminist hermeneutic.[26] As we shall see in later chapters, her work profoundly influenced nineteenth-century woman's rights advocates.[27] The texts we consider in this volume, all of which were directly or indirectly influenced by Fell Fox's work, adopt and adapt the feminist hermeneutic she developed to claim their role in churches and in the broader political arena. In so doing, as we shall see, these texts dismantled the powerful biblical arguments that supported women's confinement to the private sphere, opened up new roles and pathways for women, and profoundly impacted the development and later success of the early woman's movement.

Emergence of the Nineteenth-Century Woman's Movement

Although scholarship abounds on the nineteenth-century woman's movement, "identifying the start of the efforts for woman's rights in general and suffrage in particular is a question of definition."[28] Rather than struggling to pinpoint a date or event as the start of the movement, recent scholarship explores factors that underlay the movement's emergence. The early republic was, in the view of historian Gordon S. Wood, "the time of greatest religious chaos and originality in American history."[29] Revivals and spiritual fervor among Protestant denominations erupted in the early 1800s and ushered in a period of "unprecedented reform," which scholars term the Second Great Awakening.[30] Matt McCook observes that this religious arousal stimulated evangelical zeal throughout the country and "inspired numerous religious and moral reform efforts. Just as revivalist ministers empowered listeners by explaining that salvation was in their own hands, they also emphasized humankind's ability to evangelize the world, remedy social problems, and Christianize their culture through the activities of voluntary organizations."[31] So far-reaching and pervasive was the religious revitalization that Donald G. Mathews suggests that the Second Great Awakening was the equivalent of a social movement that mobilized hundreds of thousands of people with "profound social implications."[32]

The Second Great Awakening stemmed in part from what historian Nathan O. Hatch calls the "democratization of American Christianity." In his analysis, the American Revolution ushered in a period where values, such as freedom, equality, and individual liberty, gained salience. These values were codified in the Declaration of Independence, which boldly declared that all people were created equal and had inalienable rights. As Hatch explains, the American revolution "dramatically expanded the circle of people who considered themselves capable of thinking for themselves about issues of freedom, equality, sovereignty, and representation. Respect for authority, tradition, station, and education eroded."[33]

This spirit of egalitarianism infused every aspect of American life. Religion was no exception. In fact, heated debates about religious authority, led largely by lay people, emerged during the early Republic. These debates were characterized by "violent anticlericalism, a flaunting of conventional religious deportment, a disdain for the wrangling of theologians, an assault on tradition, and an assertion that common people were more sensitive to the ways of the divine."[34] In short, the American Revolution upended social hierarchies, including those within some churches, imbuing ordinary people with a sense of their own authority and self-worth.

Between the American Revolution and 1848, America's population grew exponentially. According to Hatch, during this time, "the population of the United States grew at a staggering rate: two and a half million people became twenty million in 70 years."[35] He argues that "amidst this population boom, American Christianity became a mass enterprise" as various denominations competed for new members.[36] As a consequence, the face of Protestant Christianity shifted, embracing evangelism and honoring intense religious experiences.[37]

Together, the fervor for evangelism and the democratization of religion opened doors for women. In the United States, hosts of women, believing they were empowered by the Holy Spirit and called by God to evangelize, began to hold prayer meetings where they exhorted and cajoled sinners to repent and reform. So powerful was their sense of moral empowerment that they braved criticism and sometimes transgressed social conventions about the "appropriate" roles and actions for women.[38]

Other socio-cultural factors also played a role. Barbara Berg contends that, contrary to the widespread belief that abolition was the primary catalyst for the woman's movement, among the deepest factors were changes in American cities during the first half of the nineteenth century. She writes: "Abolition did not inaugurate nineteenth-century feminism, nor did it generate the suffrage campaign. To be sure, some women dedicated to freeing the slaves later agitated for woman's right to vote. But many early suffragists, including Antoinette Brown Blackwell, Isabella Beecher Hooker, Ernestine Potowski Rose, and Amelia Jenks Bloomer, had little or no direct involvement with abolitionist activities." Rather than seeing the movement as linked to particular individuals, she suggests "it grew out of fundamental changes in woman's conceptions of herself, the rest of her sex, and her society. The philosophy behind the agitation for the vote shared a common etiology with the demand for expanded economic and social opportunities . . . a quest that originated and developed in American cities between 1800–1860."[39]

In the midst of these broad sociological currents, women participated in political discussions away from the public platform. They relied on socially acceptable forms of female communication such as letters and diaries. John Tinkler argues that while classical rhetorical theory focused on *contentio* or contentious oratory in the courts or deliberative assemblies, classical literature recognized another form of rhetorical activity, *sermo,* or informal discussions, conversations, and exchanges between friends.[40] Christine Mason Sutherland and Rebecca Sutcliffe observe that early woman's rights advocates made strategic use of such private and unofficial discourse, which classical rhetorical theory largely ignored. Women have, "throughout the ages," expressed their views and engaged in discussion in "letters, diaries, works of devotion, in written discourse; conversation, story-telling, social exchange of all kinds."[41] For example, while exploring family papers as part of a project about the reading habits of antebellum New Englanders, Ronald and Mary Zboray were surprised by the "frequency and depth of women's references to party politics."[42] They discovered that women, in the privacy of their homes, sometimes used their diaries as "a scratch pad for thinking through issues." In addition to recording events for later reflection, diary entries could "result in phrases or entire paragraphs destined for letters."[43] When letters were read aloud and discussed, women gained an audience for their ideas. Through letters to family and friends, women expressed opinions and created a sense of communal and intellectual intimacy.[44] As the Zborays assert, "Letters and diaries provided opportunities for writing oneself, socially, into existence, in this case being political."[45]

Noting that women were adept at using socially sanctioned forms of communication to create community, develop and test ideas, and organize, women's studies scholar Eleanor Flexner points to sewing circles, literary societies, educational societies, and parlors as venues that often became conduits for women to discuss shared concerns.[46] For instance, Lucy Stone, who would become a major figure in the movement, wrote to her brother in 1840: "It was decided in our Literary Society the other day that ladies ought to mingle in politics, go to Congress, etc., etc. What do you think of that?"[47]

In the *Beginnings of Sisterhood,* Keith Melder argues that "encouraged by the sense of common purpose inherent in the Second Great Awakening," women also organized "religious and benevolent societies" that built "bonds of sisterhood at all levels of their organized operations."[48] With the emergence of Indian removal and abolition as critical political issues, the work of women in organizing petitioning drives and later within female antislavery organizations "quickened the exchange of ideas and strengthened the loose network of women activists."[49] These networks or sisterhoods were places where women shared their experiences, honed their ideas, and grew in awareness of their mutual challenges. They were, as Campbell later describes woman's rights meetings, "ideological crucibles."[50]

The advent of the lyceum movement also provided women with an opportunity to hear discussion of issues of the day. Although the nineteenth-century lyceum was initially a "means of intellectual, moral and practical self-improvement primarily for young White men of the middle class," women could attend as spectators.[51] As Angela Ray points out, many well-known women's rights leaders such as Elizabeth Cady Stanton testified to the lyceum as formative in their activism. Later in the century, the lyceum became "one of the few public forums accessible to a broad segment of the middle class in which nineteenth-century women's voices were heard at all. . . . Debates and lectures about women drew good crowds, and lectures by women had the potential to attract the curious as well as the committed."[52]

Still, early in the nineteenth century, a broad swath of the population considered public advocacy whether from pulpit or platform as outside woman's proper sphere. In the language of Nan Johnson, pulpit and platform were gendered spaces reserved for males.[53] The strongest arguments for gendered spaces were the dominant male interpretations of scripture that seemed to prohibit women's speaking in churches and to justify their consignment to the private sphere. Powerful social conventions held that the home was the proper province for women; the public arena belonged to men.[54] To venture into the public arena, particularly to speak to a "promiscuous audience" including both men and women, jeopardized a woman's "privileged" position.[55] For many Americans, especially middle class White women, the appropriate sphere for a woman centered on hearth and home in what Barbara Welter called the cult of True Womanhood.

But as Welter notes, True Womanhood "carried within itself the seeds of its own destruction. For if woman was so very little less than the angels, she should surely take a more active part in running the world."[56] A woman's alleged moral superiority and piety were sometimes in tension with her domesticity and submissiveness.[57] In the early days of the nineteenth century, the Second Great Awakening and the emergence of controversies over Indian removal and abolition exposed the tensions. Struggling with the contradiction between their perception of their moral responsibilities and the rules that silenced them in the public arena, some women began to transgress discursive conventions so that they could fulfill their obligations as Christian women. For example, in her 1829 "Circular Addressed to the Benevolent Ladies of the United States" urging women to petition against the removal of Indian tribes from their homelands, Catharine Beecher, the prominent nineteenth century advocate for women's education, asked rhetorically: "Have not then the females of this country some duties devolving upon them in relation to this helpless race?"[58] The implied answer was, of course, that women's moral obligation as Christians prompted not only concern but action in the public arena. Although Beecher is always keenly aware of what she considers women's proper sphere of activity within the home, she justifies this exception because the Indian removal controversy is a "crisis."[59] Aware that women's engagement in this cause violated unstated, but powerful, discursive rules, Beecher believed that women's responsibilities as Christians were paramount.

These petition drives inevitably and irrevocably changed the self-perceptions of participants. Susan Zaeske observes that over time the tenor of petitions changed from one of humility and supplication to one of assertiveness, reflecting a "transformation of the political identity of signers from that of subjects to that of citizens."[60] Elaborating further, she points out that "not only signing but also circulating petitions effected a transformation in women's political identities, for it provided practical experience in carrying out a campaign to influence public opinion."[61] The result of these antislavery petitions was that they "provoked what was perhaps the first sustained discussion of women's political rights and the status of women as citizens in the history of the U.S. Congress."[62] Alisse Portnoy concurs, noting that in and through the petitions, women "discursively constructed" their identity as agents "empowered to intervene in U.S. national policy."[63]

The quick and widespread disapproval of outspoken women catalyzed reactions. Newspaper coverage where it occurred was often negative and even caustic.[64] But "when critics claimed that speaking to mixed audiences [of men and women] violated female propriety, reform women responded that they were fulfilling their womanly duty by speaking in defense of the slave and other downtrodden souls."[65] In short, women were proposing significant changes in their roles and responsibilities, "in societal norms and values," that would inevitably generate opposition in a moral struggle.[66] Robert Cathcart elaborates: "When . . . a collective experiencing alienation and frustration, employs a rhetoric which accesses experience in a different way—i.e., questions the old forms and creates new symbols—a rhetorical clash is produced. If and when this clash becomes a matter of essence and principle, we have a dialectical enjoinment. This enjoinment raises questions not about means and ends, but about the social reality we have been conditioned to accept."[67] In this case, that moral enjoinment exposed fissures in the discursive rules that governed women's behavior.

The Focus and Contribution of This Project

The goal of this project is to build on the work done by previous scholars on the nineteenth-century woman's movement and its leaders.[68] Rhetorical scholars have approached the woman's movement from a variety of perspectives. Some offer historical accounts, others recover overlooked or undervalued work by women, and still others provide insight into the strategies women used to advocate for their rights.[69] Some investigate individual women[70] or pivotal events.[71] A few consider the movement as a whole.[72]

Our approach is unique in tracing a strand of argument, grounded in the Bible, that permeated the movement from its inception and was crucial for the movement's development and success. We focus on how women developed and employed a distinctive feminist hermeneutic to challenge what they perceived as the most significant obstacles to achieving their fullest, God-given potential: male interpretations of scripture. Exploring key texts, we argue that with and through a feminist hermeneutic, women developed a distinct argument from moral agency, strategically adopted a posture of dissent, and positioned themselves as prophetic voices calling for the implementation of God's divine plan on earth.

Significantly, each of the texts analyzed in this volume engages with a larger conversation about women's role in public life that occurs throughout the nineteenth century. Moreover, each text enters the controversy about women's rights at a critical juncture, drawing on biblical arguments derived from scripture and interpreted through a female lens. Thus, and through a feminist hermeneutic, the texts literally write women into consciousness of themselves as moral agents and provide women advocates with an arsenal of arguments warranted in scripture to defend their rights.

A Third Strand of Argument in the Early Woman's Movement

Most scholars have adopted Aileen Kraditor's assertion that two arguments undergirded the suffrage movement: the argument from justice and the argument from expediency, with the former fading away as the other developed over the course of the century.[73] The justice argument, she suggests, grew out of the natural rights philosophy articulated in the thinking of the Declaration of Independence. That is, women have the same natural and inalienable right as men to vote. By the end of the century, however, Kraditor contends that women put more emphasis on expediency, or the beneficial impact of their votes as a result of their feminine nature. That is, societal perceptions of women were that they were more pure, moral, and pious than men and therefore, women would bring these traits to bear in the political realm.

Challenging Kraditor's assessment, Zaeske argues that "contrary to accepted wisdom . . . early women speakers did not ground their defenses in appeals to justice, law, equity, or constitutionalism." Rather, she asserts, in order to claim the public platform, women "employed a rhetoric of gendered morality that emphasized the special nature of female benevolence and the social utility of exercising that benevolence to the spoken word."[74] As evidence, she points to prominent women's rights leaders such as Angelina and Sarah Grimké, Lucretia Mott, and Abby Kelley, all of whom wielded moral arguments grounded in scripture to warrant their right to speak. The challenge to women's rhetoric, therefore, "was not to show that speaking in the public sphere was consistent with natural law or guaranteed by the U.S. Constitution, but to demonstrate that it was consistent with woman's special virtue and moral authority."[75] Zaeske's observation about the deployment of scripture as a basis for their actions hints at the strand of argument and the cache of rhetorical strategies emanating from it that are the focus for this volume. She does not, however, explore that thread of argument.

Building on Zaeske's insight, we believe that a third, overlooked strand of argument percolated throughout the early woman's movement. This third strand of argument—the argument from moral agency—was grounded in scripture and emphasized women's responsibilities as moral agents. A sense of personal moral agency derives from a perception of having a distinctive role in the working out and implementation of some transcendent values and principles in the world. For the women in this volume, moral agency emerged from their understanding of their distinctive roles and obligations as Christian women, particularly as wives and mothers, to advance God's kingdom in the world.

This argument from moral agency is distinct from the two threads of argument Kraditor identifies. The argument from moral agency does not emphasize inherent or natural rights but rather focuses on the divinely ordained identity of women and the moral obligation that entails. In fact, the women in this volume repeatedly express their reluctance to become engaged in political activity but claim that moral, divinely inspired obligation motivates them. In contrast to the argument from expediency, the argument from moral agency is not on the beneficial impact of women's activity by virtue of their feminine qualities such as piety. On the contrary, the argument from moral agency is based on women's fulfillment of their role as Christians and as agents in God's redemptive work. This argument from moral agency, derived from scripture seen through a feminist hermeneutic, was a key to women's claims of legitimacy and it also had a strong persuasive appeal for potential supporters. When women saw themselves as moral agents, they were able to connect to strong cultural values, including the Bible and the notions of feminine piety, even as they became prophetic voices, harkening American society to much needed reforms.

A Posture of Rhetorical Dissent

Second, we will elucidate how women's hermeneutical strategies allowed them to dissent decorously. Although the term "dissent" can have negative connotations, in legal and rhetorical discourse it refers to offering alternative understandings and interpretations which, nonetheless, are grounded in and derive from the same key principles as the position from which they differ. Thus, a Supreme Court dissenting opinion shares allegiance to the Constitution and the rule of law as the majority opinion but draws different conclusions from those shared allegiances. Rhetorical theorist Robert L. Ivie defines dissent as "advancing a significant difference of opinion or expressing a substantial disagreement without making a complete break with the prevailing viewpoint."[76] Dissent occurs when the "taken-for-granted rules, topics and norms of public deliberation are contested, opposed, or transgressed."[77] Because dissent does not break completely from dominant discourses, strategically it provides rhetors with "a sharp edge for cutting through political orthodoxies" while maintaining "a solid footing in public culture." Thus, dissent "participates in a transformation performed within 'an existing web of power and knowledge.'"[78] Moreover, the beauty of dissent is that it can advance "a politically unconventional position without demonizing adversaries (or making oneself a demonized subject)."[79] As Ivie concludes, "there may be no more quintessentially democratic discourse than that of dissent."[80]

The texts we analyze here employ the rhetorical strategy of dissent to position women's actions as consistent with their womanly piety.[81] They argued for enlarging woman's sphere of influence to include preaching and voting so that they could protect their homes and families and fulfill their duties as Christians. These texts adroitly connect progressive reform ideas to the Protestant religious tradition and values. At the same time, in and through their texts, the women avoided completely rejecting prevailing views of femininity. On the contrary, in both rhetorical approach and appearance, these women sometimes accentuated and affirmed their femininity. A rhetorical posture of dissent enabled the women to "cut through political orthodoxy" without "becoming alienated from the mainstream public culture." With considerable skill, their texts challenge "rigidified conventions, habits and practices"[82] and argue for change by speaking "*against* the dominant ideology, but from *within* its own vocabulary."[83] As these women challenged the rules that prohibited them from speaking, advocating on behalf of others, and preaching, they had varying degrees of success. But with each success, they altered the dominant discourse, paving the way for future women to further advance woman's rights.

A Prophetic Vision

Third and finally, our analysis will argue that, in adopting the strategy of dissent, the women assumed the prophetic persona, a powerful force in the Judeo-Christian tradition.[84] Popular views of prophecy often understand it as foretelling the future. However, within the Judeo-Christian culture, prophets are spokespersons for the Divine and their role is both to remind the faithful of shared communal values and principles while simultaneously pointing out where they have failed to live into and with these values and principles. While prophets can be harsh in pointing to failures and lapses within the community, they can also offer hope of restoration and fulfillment when the community returns its allegiance to the rules established by the Divine. In this sense, "prophetic speech is not merely predictive, but combines aspects of memory, tradition, and hope to awaken vision and resistance. . . . Prophets were, therefore, both conservators and innovators. They worked on the basis of prior religious traditions and revamped them in new circumstances."[85] Because the prophet is a messenger of Yahweh, and usually a reluctant messenger, "his activity is not only justified, but mandated."[86] As Joan Chittester aptly concludes: "In every period, the prophetic task was the same: to interpret the present in light of the Word of God so that new worlds could be envisioned and new attitudes developed that would eventually make the world a better place."[87]

Indeed, the texts analyzed in this volume draw on an argument grounded in scripture to point out how the faithful have strayed from God's divine plan. The texts employ the three interrelated parts of what Sacvan Berco-vitch termed the American Jeremiad, a form extensively used in American political discourse.[88] They deplored the status of women, suggested it devi-ated from the original divine plan, and rebuked those who opposed their efforts. The women who authored these texts saw themselves, like prophets always do, as playing a critical role in "God's great redemptive plan for the world."[89] As Ruether explains, "Redemption in Christ was then defined as restoring this original equality in the image of God for women equally with men."[90] In different contexts and in different ways, the texts studied in this volume make this claim.

Achieving Legitimacy and Attracting and Empowering Followers

The persistence and ultimate success of the early woman's rights movement required its leaders to achieve legitimacy for the movement while simultane-ously attracting and empowering followers. As Stewart, Smith, and Denton note, achieving legitimacy "is the principal goal or demand of social move-ments, the primal challenge of movements to institutions, and the most central obstacle leaders of movements must overcome.[91] To achieve that goal, "social movements must identify with fundamental norms and values to transport themselves from the margins of society to the centers where legitimacy resides."[92] Social change advocates can "employ a strategy of tran-scendence by identifying themselves with what is large, good, important and of the highest order in society."[93] Thus, "activists are wise to identify with the moral symbols, sacred emblems, heroes, founding fathers, and re-vered documents of society rather than to attack or to disparage them."[94] Indeed, that is precisely what women in the early woman's movement did. With and through the feminist hermeneutic, they were able to ground their views in scripture. Doing so allowed them to keep their "footing in public culture" while simultaneously challenging "taken-for-granted rules" about their proper sphere.

The argument that women developed and employed was attractive and comfortable for potential supporters because it created what rhetorical the-orist Kenneth Burke termed "identification" between the women and their audiences. Burke writes: "You persuade a man [*sic*] only insofar as you can talk his language by speech, gesture, tonality, order, image, attitude or idea, identifying your way with his."[95] This argument from moral agency, coupled with a posture of dissent and a prophetic ethos, was critical to achieving a major goal of all social movements, which is to increase the size and scope of membership. In his essay on the second persona, Edwin Black argues that all discourse implies an auditor, that is "a model of what the rhetor would have his real auditor become."[96] In other words, every piece of discourse conveys a sense of the values, attitudes, and characteristics of an implied audience, or second persona. Black's interest was enabling a rhetorical critic's moral judgment of discourse on the basis of an implied audience. Within a social movement framework, the second persona refers to an identity or role that the rhetor invites potential followers to assume. The Bible was the cornerstone of Protestant belief. When interpreted from women's perspective, it offered a socially acceptable role for women as moral agents.

Building on Black's argument, Maurice Charland elucidates how rhetoric literally calls into being an audience with a history and motives that transcend individual interests.[97] His analysis of the case of the "Peuple Québécois" reveals how rhetorical discourse can create its own audience rather than simply appeal to an existing group. In other words, rather than being targeted at a preexistent group, discourse can call an audience into being, influencing its recipients to see themselves as part of a community that had not been previously perceived. He calls this process interpellation. Such constitutive rhetorics "have power because they are oriented towards action . . . not merely because they provide individuals with narratives to inhabit as subjects and motives to experience, but because they insert 'narrativized' subject-as-agents into the world."[98] When rhetors craft an appealing and comfortable identity, recipients are more inclined to accept a rhetor's argument and viewpoint.

Similarly, the texts analyzed in this volume construct an appealing identity or subject position that creates a space for individual women to see themselves as part of a larger community with shared concerns and a shared future. Charland explains that successful constitutive rhetorics, like the texts we examine here, "offer new subject positions that resolve, or at least contain, experienced contradictions."[99] In this case, Jarena Lee, Sarah Grimké, Lucretia Coffin Mott, and Frances Willard craft narratives that are supported by an argument from moral agency. Their narratives skillfully resolve the tensions between piety and domesticity so that new movement adherents can see themselves as both women with responsibilities to home and hearth and moral agents with Christian obligations to act in the public sphere. Indeed, the role of women that movement leaders discerned in scripture and called into being through their texts was not only acceptable, but compelling.

A feminist hermeneutic enabled women to argue from moral agency, to adopt a rhetoric of dissent, and to assume a prophetic ethos. In so doing, these women enacted the new version of empowered but still feminine womanhood as they crafted a compelling argument for their own and other women's empowerment. Their texts helped evolve a social movement to gain a more expansive role for women in religious circles and in American political life. They were not revolutionaries or radicals bent on destroying or drastically altering the status quo as their opponents sometimes claimed. Rather by carefully positioning themselves as restorers of God's divine plan, they enabled other women to see themselves as in the vanguard of Christian perfectionism. These strategies were, we believe, key to their gaining adherents and achieving, after much effort, woman suffrage, a critical step in women's advancement.

TWO

Jarena Lee's *Religious Experience and Journal*

A Nascent Feminist Hermeneutic

If a man may preach, because the Savior died for him,
why not the woman?

—JARENA LEE, *RELIGIOUS EXPERIENCE AND JOURNAL*

In 1844 when Jarena Lee applied for permission to publish an updated version of her autobiography, the members of the Book Concern of the African Methodist Episcopal Church (AME) denied her request.[1] The rejection was surprising and even painful because just one year earlier the AME General Conference honored her, recommending that the denomination publish the autobiography.[2] Still, this rejection reflected the repeated challenges Lee faced as a Black woman in her struggle to live into what she believed to be her divine call and even mandate to preach. As Anna Carter Florence observes: "Lee felt she had been publicly humiliated. Once again, to keep silent when her ministry was demeaned by those who had formerly welcomed (and benefited by) it was to deny the home she had made for herself through decades of constant travel. This time, however, Lee knew there was more than one way to preach this sermon. She took her expanded story to print, believing that "'the Lord gave his handmaiden the power to speak.'"[3]

Lee's *Religious Experience and Journal* was to have profound reverberations in the Methodist community and beyond. It "launched black women's autobiography in America with an argument for women's spiritual authority . . . [and] plainly challenged traditional female roles as defined in both the free and slave states, among whites as well as blacks."[4] In *All Bound Up Together: The Woman Question in African American Public Cultures, 1830–1900*, Martha S. Jones contends that Lee's *Religious Experience and Journal* "ignited a debate about the standing of women within the religious realm"

: 19 :

and her struggle "took on institutional significance as Methodists debated whether women should be granted licenses to preach."[5] Like the women to follow—Sarah Grimké, Lucretia Mott, and Frances Willard—Lee necessarily turned to scripture to develop a defense of her actions. With them, she found inspiration and warrant in the prophet Joel's prediction: "And it shall come to pass afterward, that I will pour out my spirit upon all flesh; and your sons and your daughters shall prophesy, your old men shall dream dreams, your young men shall see visions. And also upon the servants and the handmaids in those days will I pour out my Spirit."[6] Lee's *Religious Experience and Journal* is a sustained narrative argument to demonstrate that God had poured out his spirit on her and had indeed called her to preach.

The Life of Jarena Lee

Lee's early life, about which we know very little, gave no indication of her future direction.[7] She was born on February 11, 1783, in Cape May, New Jersey to parents who were free but impoverished. About her childhood she writes that her family was "wholly ignorant of the knowledge of God."[8] At seven, she was hired out as a maid, an arrangement one scholar calls "effectively, a legalized form of slavery."[9] By her own admission, she had no more than "three months of schooling."[10] Keenly aware of her lack of formal education, Lee writes in her published narrative: "Please pardon errors, and excuse all imperfections, as I have been deprived of the advantages of education (which I hope all will appreciate) as I am measurably a self-taught person."[11]

In 1804, having explored other denominations and after hearing Richard Allen preach, Lee affiliated with a community that would evolve into the AME.[12] Seven years later, after considerable spiritual struggle, she told Allen that she believed she was called to preach.[13] "As to women preaching," she recalls, "Allen said that our discipline knew nothing at all about it—that it did not call for women preachers."[14] In fact, in 1803 the Methodist Episcopal Church, of which Allen's congregation was still a part, had explicitly banned women preachers in its bid for respectability.[15]

When she returned to Philadelphia in 1818, a widow with two young children and few resources, Lee reminded Allen, recently ordained and now bishop of the newly created AME, of her calling. He gave her permission to hold prayer meetings and to exhort.[16] According to John H. Wigger: "Methodists drew a technical distinction between exhorting and preaching, local and itinerant preachers. In theory, exhorting consisted simply of telling one's testimony of conversion or relating real life experience in the faith, with the goal of imploring one's listeners toward greater holiness and fuller service. . . . Only licensed preachers were supposed to exercise the privilege of taking a text."[17] That distinction, however, was difficult to maintain in prayer meetings and other gatherings outside the church proper.

Lee spent the next fifteen years as an itinerant evangelist in the Mid-Atlantic, Northeast, and Canada, holding prayer meetings, exhorting, and, when invited, preaching. Buoyed by Allen's invitations to preach, she felt he endorsed her call and acknowledged her skills.[18] In fact, Allen never issued her a license to preach, but "he did however endorse her as a traveling exhorter," which "did not guarantee that Lee would be well received by clergymen she encountered on her travels" but may have "helped open church doors and attract larger audiences to hear her preach."[19] In an era of religious fervor in a newly formed denomination that prized evangelism, Lee believed her successes not only benefited the church but also proved her call.

The challenges Lee encountered and the growing debate surrounding women's preaching prompted her to publish her story. Her choice of a medium was shrewd. Penning a spiritual autobiography was a natural part of her life as a Methodist. Collins observes "the discipline of journal writing was central to the 'method' of individual spiritual growth in Methodism."[20] As Katherine Bassard explains, "By writing her *Journal,* however, Lee was being not only dutifully Christian, but dutifully *Methodist,*" because "John Wesley himself had published his journals, which spurred many American Methodists to begin writing spiritual journals."[21] In defending the publication of her *Journal,* Lee recounts that such effort "though much opposed . . . is certainly essential in life, as Mr. Wesley wisely observes."[22]

In 1836 at her own expense, Lee published 1,000 copies of a pamphlet, *The Life and Religious Experience of Jarena Lee, A Coloured Lady, Giving an Account of Her Call to Preach the Gospel,* and reprinted an additional 1,000 in 1839. In 1849, smarting from the AME Book Concern's refusal to print an updated, expanded version, she published, again at her own expense, *Religious Experience and Journal of Mrs. Jarena Lee: Giving an Account of Her Call to Preach the Gospel,* which she sold and distributed at meetings and religious gatherings.[23] One of the first people who purchased her book was Sarah Allen, Richard Allen's widow.[24]

Within the AME, Lee's path as an itinerant preacher was not smooth. As Carla Peterson notes, "conditions for women preachers in the AME deteriorated further after Allen's death" in 1831.[25] Nevertheless, Lee continued to serve as an itinerant preacher, attending and even speaking at the denomination's annual meetings and conferences.[26] Following the AME's strong commitment to abolitionism, she also attended an antislavery meeting in Buffalo in 1834 and in 1840 she joined the New York Anti-Slavery Society. In 1853 at age 70, with her fellow preacher Sojourner Truth, she spoke against colonization at the American Anti-Slavery Convention.[27]

Context and Influences

Lee's ministry emerged in the context of dynamic change both in American society and in religion embodied, in part, in the Second Great Awakening. Three factors in that context shaped her thinking and influenced her development: (1) Methodist theology; (2) the development of Wesleyan Methodism in the United States; and (3) the emergence of the AME itself.

Methodism and Jarena Lee's Spiritual Journey

Methodist theology informed Lee's understanding of her own spiritual journey and her certainty about her call to preach in at least three ways. First, John Wesley's concept of the "inward witness" or "a believer's personal experience of the presence of God" undergirded Lee's sense of her call.[28] In a letter he wrote about his father's death, Wesley recalls: "'The inward witness, son, the inward witness,' said he to me, 'that is the proof, the strongest proof, of Christianity.'"[29] His father's testimony about "the inward witness" and his own life, including the strange warming of his heart at a Moravian gathering at Aldersgate in London, convinced him that lived experience was an important element in spiritual discernment. Thus, his theological perspective emphasized four pillars of religious authority: scripture, tradition, reason, and experience.[30] Although all four elements helped believers work out their faith, Wesley privileged experience, believing that all truth, including the word of God, should be tested by one's own experience. Like the Quaker notion of the inner light, this theological principle emphasizes the primacy of an individual's perception and experiences in the process of spiritual discernment.

Second, Wesley evolved a notion of the spiritual life as an ongoing process through predictable stages. While at Oxford, Wesley embraced the concept of "holy living as a lifelong quest."[31] In time, he outlined an "Order of Salvation" that began with a sense of conviction when one recognized that all people were sinful and acknowledged one's own sinfulness. With acceptance of one's brokenness and God's grace, a person could experience "justification," the state of being restored to a right relationship with God. Finally, empowered by this process, a faithful believer could begin "sanctification," a lifelong quest for Christian perfection.[32] By studying scripture, relying on reason, and (most of all) attending to experience, an individual could move from conviction to sanctification.

Sanctification was not only an end goal in one's spiritual life, but it also "resulted in personal inward and outward purity as well as the desire to grow in Christian maturity and love. Another consequence of sanctification was power . . . the empowerment of the Holy Spirit . . . [which] enabled Wesleyan/Holiness women to possess a self that successfully countered the weak, dependent self that society sought to impose on them."[33] For three early African American women autobiographers, including Lee, Andrews observed: "The experience of sanctification liberated [them] . . . from the sense of personal inadequacy that their perception of their own sinfulness had place on them. Belief in the Wesleyan version of sanctification freed them to trust the promptings of their innermost selves because of their conviction that what came from within was of the Holy Spirit, not the corrupt ego."[34]

An emphasis on an individual's moving through this Order of Salvation stimulated personal narratives in which individuals shared stories of their own progress toward sanctification. Ann Taves explains that Wesley encouraged sharing narratives at "experience" meetings because they "provided occasion for recounting (or witnessing to) one's experience and thus provided models of authentic experiences for others."[35] Spiritual autobiographies were another way to trace progress through the Order of Salvation. Because sanctification brought not only a "new birth" but also "an increased sense of power to a Christian," spiritual narratives could convey one's "realization of one's true place and destiny in the divine scheme of things."[36]

Third, in contrast to Anglicanism, Methodism emphasized evangelism. Methodists, including women, "learned from the Wesleys that authentic Christianity is mission, and sincere engagement in God's mission is true religion. Evangelism was the heart of this missionary vision, fueled by the desire to share the good news they had experienced in Christ with others in both word and deed."[37] Spreading the good news by vigorous evangelism was an integral part of Methodist life. The Second Great Awakening intensified this impetus.

In its early days, Methodist evangelism depended not only "on Wesley's own energetic itinerant preaching" but also "on the preaching of nonordained itinerant clergy who attracted the curious and the faithful to spirit-filled gatherings."[38] As Chilcote writes: "It was ordinary people in community rather than the high-profile leader, who exerted the most influence both inside and outside the movement as they attempted to put their faith into practice in the daily round of life."[39] Reluctant at first to embrace lay preachers because that practice was at odds with Anglicanism, Wesley soon became a staunch defender because their efforts were often quite successful.[40]

Such an evangelical emphasis had significant ramifications for women.[41] In his "Sermon on the Sick," Wesley expresses his sense of the equality of women in the eyes of God: "You, like them, were made in the image of God; . . . you too are called of God, as you have time, to 'do good unto all men.'"[42] In 1771 Mary Bosanquet wrote Wesley to answer objections to her activities: "I do not believe every woman is called to speak publicly, no more than every man to be a Methodist preacher, yet some have an extraordinary call to it, and woe be to them if they obey it not."[43] In his response, Wesley adopted her notion of an "extraordinary call" and admitted that women could be authorized as lay preachers, noting that even St. Paul made allowances for female lay preachers.[44] Although Wesley "never permitted women's preaching to become a general practice," he did increasingly admit that some women could be divinely called to preach.[45]

In sum, Methodism's evangelistic spirit, the denomination's emphasis on an individual's spiritual journey, and Wesley's support for women's extraordinary call all contributed to an environment where women like Lee could explore roles within the Church. This context undoubtedly influenced Lee's decision to write an autobiographical narrative that both testified to her spiritual journey, highlighting her successes, and aimed to shape the AME's views on women.

The Development of Wesleyanism in the United States

The development of Wesleyanism in the United States also influenced Lee's thinking. Initially, Wesley envisioned the Methodist movement as a renewal effort within the Church of England. In 1763 in their first *Discipline,* a guide to their principles and practices, the fourth question in a catechism they developed asked: "What may we reasonably believe to be God's design, in raising up preachers called *Methodists*?" The answer was clear: "To reform the Nation, particularly the Church; and to spread scripture holiness over the land."[46] To facilitate these goals Wesley deployed lay leaders to guide small groups. When they proved successful, he expanded their charge to include preaching.[47]

As interest in Methodism grew in North America, lay leaders there pleaded for ordained clergy to help with their work. Wesley tried to persuade the Bishop of London, the Anglican prelate in charge of North America, to ordain men to serve there.[48] When the Bishop refused, Wesley took matters into his own hands, ordaining men and sending them "to implement the transition of a reform movement into a church. By his several acts and literary conveyances, he created, in effect, a new 'Methodist' Anglicanism in the new nation."[49]

The American Revolution opened an opportunity for Wesley to guide the creation of a new, independent denomination, free from the oversight of the Church of England and the government. In September 1784, Wesley wrote to some Methodist leaders: "As our *American* Brethren are now totally disentangled from both the State, and from the *English Hierarchy,* we dare not entangle them again, either one with the other. They are now at full liberty, simply to follow the Scriptures and the Primitive Church. And we judge it best that they should stand fast in that Liberty, wherewith God has so strangely made them free."[50] Encouraged by Wesley and sensing a need to organize themselves, in December 1784, American Methodists met in the so-called "Christmas Conference" in Baltimore to establish their denominational identity. They officially founded the Methodist Episcopal Church.

The egalitarianism growing from the American Revolution reverberated within the Methodism in the United States and led it further away from its Anglican roots. "Methodism emphasized class meetings (with rigorous attention paid to biblical texts rather than ministers' erudition), camp revivals (where congregants visually displayed the power of God's saving grace), and expansive preaching circuits (which extended deep into the North American countryside)."[51] In his history of the African Methodist Episcopal Church, Dennis C. Dickerson contends that "egalitarian tendencies were deeply anchored in Methodist evangelism in British North America. The revivals and camp meetings, which regularly attracted large crowds, provided equal access to all."[52] The frequently lay-led meetings, where both White and Black men could preach, "linked authenticity to observable 'fruits' rather than nuanced philosophical distinctions."[53]

During the Second Great Awakening, the Methodist Church was the most successful denomination at attracting and converting people. Compared to other denominations, the growth of Methodists was "off the chart in a class all of their own." Methodism quickly became "the most pervasive form of Christianity in the United States."[54] Hatch notes that "Methodism in America grew at a rate that terrified other more established denominations. By 1820 Methodism membership numbered a quarter million; by 1830 it was twice that number."[55] In large part, Methodism's success in North America stemmed from Wesley's decidedly unorthodox approach in

England, including his empowerment of lay leaders and encouragement of itinerant preaching. In a burgeoning denomination, women, including Lee, discovered leadership opportunities within the Church in roles like exhorting and itinerant preaching.

The Emergence of the African Methodist Episcopal Church

A third influence on Lee was her relationship with Richard Allen, the founder and first bishop of the AME. Allen converted to Methodism while still a slave after hearing an itinerant preacher. Indeed, his Methodism became the venue for his arranging to purchase his freedom. Proving himself a model slave, he prevailed on his master to invite a Methodist evangelist to visit his home. Deeply affected by the experience, the master signed an agreement to allow Allen to gradually purchase his freedom.[56]

Once he was free, Allen became an itinerant preacher. Over time he became a well-known figure at camp meetings and other venues. He also became fast friends with Francis Asbury, an ordained Anglican clergyman, whom Wesley sent to North America to nurture Methodism.[57] After the Christmas Conference, which he attended, Allen "decided that someone must convert blacks into a powerful Afro-Christian community."[58]

Fortuitously, in February 1786 Allen was invited to return to his hometown, Philadelphia, to preach to Black members at St. George's Church. He reported: "I soon saw a large field open in seeking and instructing my African brethren."[59] As Richard S. Newman reports, Allen preached as often as he could, "wherever I could find an opening." Believing "the freed blacks needed religious guidance to navigate through the rough waters of freedom in late-eighteenth-century Philadelphia," he "also created prayer meetings for black congregants. Although they were compelled to meet at 5 a.m., his small flock grew. His diligence and dedication paid off. Within a year of coming to Philadelphia, he had built 'a society of forty-two [Black] members.'"[60]

During this period, he and Absalom Jones, who had also been involved in the Free African Society, a benevolent self-help group, and who also attended St. George's, began to raise money to build a free-standing church for African Americans.[61] Then, sometime in the 1790s, an incident at St. George's compelled them to act. In a reversal of practice, White elders insisted that Black members, who had mingled freely in the congregation, must sit in a segregated balcony. In Allen's report, elders pulled Jones from where he was kneeling to move him into the segregated area. When the prayer was finished, Allen, Jones, and all the Black members rose as one and left the church.[62] Allen wrote of the event: "Here was the beginning and rise of the first African church in America."[63]

Resisting pressure from the White community, Allen and others persisted. They rented a space and began to meet. In March 1793 they broke ground for an African church that was to become St. Thomas's African Episcopal Church. However, Allen and Jones disagreed over the appropriate affiliation for the new congregation, with Allen preferring the Methodist Church and Jones the newly formed Episcopal Church, in which he became the first African American priest.

In 1794, Allen and his Methodist-leaning followers moved a blacksmith's shop to a plot they had purchased. That shop became Bethel Church. On July 29, Asbury came to the dedication in a show of support.[64] From its inception, Allen limited membership to "descendants of the African race" and declared that the majority of members could "call any brother that appears to us adequate to the task to preach or exhort as a local preacher, without the interference of the Conference or any person or persons whatsoever."[65] This full independence proved more difficult to achieve than simply to declare.

Finally, in 1815, after years of legal wrangling, White Methodists wrested control of Bethel and summarily put the church on the auction block in a sheriff's sale. Allen and his followers, who had been amassing funds over the years, purchased the property, much to the surprise of their opponents.[66] In April 1816, Allen and his sympathizers met at Bethel to form the AME as an independent denomination. Allen was elected bishop, with his long-time friend and now Episcopal clergyman Absalom Jones as one of those who laid hands on him in the ordination.[67]

Allen and other members of the AME retained the key tenets of their Methodist roots. At the same time, Allen shared Wesley's ambivalent sentiments about women preaching. Earlier in 1803, when Dorothy Ripley approached him about preaching, at that point himself un-ordained and struggling for some independence from the White Methodists, he denied her request.[68] Lee's first approach to him in 1811 came as he, still challenging control by Whites, probably had little appetite for an additional bone of contention. Later, when he had achieved his long-sought independence and had established the AME, Allen valued Lee's demonstrated effectiveness as an asset in efforts to grow his fledging denomination. His support was critical to Lee's success as an exhorter and probably emboldened her to seek the right to preach.

Autobiographical Narrative as Argument

The inward witness . . . Is the strongest proof of Christianity.

—JOHN WESLEY, *LETTERS*

A typical spiritual autobiography, Lee's work is also a complex text that both defends her itinerant preaching and offers a prophetic evangelistic witness. As Donna Giver-Johnston observes, Lee's autobiography is "a work of theological interpretation, rhetorical strategy, agency claim, and narrative construction" that challenges "the prevailing interpretation of the call to preach."[69] Her *Religious Experience and Journal* uses a feminist hermeneutic to make a four-pronged argument.

First, through implicit and explicit biblical exegesis, she proves that God does, indeed, call some women as preachers. This is an essential starting point for her argument because it establishes an unassailable divine precedent for women's preaching. Second, after first tracing her progress through the Order of Salvation, her narrative limns her call story, implicitly linking it to the biblical pattern of God's calling and empowering of prophets. This ordering is critical—achieving sanctification and then discerning call—because in Wesleyan theology sanctification brought with it the ability to identify and enact God's will from one's life. Third, drawing on Matthew's notion that true prophets are known by the fruits they produce, Lee insists that her successes affirm her divinely sanctioned call.[70] Finally, Lee's narrative implicitly depicts her as an evangelical preacher, displaying all the talents and skills requisite to that role. In essence, Lee asserts boldly and confidently that God, not ecclesial authority, is the source of her call to preach and then, through enactment displays her skills.

God's Call to Women to Preach

To make her case, Lee strategically chooses Acts 2:17 as the epigraph for the narrative: "And it shall come to pass . . . that I will pour out my spirit upon all flesh; your sons, and your *daughters* shall prophecy"[71] Here Peter, defending the disciples, men and women, who are speaking in tongues on the day of Pentecost, quotes Joel 2:28. In Joel, these lines culminate a typical prophetic paradigm of excoriating the Israelites for their failings before reassuring them of Yahweh's ultimate reconciliation. After his stern denunciation of lapses of the Israelites, Joel describes the coming of the "Day of the Lord," a time of restoration and renewal. Adapting Joel, Peter is implicitly suggesting that Jesus's ministry and the descent of the Holy Spirit are the coming of the "Day of the Lord" that the prophet envisions.[72] In using Acts as her epigraph, Lee suggests that the present moment is a time of divine restoration and that she is one of the "daughters" called to prophesy to enable God's restorative efforts. God has sent the spirit on her as on the disciples at Pentecost. She, like them, is empowered to preach the good news to all people.

Convinced by a vivid vision of God's commanding her to preach, she seeks biblical evidence that God has empowered past women to fill that role. She finds a compelling example in the story of Mary Magdalene in John 20:17–18. There Jesus encounters Mary alone in the Garden of Gethsemane on the morning of the resurrection. When she does not recognize his changed appearance, he calls her by name. Then he charges her: "Do not hold on to me, for I have not yet ascended to the Father. Go instead to my brothers and tell them, 'I am ascending to my Father and your Father, to my God and your God.' Mary Magdalene went to the disciples with the news: 'I have seen the Lord!' And she told them that he had said these things to her."

Theologians have long recognized the significance of this passage. By proclaiming the good news of the resurrection to the others, medieval theologian Thomas Aquinas contends, Mary became an apostle: "she had the office of an apostle; indeed, she was an apostle to the apostles insofar as it was her task to announce our Lord's resurrection to the disciples. Thus, just as it was a woman who was the first to announce the words of death, so it was a woman who would be the first to announce the words of life."[73] Bart Ehrman, a distinguished biblical historian, labels her "the original apostle" and credits her with founding Christianity: "Technically speaking, Christianity could not begin until someone proclaimed Jesus raised from the dead. It appears that Mary Magdalene was the first to do so. If so, Mary . . . really is the one who started Christianity."[74]

In an artful exegesis, Lee argues that Mary's testimony was, in truth, preaching:

> Did not Mary *first* preach the risen Saviour, and is not the doctrine of the resurrection the very climax of Christianity—hangs not all our hope on this, as argued by St. Paul? Then did not Mary, a woman, preach the gospel? For she preached the resurrection of the crucified Son of God.
>
> But some will say, that Mary did not expound the Scripture, therefore, she did not preach, in the proper sense of the term. To this I reply, it may be that the term *preach* in those primitive times, did not mean exactly what it is now *made* to mean; perhaps it was a great deal more

simple then, than it is now—if it were not, the unlearned fishermen could not have preached the gospel at all, as they had no learning.

To this it may be replied, by those who are determined not to believe that it is right for a woman to preach, that the disciples, though they were fishermen, and ignorant of letters too, were inspired, yet that inspiration did not save them for showing their ignorance of letters, and of man's wisdom; this the multitude soon found out, by listening to the remarks of the envious Jewish priests. If then, to preach the gospel, by the gift of heaven, comes by inspiration solely, is God straitened; must he take the man exclusively? May he not, did he not, and can he not inspire a female to preach the simple story of the birth, life, death, and resurrection of our Lord, and accompany it too, with power to the sinner's heart.[75]

Clearly, then, Lee argues that the inspiration and empowerment to preach come not from ecclesial approval but rather from God. As she declares, "If the man may preach, because the Savior died for him, why not the woman?"[76] Unlike the other women in this volume, she is not concerned with women's rights in general or with women's roles as public advocates. Her focus is solely on proving God's empowerment of some women to preach. As a result, Lee does not, as other women in this volume will do, delve deeply into biblical exegesis to discover other examples of women empowered by God or to contest problematic passages. With a sharply focused feminist hermeneutic, she finds a key example of God's choice and empowerment of a particular woman to be an evangelist. The case of Mary Magdalene and her choice of Joel 2:28 ("your sons, and your *daughters* shall prophecy"[77]) are sufficient to prove her case.

The Rocky Path through the Order of Salvation

In writing her autobiography, Lee intended to demonstrate "how the Lord called me to his work, and how he has kept me from falling from grace, as I feared I should."[78] With the backdrop of Mary Magdalene as irrefutable proof that with God all things are possible and that God does empower some women to preach, her narrative first traces her progress through the Order of Salvation. For an AME audience, spiritual maturity, as evidenced by progress through the Order of Salvation, was a prerequisite for a legitimate call.

Her earliest sense of conviction, the first step in spiritual maturation, came at age seven when, as a maid, she lied to the lady of the house. The spirit of God "told me I was a wretched sinner."[79] Her sense of guilt was so strong that "I promised in my heart that I would not tell another lie."[80] Despite her failures, "the spirit of the Lord never forsook me, but continued mercifully striving in me, until his gracious power converted my soul."[81] This striving comes to fruition in 1804, when she hears a Presbyterian missionary preach. The reading of the psalms stirs her soul. She sums up her feelings with a verse from a hymn by Isaac Watts based on Psalm 51: "Lord, I am vile, conceived in sin; Born unholy and unclean. Sprung from man, whose guilty fall Corrupts the race, and taints us all. As she recalls these words, Lee notes that recognizing her dire condition "made me to feel in some measure, the weight of my sins, and sinful nature."[82] However, with no idea how to improve her situation, she "was driven of Satan, in the course of a few days, and tempted to destroy myself."[83] But "the unseen arm of God . . . saved me from self-murder."[84]

Having tried other denominations, she is drawn by Allen's preaching and finds her spiritual home in the AME. When he invites those "who felt a desire to flee the wrath to come, to unite on trial with them," Lee recalls "I embraced the opportunity."[85] Just three weeks later her soul "was gloriously converted to God." A verse from Acts 8:21—"I perceive thy heart is not right in the sight of God"[86]—produces her strong sense of conversion and justification. Her depiction of her reaction to this verse is, again, vivid and deeply emotional. "That day was the first when my heart believed, and my tongue had made confession unto salvation. . . . For a few moments I had power to exhort sinners, and to tell the wonders of the goodness of him who clothes me with his salvation. During this, the minister was silent, until my soul felt its duty had been performed, when he declared another witness of the power of Christ to forgive sins on earth, was manifest in my conversion."[87] Notably, at the moment of her conversion, she is moved to exhort, offering her testimony of God's actions in her life to her hearers. The attention she generated and the minister's spontaneous endorsement affirmed her call.

For three months, her experience of conversion gives her a sense of peace. At that point, a man named William Scott visits Lee and asks if she has experienced justification, the state of being forgiven of her sins. When she agrees that she has, he asks her about sanctification. Finding her ignorant of that, he instructs her in the order of salvation, which immediately appeals to her. In the following months, "by the increasing light of the spirit," she senses that "pride, anger, self-will, with many evils" continue to lurk in her soul and she begins to fear she's been deceived in her sense of justification. After retiring to a "secret place" for intense prayer, she hears a voice whispering "Pray for sanctification."[88] Retreating to pray for sanctification, she hears a spirit voice saying, "*Thou art sanctified!*" as she stands with hands outstretched and face gazing toward Heaven.[89]

For Lee, moving toward spiritual maturity in sanctification is a traumatic process. At every stage, her descriptions of her spiritual anguish and her times of despair are poignant. Her visions, internal voices, and emotional turmoil mark her journey as deeply personal and profoundly challenging. At the same time, her depictions help establish both her ethos and the legitimacy of her call.

Discerning God's Call

Significantly, her depiction of her process toward sanctification precedes her discussion of her call to preach. Through sanctification, as Anderson explains, women like Lee "believed that they had recovered their true, pristine identity in Christ. It was their religious duty, therefore, to be faithful to that renewed and purified self. If this meant challenging, even disobeying ecclesiastical or social authorities, then these women were prepared to do so." At the same time, "they felt obligated to cite from the Bible some precedent or verse that would authorize their convention-shattering views or behaviors."[90] Of course, Lee has used a version of Joel's pronouncement as the epithet for her entire narrative. The bulk of her narrative unfolds her call story in chapters titled: "My Call to Preach the Gospel," "My Marriage," "The Subject of My Call to Preach Renewed," "The Vineyard of the Lord Before the Laborer Dies." Clearly, her call, not the details of her personal life, are the focus of her narrative.

Her narrative follows the pattern laid out in Hebrew scripture when Yahweh calls leaders and prophets for the Israelites. First, a divine call interrupts a life. Moses, for example, is a shepherd for his father-in-law in Moab when he encounters the burning bush.[91] Second, those called are always hesitant to agree. Moses, who fled to Moab to escape punishment for killing an Egyptian soldier who was beating an Israelite, responds to Yahweh's instructions to demand the release of the Israelites: "Who am I that I should go to Pharaoh and bring the Israelites out of Egypt?"[92] Third, without exception, those called plead their inadequacy for the task. Moses insists he is "slow of speech and tongue."[93] In response, Yahweh assures those called that they will not be alone. Yahweh tells Moses: "I will be with your mouth and teach you what to speak."[94]

Lee's narrative follows a similar pattern with God calling her throughout her lifetime, her resisting, and then receiving affirmation of her calling.

After several years, she reports: "But to my utter surprise there seemed to sound a voice which I thought I distinctly heard, and most certainly understood, which said to me, "Go preach the Gospel!" I immediately replied aloud, 'No one will believe me.' Again I listened, and again the same voice seemed to say 'Preach the Gospel; I will put words in your mouth, and will turn your enemies to become your friends.'"[95]

Even this brief passage reveals the key features of the calls found in scripture: a summons that surprises the recipient, self-doubt and initial hesitancy to accept the responsibility, and a promise by God to aid the reluctant chosen one. Significantly, her description of her call is replete with biblical allusions. At one point, Lee explicitly likens herself to Jonah, who fled when the Lord called him to go to Nineveh. She confessed that she "lingered like him [Jonah], and had lingered to go at the bidding of the Lord, and warn those who are as deeply guilty as were the people of Ninevah [sic]."[96] When she expresses her fears that no one will believe if she preaches, she hears the voice in her head assuring that God will provide guidance.[97] This echoes God's response to Jeremiah when he expressed trepidation over receiving God's call: "Then the LORD put forth his hand, and touched my mouth. And the LORD said unto me, Behold, I have put my words in thy mouth."[98]

Lee spends considerable time discussing her reluctance and resistance to accepting God's call to preach. Imagining that her sense of call is a trick of Satan, she goes into private to pray "to know if he had called me to preach, and whether I was deceived or not; when there appeared to my view the form and figure of a pulpit with a Bible laying thereon." During the following evening, she dreams with such force that she is preaching from a text that she is awakened by the sound of her own voice. This dream and call then propel her to speak with Allen about pursuing God's plan for her. She apparently tells him, again in a form typical of the divine call, that "the Lord had revealed it to me, that I must preach the gospel."[99]

In her study of Lee's autobiographies, Carla Peterson carefully charts how Lee weaves in the "traditional Christian iconography of the New Testament" into her narrative.[100] Her skill at weaving these allusions into her narrative suggests her deep familiarity with scripture, which also enhances her credibility. "By anchoring her narrative in scriptural precedent, she tried to weave her personal story into the fabric of sacred history, grafting her life onto the Bible."[101] In short, Lee positions herself as one of the prophets Joel foretold.

As do many women in what Stanley terms the Wesleyan/Holiness tradition, Lee elides the details of her personal life to focus intentionally on her ministry.[102] This omission also permits her to focus on how God used her as a vehicle for spreading the Word. Her candid personal story will, she hopes, be instructive to others. Offering her story to help and inspire others is solidly in the Methodist tradition of evangelism: all Christians should work to spread the Good News.

Bringing Forth Good Fruits

If her emotional and vivid narrative suggests the authenticity of her call, her successes affirm its validity. Her years of work have provided her with an arsenal of examples of her success. Her third strategy, then, is an implicit argument that the success of her work proves her call. In so doing, Lee strategically draws on Matthew 7:12–20, a portion of the Sermon on the Mount, a widely known text: "Beware of false prophets, who come to you in sheep's clothing but inwardly are ravenous wolves. You will know them by their fruits. Are grapes gathered from thorns, or figs from thistles? In the same way, every good tree bears good fruit, but the bad tree bears bad fruit. A good tree cannot bear bad fruit, nor can a bad tree bear good fruit. Every tree that does not bear good fruit is cut down and thrown into the fire. Thus you will know them by their fruits." Knowing that her audience would be familiar with this passage, she refers to it obliquely, but it is crucial to her argument. Because she converts many, her effective preaching must be a good thing. Lee avers: "As for me, I am fully persuaded that the Lord called me to labour according to what I have received, in his vineyard. If he has not, how could he consistently bear testimony in favour of my poor labours, in awakening and converting sinners?"[103] In discussing the evidence that one might have a call to preach, Allen himself lists "fruits" as a critical criterion: "Have they fruit? Are any truly convinced of sin and converted to God by their preaching?"[104] In essence, then, two sources important to her readers, scripture and Allen, affirm the standard she offers to judge her efforts and her call.

Notably, one of her first fruits was Allen himself. The details of that event are significant. In 1817, Lee attends a Sunday service at Bethel Church, where the Reverend Richard Williams is preaching on a portion of Jonah 2:9: "Salvation is of the LORD." She reports: "But as he proceeded to explain, he seemed to have lost the spirit. I sprang, as by an altogether supernatural impulse, to my feet, when I was aided from above to give an exhortation on the very text which my brother Williams had taken. . . . During the exhortation, God made manifest his power in a matter sufficient to show the world that I was called to labour according to my ability, and the race given unto me, the vineyard of a good husbandman."[105] Observing this, Allen "rose up in the assembly and related that I had called upon him eight years before. . . . and that he had put me off; but that he now as much believed that I was called to that work, as any of the preachers present."[106] Strengthened by these remarks, she experienced serenity and "a holy joy of a peculiar kind, untasted in my bosom until then."[107]

As her efforts continue, she chronicles her successes. She tells of doctors, lawyers, church elders, an "aged slave holder who . . . walked about three miles to hear me," unbelievers, American Indians, people who are "averse to a woman's preaching," people from different denominations, all of whom are deeply moved by her preaching.[108] Some convert to Christ, others overcome prejudices, and still others acknowledge that her spiritual gifts are equal to male preachers. At the end of this recital, she reports returning to Cape May after ten years and meeting a "white lady of the first distinction, a member of the Methodist society" who told her "at the same school house, ten years before, under my preaching, the Lord first awakened her." This was, Lee adds, "bread cast on the waters, seen after many days."[109] Her success proves she is bearing "good fruit" and validates her call.

In the much fuller list of her activities in her 1849 *Religious Experience and Journal,* she observes at one point: "I have travelled, in four years, sixteen hundred miles and of that I walked two hundred and eleven miles, and preached the kingdom of God to the falling sons and daughters of Adam, counting it all joy for the sake of Jesus. Many times cast down but not forsaken; willing to suffer as well as love."[110] In her accounts, Lee not only details her successes but also reveals her unrelenting ardor for the work she feels called to do. At one point, she observes: "In Philadelphia, N. York, Baltimore, and all the principal cities, from 100 to 1000 miles distant, as I travelled under the reign of the first Bishop Rt. Rev. Richard Allen, I have been instrumental in the hands of God of gaining many hundreds of dollars for the connexion, by raising societies where there never had been any, since which time they have grown to such a mass as to build large churches, and that in different places, and likewise have spent hundreds, but don't regret it, as I was about the work of Him that sent me, for which my reward is promised if I but hold out faithful."[111] Her sacrifices are unimportant to her because she has persisted in following her divine mandate to spread the Gospel.

This expanded version with its extensive list of her travels and successes makes her work implicitly prophetic. As the church hierarchy dithers and debates whether to allow women to preach, Lee's track record serves as an indictment of the opposition. Both the founder of the AME and scripture established a criterion for "true" prophets; her efforts fulfill that. By implication, the opposition is benighted, refusing to perceive the work of the Holy Spirit in their midst. Like Joel had done, she is pointing out the sins of the church leadership in ignoring and even thwarting her, and other women's, evangelistic successes.

The Evangelistic Preacher

Finally, Lee's narrative, structured in sermonic form, allows her to adopt the persona of a preacher. In 1819, in *The Doctrines and Disciplines of the African Methodist Episcopal Church,* Allen and Tapisco specify that morning, afternoon and evening services should include singing, prayers, the reading of scripture, and preaching.[112] They are quite clear that the minister's two primary responsibilities in these services are to choose an appropriate text to explicate in a sermon and to select suitable hymns to complement the message. With great skill, through her narrative, Lee delivers a "spiritually convincing" sermon, replete with hymns as she enacts the role of an evangelical preacher, called by God.

First, the overall structure of Lee's *Religious Experience and Journal* reflects the sermonic pattern typical of the AME practice of choosing a text to expound on. Framing her narrative with Joel's declaration that "your sons, and your daughters shall prophesy," she unfolds her life story as a homiletical gloss on that passage.

Arguing that the 1836 *Life and Religious Experience* was "an excerpt from the Journal," Bassard concludes that the earlier work is, in a sense, "a text within a text" that "figures the writing and publication of the earlier narrative as an *event* with the narrative line of the second."[113] The *Religious Experience and Journal* "chronicles an exhausting list of dates, times, locations, audiences, and scriptural texts" interspersed with brief transitions that focus on her movement from place to place.[114] Taken together, then, "the narrative line centers on Lee's 'call' from God, for which both her bold itinerant ministry and her text(s) serve as a response."[115] At every turn, Lee highlights her successes as a minister in bringing new souls to God. In tandem, the two texts are a demonstration of her initial epigraph: she is, indeed, a daughter called to preach. Thus, together, the first and the expanded version preach a sermon that supports and elucidates the epigraph from Joel.

Within the narrative, she also adopts the sermonic pattern of taking a text and offering exposition of it to interpret the individual events of her life. For example, early on, having described how some divine power saved her from self-harm, she turns to Isaiah 65:1–2: "I am sought of them that asked not for me; I am found of them that sought me not."[116] Reflecting on her experience of justification, she quotes Psalm 103:12: "God had separated my sins from me, as far as the east from the west."[117] In depicting her experiences, Lee draws on scripture to interpret or explain events much as a sermon would do. Individual episodes in her life, viewed through the lens of scriptural passages become, in effect, sermons in miniature.

Second, Lee also interweaves hymns into her narrative just as an evangelical preacher would intersperse them in a service. In the 1829 instructions about conducting services, Allen and Tapisco dictated that only a minister should give out the words of a hymn deemed "proper for the congregation," which should be familiar and singable to encourage all members to sing.[118] Focusing on the function of hymns in Lee's work, Minifee argues that "her strategic inclusion of hymns catered to specific experiences during her spiritual journey reveals another skill that corroborates her ministerial qualifications,—choosing the 'right' hymns for the right occasions."[119] Lee proves herself expert at this task.

Her narrative is replete with verses from hymns familiar to her readers that drive home a point she is making. Early on, when she obsesses with thoughts of suicide, something holds her back. Reflecting on this experience, she writes "how appropriately can I sing:

> Jesus sought me, when a stranger,
> Wandering from the fold of God;
> He to rescue me from danger,
> Interposed his precious blood."[120]

A few paragraphs later, she recalls "the latter part of my state of conviction," finding "the beautiful words of the poet" fit her situation perfectly:

> The more I strove against its power,
> I felt its weight and guilt the more;
> Till late I hear'd my Saviour say,
> Come hither soul, I am the way.[121]

Throughout her works, Lee offers bits of hymns to catch the spirit of her situation, much as congregational singing might reinforce and highlight the readings and the sermon in a church service. Bassard argues that her inclusion of hymns enabled her "to tell a complex and multifaceted life story succinctly."[122]

Minifee also suggests that Lee's "excerpts of the nineteenth century's most popular hymns create an aural ambience reminiscent of a worship service that engages her Christian readers' pathos and sense of piety in order to disengage their prejudice against her race and gender."[123] By including hymns familiar to both Black and White Christians, she is "conjuring the corp-aural communion of a multiracial congregation worshipping together."[124]

Much as a preacher might conclude a service with a suitable hymn, at the end of her *Religious Experience and Journal,* Lee draws her story to a close by highlighting her persistent faithfulness in continuing to live into her call. Referring to her "impaired" health, she then quotes a hymn, written by Thomas Olivers, another Methodist itinerant preacher who served as Wesley's assistant:

> Though Nature's strength decay,
> And earth and hell withstand-To Canaans land
> I'll urge my way,
> At HIS Divine command.[125]

Her practice of offering texts on which she expounds and her insertion of appropriate hymns, echoing a sermon within a service, would have been familiar both to the audiences to whom she spoke and to her readers. This "sermonizing" connects her to the African American faith community that was her primary audience and gives her voice "persuasive force."[126] This skillful and adept spiritual autobiography, which functions as sermon, not only proves the legitimacy of her call, but also reveals her skill in the very role she longs to fill.

If her record of success is not sufficient to convince her readers, her enactment of the role makes her gift in preaching clear. Through her narrative, she unequivocally demonstrates her skill in being the preacher she is called to be. She can and does take a text to expound on it. And that is the work of an AME preacher.

Enjoining the Debate

There is neither Jew nor Greek, there is neither bond nor free, there is neither male nor female: for ye are all one in Christ Jesus.

—GALATIANS 3:28

Like other spiritual autobiographers in the Methodist tradition, Lee intended her *Religious Experience and Journal* to inspire and enlighten others. Brekus notes: "She became an autobiographer out of a conviction that the record of God's work in and through her would help lead others to

Christ."[127] Her *Religious Experience and Journal* was, then, an extension of her evangelistic efforts. As she writes near the conclusion: "I hope the contents of this work may be instrumental in leaving a lasting impression on the minds of the impenitent; may it prove to be encouraging to the justified soul, and a comfort to the sanctified."[128]

On another level, however, Lee's narrative was a catalyst for and participant in ongoing conversations within the AME about the licensing of women to preach. As Giver-Johnston observes: "Jarena Lee wrote and published her autobiography as an interruption to the dominant narrative that denied women their call to preach with ecclesial authority. . . . Her narrative described a private experience; and yet, her rhetoric was intended for a public audience."[129] She very much hoped not only to inspire and encourage other women, but also to influence male decision makers.

The timing of Lee's decision to publish her expanded version makes this clear. Lee published the first iteration of her autobiography in 1836 and a revision in 1839. In 1844 Lee applied for formal permission to publish the updated version of her autobiography. Although the Book Concern of the AME asserted it was "written in such a manner that it is impossible to decipher much of the meaning contained in it," their assessment rings hollow.[130] In fact, Lee's autobiography was an unambiguous and resounding call for women's divine right to preach and a bold contradiction of the AME's growing rejection of women preaching. That same year, Nathan Ward, "an ordained clergyman at the AME General Conference in Boston formally presented a petition requesting that women be allowed to preach."[131] Julia Foote, who was in her early 20s, attended that conference. She recalled: "The Conference was so incensed at the brother who offered the petition that they threatened to take action against him."[132] This petition failed.

During this time, David Payne, who would eventually become the third bishop of the AME Church, joined the Bethel AME church and quickly became a powerful voice in the denomination's discussion over women's appropriate roles, including preaching, and over the proper preparation of ministers. Both issues had significant implications for Lee and other itinerant preachers. Apparently, perhaps in an effort to gain legitimacy, Payne embraced the Cult of True Womanhood, or what Jean Miller Schmidt terms the "true Methodist woman," extolling the virtues of women who recognized their place in the home as mothers and domestic educators.[133] As Newman reports, Payne "published several treatises on free black women's domestic roles. His ideas resonated in broader debates over women's place in American culture. Black women, the powerful Payne declared, must become guardians of the home, domestic educators of black youth, and matriarchs of respectability. This would not only help uplift the race on its own merits but appeal to respectable whites as well."[134] In addition, in 1842, Payne introduced a resolution at the Philadelphia and the Baltimore Conferences to require formal education of clergy including exhorters. Shortly thereafter, Payne wrote several letters to the *African Methodist Episcopal Church Magazine* "in which he called upon the General Conference of 1844 to act decisively to upgrade educational standards for the AME ministry."[135] David Wills argues that "Payne's campaign for a learned clergy inevitably impeded the efforts of Jarena Lee—and lesser-known figures as well—fully to legitimate on a charismatic basis the ministry of women in the AME Church."[136]

Four years later in 1848, the General Conference rejected another petition for women to preach.[137] Reflecting several years later on this "encroachment of female preachers on male prerogatives," an editorial in the *Christian Recorder* stated that in 1848, "the subject of licensing came up for consideration before the General Conference in the form of a petition from the Daughters of Zion. It then went so far in their favor that they were granted permission to preach in our churches, but not to receive licenses from the Conference."[138] Payne recollects in his *History of the African Methodist Episcopal Church* that "the origin of the question (licensing women to preach) is found in the fact that certain women members of the A.M.E. Church, who believed themselves divinely commissioned to preach by formal licenses, subsequently organized themselves into an association with the avowed intention of laying out a field of usefulness of the themselves, and making out appointments for such a field after the manner of our Annual conferences. They held together for a brief period, and the fell to pieces like a rope of sand."[139] In 1849, "despite the fact the church had already forbidden traveling preachers to publish books or pamphlets without formal approval," Lee republished an expanded version of her initial narrative with a more extensive discussion of her travels and her evangelical successes.[140] Clearly, she hoped to influence these debates. One year later at the 1850 Philadelphia Conference of the AME Church, a group of women "who believed they were divinely commissioned to preach regardless of whether the church hierarchy chose to license them," organized to make their own appointments. Andrews opines that Lee was "very likely" among this "group of ecclesial insurgents."[141]

Despite this setback, women persisted. "They again petitioned this [1852] General Conference to grant their license in all respects as men are licensed, and so to graduate up to the highest office in the church."[142] Payne reports: "the question of licensing women to preach . . . was discussed with a great deal of judgment and spirit. Rev. Thomas Lawrence moved that license should be granted them. The motion was put and lost by a large majority."[143] Still later in 1864, "the General Conference let a resolution to license women to preach die."[144] By the 1870s, around seventy women had received local preachers' licenses, but the General Conference did not officially recognize them. For example, in 1874, Bishop Stephen Merrill who presided over the California Conference, ruled "that lower judicatories had no right to grant women licenses to preach."[145] An appeal of Merrill's decision to the 1876 General Conference failed. Despite these disappointing outcomes, Lee's story became iconic in the AME tradition.

Moral Agency, Dissent and Prophetic Vision in Lee's *Religious Experience and Journal*

Jarena Lee was not the first woman to struggle for the right to preach. Brekus, who identified more than one hundred women who preached between 1740 and 1845, observes that "several generations of women struggled to invent an enduring tradition of female religious leadership."[146] Dodson acknowledges that in the period between the AME church founding and Jarena Lee's 1849 *Religious Experience and Journal,* "a number of black women were actively preaching across the land," including Rachel Evans, Sophie Murray, Elizabeth Cole, Rachel Evans and Harriet Nelson Taylor.[147] Several other Black female exhorters gained renown as "charismatic religious leaders" even without formal recognition by the AME Church. At least two, Julia Foote and Zilpha Elaw, published spiritual autobiographies on the heels of Lee's narrative. Sadly, as Brekus surmises, many of these Black women preachers remain unidentified and unnamed in the historical record.[148]

In the context of these women's struggles, Lee's autobiography emerged at a delicate point because the AME was fully engaged in a discussion of women's roles. Clearly, she hoped not only to attract supporters but also to respond to opponents. In contrast to other texts in this volume, Lee's *Religious Experience and Journal* has both a relatively narrow focus and a well-defined audience of AME members. The choices she made in crafting her narrative, which we have discussed above, were, in our view, strategically shrewd.

Her selection of a journal to share her message has several rhetorical advantages for her. For example, by avoiding direct argument, she sidesteps being seen as overtly confrontational. She makes her case indirectly, following the well-established Methodist tradition of spiritual autobiographies. In addition, an autobiography also enables her to "relive" her progress through the Order of Salvation, highlight her call story, and build her ethos as a prophetic voice. As a prophet, empowered by God to preach the Gospel, she is a moral agent sent not only to instruct and convert her hearers, but also to enable church leaders to understand how God can use women as well as men in efforts to redeem the world. Her vivid descriptions of her emotional and spiritual struggles as she progresses through the Order of Salvation, particularly her experience of sanctification, invite her readers to judge her sincerity and authenticity. Her call story, which reflects so clearly the pattern of Judeo-Christian prophetic calls, especially in her resistance and disbelief that God could be calling her to preach, adds weight to her claims. Further, her narrative follows the well-established Methodist tradition of spiritual autobiographies, evincing her commitment to following the path Wesley laid out for his followers. In essence, Lee masterly connects her story and her argument to experiences that are central to the lives of her Methodist readers.

As a result, Lee builds identification with her audience because, as rhetorical theorist Kenneth Burke advises, she is speaking their language. In and through the narrative, Lee reveals that she, like other women, is "devoutly religious" and "supremely ordained to carry out" a call "to preach the gospel of Christianity."[149] In short, Lee connects her divine call to scripture, precedent, and religious tradition. Arguing for her right to preach, Lee proves the validity of her call. As she repeatedly claims, her status as a moral agent is affirmed by her success in stirring and converting hearers.

Second, Lee embodies dissent by affirming Methodist traditions even as she advocates for women's right to preach. Her agenda does not call for radical change or new patterns of behavior; rather, she upholds traditional values and ideals. Significantly, she is not arguing for the spiritual or political equality of women. She is not arguing for or even addressing the ordination of women. Instead, she seeks to establish that God can call and empower certain women to preach and to evangelize. As Giver-Johnston explains: "Feminist claims for equal rights for all women did not drive" women like Lee; "rather, a divine call so compelled and strengthened them to challenge the male domination of the church, even the pulpit."[150] Lee implicitly endorses Wesley's notion of the extraordinary call. Her rhetoric is progressive and forward looking, not completely breaking with the past but rather affirming tradition.

Another part of her strategy of dissent is to locate her story in the nexus of three well-known passages in scripture: (1) Peter's words to the crowd on the feast of Pentecost, an adaptation of a passage by Joel; (2) the story of

Mary Magdalene; and (3) a portion of the Sermon on the Mount addressing true versus false prophets. Each passage powerfully connects her position with significant Christian stories and values. By framing her narrative with Peter's words on the day of Pentecost, she situates her story in the context of the very beginning of Christianity. With the descent of the Holy Spirit as tongues of flame and a rush of wind, all those assembled, men and women, were empowered to speak in tongues. That day was a fulfillment of Joel's prophesy and opened up full participation to women as well as men. Pentecost, sometimes referred to as the birthday of the church, heralds a new era where all people are to proclaim the Gospel.

Jesus's empowerment of Mary Magdalene on the day of his resurrection is unimpeachable evidence of God's intention to use women, as well as men as evangelists. In fact, in the case of Mary Magdalene, Jesus specifically instructs her to proclaim the resurrection to men. Women's preaching, then, corresponds perfectly with Jesus's actions in empowering his disciples to be evangelists.

Finally, Lee's emphasis on her effectiveness as proof of her call is grounded in Jesus's words to the crowd in the Sermon on the Mount: "By their fruits, ye shall know them."[151] Her revised autobiography, published in the midst of the consideration of women's preaching in the AME, greatly expanded her discussion of her successes, the fruits of her labors. And her account is impressive. With those details, Lee emphasizes the "good fruits" she had produced, which prove that she is a "good tree." But more than that, the Matthew passage implies that those who oppose her fruitful works are "false prophets" who come in sheep's clothing to delude followers. Her reliance on this passage, then, connects her successes to the standard Jesus himself laid down. Her effectiveness is proof that she is a good tree.

Outside the text, Lee is also careful to present herself as decorously feminine, another dimension of her posture of dissent. When he began authorizing women to preach, John Wesley himself, aware that many would find their behavior unacceptable, advised women to "present themselves modestly," even giving advice on modulating their voices.[152] The challenge to Black women was clearly exacerbated by racist stereotypes. As Nell Painter observes, a "Black woman as lady went against the commonplaces of nineteenth-century American culture." By mid-century, however, photographs enabled Black women like Lee to claim "womanhood for a black woman" through dress and appearance.[153] In her study of Sojourner Truth, for example, Painter discusses how Truth commissioned and distributed portraits of herself to build and control her public image.[154]

Similarly, as Truth did, in her 1849 *Religious Experience and Journal,* Lee includes a picture of herself on the frontispiece. Like many female Methodist ministers, Lee takes care to present herself as a demure, respectable woman—a True Woman. Lee wears a simple bonnet and has a shawl draped over most of her body, as she sits at a desk, pen in her hand, and a Bible nearby. As religious historian Catherine Brekus observes: "Frozen in time for the American public, she does not look uneducated, or uncouth, but scholarly, genteel, and utterly feminine."[155] Carol Mattingly explains in *Appropriate[ing] Dress: Women's Rhetorical Style in Nineteenth-Century America,* that though dress was a "way of disciplining women, it also provided an effective means of resistance."[156] Clearly, Lee, in her dress, adheres to socially constructed appearances of femininity even as she challenges the restrictions on women's preaching. This strategic stance of dissent allows Lee to accentuate her allegiance to traditional notions of womanly decorum even as she urges a broadening of their social roles.

Third, Lee's *Religious Experience and Journal* has a prophetic dimension. As mentioned earlier in this chapter, her account is replete with examples of her successes. Page after page recounts her extraordinary accomplishments in strengthening the faithful and converting others who come from all walks of life. Traveling thousands of miles to share God's good news is an implicit indictment of the Church authorities who would rob people from hearing God's word and who would prevent anyone, man or woman, from exercising their spiritual gifts. God's call is at odds with church practices, she asserts, noting that women do "not need the Church's sanction, because their ministry [is] authorized by a power beyond the Church, namely God, who spoke to them through the Holy Spirit."[157] Like the prophets of old, some women experience a direct mandate to spread the Gospel, despite social conventions that disbar them from such work. Throughout her narrative, Lee is calling her audience to respect the divine prerogative to choose whomever to do whatever work in the world.

Also, like the Hebrew prophets, Lee strongly suggests that church leadership is ignoring and even rejecting the movement of the Holy Spirit. Adopting a prophet's "uncompromising," "excoriating stance," Lee rebukes her audience for following the customs of a man-made church government that are clearly at odds with God's vision for women.[158] She argues: "Oh how careful ought we to be, lest through our by-laws of church government and disciplines, we bring into disrepute even the word of life. For as unseemly as it may appear now-a-days for a woman to preach, it should be remembered that nothing is impossible with God. And why should it be thought impossible, heterodox, or improper for a woman to preach? [S]eeing the Savior died for the woman as well as the man. If the man may preach, because the Saviour died for him, why not the woman? [S]eeing he died for her also. Is he not a whole Saviour, instead of a half one? [A]s those who hold it wrong for a woman to preach, would seem to make it appear."[159] Lee contrasts the limited view of opponents with her divinely inspired interpretation of scripture. She wields scripture and the word of God to critique naysayers and to position herself as God's messenger and prophet.[160]

Lee's *Religious Experience and Journal,* through personal examples and a feminist hermeneutic that juxtaposes divine law with man-made customs, calls church leadership to realign its actions and attitudes to reflect more fully divine autonomy. Unlike other women discussed in this volume, she does not argue for the spiritual equality of women, but her narrative envisions an ecclesial structure that reflects more fully and well an acknowledgment and acquiescence to God's authority. Her view is, thus, prophetic both in its recognition of the shortcomings of the church's decisions and in its hopeful anticipation of progressive change.

Her insistence that God calls women, including her, to preach is, on the surface, controversial, even radical. Grounding her call in scripture opens a new perspective for her readers, who hold that source to be the foundation of their beliefs. With this approach, she becomes a prophetic voice, not challenging God's divine plan, rather instead pointing the way to its fuller, truer realization. This posture of dissent—affirming the centrality of Biblical truth while calling for dramatic reforms of traditional attitudes—positions her viewpoint as a beginning of the unfolding of God's kingdom on earth. Those who respond to and support her view can help bring about a new order that honors God's decisions and power. Lee's *Religious Experience and Journal* both inspired and empowered followers.

Beyond its influence in the AME, Lee's *Religious Experience and Journal* participated in a larger conversation about women's proper roles in American life. Unequivocally establishing a link between Lee and the other women in this book is difficult. However, the overlap of interests, especially abolitionism, and concerns, particularly women's right to be involved in ministry, makes at least some level of relationship highly likely. Frederick Knight outlines one concrete possibility. Lee was active in abolitionist circles, attending at least two antislavery meetings in Boston in 1834 and in New York in 1840. Sarah and Angelina Grimké did a lecture tour in Massachusetts and New

York in the 1830s and Sarah Grimké's *Letters on the Equality of the Sexes* were sent to Mary S. Parker, who was president of the group at the time and had been active before being elected. Quite possibly, they encountered Lee.[161] Moreover, the work of both Grimké sisters was widely distributed in abolitionist circles. Since Sarah Grimké encountered male resistance to her sense of a call to ministry and since both sisters faced opposition to their public advocacy, their experiences resembled Lee's. In the relatively small world of abolitionists in the 1830s and the various women's antislavery activities, the chances of their encounter seem remarkably high. We do know that in 1853, Lee, William Lloyd Garrison, Lucretia Mott, and Sojourner Truth all attended the Convention of the American Anti-Slavery Association in Philadelphia.[162]

Moreover, during her years as an itinerant preacher, Lee used Philadelphia as her home base. Mott lived and was active in that area. Again, they may have met and interacted. These possible connections are, sadly, lost in the mists of history, but since abolitionist circles were overlapping and active, it seems reasonable to assume that at least Grimké and Mott knew of her work and may have even shared their common concerns.

Although her narrative was not immediately successful in securing a place for women as preachers in the AME, the argument she presents catalyzed and enjoined discussion among her religious community about women's roles, a debate that would continue with vigor throughout the nineteenth century. By the 1880s and building on the efforts of women like Lee, Zilpha Elaw, and Amanda Berry, two women—Sarah Ann Hughes and Amanda Wilson—began to "expand the boundaries of women's ministries" by "seeking compensation and titles equivalent to those of their ministerial brethren."[163] In 1884, the General Conference agreed that women could be granted local licenses to preach. But as Stephen Angell points out, George Sampson, the man who brought the resolution to license women preachers, did so to have control over women's ministries.[164] Later, in 1886, Methodist bishops debated the General Conference's licensing of women to preach in the *AME Church Review*. Bishop John Mifflin Brown spoke in favor of women's ordination, "point[ing] to women whom he deemed to be among the leading thinkers of the day," and specifically naming Jarena Lee as an influential and "excellent 'pastor.'"[165] Not until the 1890s were two women, Julia A. J. Foote and Mary Small, ordained as deacons in their denominations.[166] At the 50th Quadrennial session of the AME's General Conference in 2016, Lee was posthumously ordained "208 years after she acknowledged her call; 207 years after her call was denied; 198 years after she was licensed;

and 16 years after the AME/WIM's [Women in Ministry] unsuccessful attempt to have her call to ordained ministry affirmed at the 2000 General Conference."[167] She is now the Reverend Jarena Lee and women ministers in the AME regard her as their foremother. In a sense, Lee lost the battle but won the war.

THREE

Sarah Moore Grimké's

Letters on the Equality of the Sexes

The Bible through a Woman's Eyes

Thine for the oppressed in the bonds of womanhood

—SARAH M. GRIMKÉ, *LETTERS ON THE EQUALITY OF THE SEXES*

In 1821, Sarah Moore Grimké made a momentous decision. She left her home and family in South Carolina to live in Philadelphia. This move was "scandalous for a woman of her background. . . . Sarah was planning to leave home, family and church to live alone and unprotected in a strange city and become a Quaker."[1] She had, however, sensed "an unmistakable call, not to be disregarded" telling her to move North.[2] Once there, she lodged in the home of Israel Morris, a prominent leader in the Quaker community whom she had met earlier. Later she moved to live with his sister Catherine Morris.[3]

Two years later, after intense questioning by the admissions committee, she was admitted as a member of the Fourth and Arch Street Quaker meeting, where she hoped to find a spiritual home after years of turmoil.[4] Despite her earlier trepidations about the Quakers and their style of dress, she admitted that changing into plainer clothes "was accompanied by a feeling of much peace."[5]

A Slave Holder's Daughter Becomes an Abolitionist Activist

Joining that meeting brought an additional benefit. There, she encountered Lucretia Mott, who was "a highly effective and respected minister" in that community. A woman minister was, of course, an anomaly for Sarah. As Gerda Lerner observes, "Sarah must have been impressed and encouraged

: 49 :

by hearing her speak."[6] Confirmed as a minister in 1821, Mott had already gained attention for "her 'peculiar testimony' on 'female elevation' and 'woman's responsibility as a rational and immortal being.'"[7] Over the next decade, when Sarah would have been an active part of that meeting, Mott herself moved from being "a respectable Quaker minister" to being a notable public activist, particularly for abolition.[8]

For the next few years, although she felt she had been called to join the Quakers, Sarah struggled to find her identity and appropriate role in that community. Declining two marriage proposals from Morris, she visited prisons and taught in charity schools. With the encouragement of Catherine, she discerned and struggled with her sense of a calling to become a minister. Suitability for that role in Quaker circles stressed an ability to speak extemporaneously from inspiration in a meeting, and "Sarah's alternately halting and hasty delivery inevitably created a bad impression."[9] Although Sarah was discouraged on that front, the arrival of her sister Angelina in 1829 set her on a path to discover her life's work as an abolitionist and woman's rights advocate.

Published at the height of Sarah's fleeting but influential public career, *Letters on the Equality of the Sexes* deployed a fully developed feminist hermeneutic to refute contemporary social views of women's proper role and to argue for Christian women's true identity as moral agents. Seeing scripture through a feminist lens, Sarah maintained that women had a responsibility to engage in public life especially when moral issues were at stake. Her *Letters on the Equality of the Sexes* had an immediate, dramatic impact on some women of the time. Lucretia Mott said the letters were "the most important work since Mary Wollstonecraft's *Rights of Women*," a work she deeply admired. Lucy Stone, an important force behind the 1848 Seneca Falls Convention and a strong advocate for both abolition and woman's rights, called Grimké's work "first rate" and suggested it confirmed her determination "to call no man master." Abby Kelley and Elizabeth Cady Stanton freely "acknowledged the impact of her work on their own development."[10] In short, like-minded women of her day found her letters inspiring, enlightening, and empowering. As we will demonstrate, her *Letters on the Equality of the Sexes* provided a full-blown feminist hermeneutic for women who followed that not only shaped their thinking but also provided them with resources for their own advocacy.

Grimké's *Letters on the Equality of the Sexes* was the culmination of many years of spiritual struggle and continuing frustrations she encountered because of her gender. The roots of her aversion to slavery and her commitment to improving the situation grew out of her early years in South Carolina. These experiences were formative. As an adult, the growth of abolitionist fervor, the tenets of the Quaker faith, and the larger social and political context shaped her thinking and catalyzed her writing.

Childhood Experiences

Born in 1792, Sarah was the sixth child and second daughter of John and Mary Grimké, a prominent South Carolina slave-holding family. For a female from an affluent family in Charleston, the social expectations were clear: marriage, a family, and a home staffed with slaves. Nevertheless, four factors in Sarah's environment shaped her development and thinking, moving her in directions no one would have anticipated.[11]

First, in her earliest years, Sarah confronted the horrors of slavery. At four, she reportedly reacted strongly to seeing a woman being beaten for some offense.[12] She was so upset that "a half hour later her nurse found her on one of the wharves, trying to convince a captain to take her away to someplace where such things did not happen."[13] Although having slaves was a normal part of life for her family, she struggled, as her much younger sister Angelina would, with the realities of the institution and the abuses she witnessed. She reported to a friend that "Slavery was a millstone about my neck, and marred my comfort from the time I can remember myself."[14] At eleven, she carried her convictions into action, defying her much admired father as well as South Carolina law to teach her young slave companion to read. Her usually tolerant father, unable to abide such actions, quickly ended her activities.[15] She managed, however, to circumvent her father's wishes a bit by teaching a special Sunday school class for slave children, encouraging them to look over her shoulder as she read from the Bible.[16]

Deeply distressed with the conditions and treatment of slaves, Sarah discussed slavery at length with her brother Thomas, with whom she would remain close for the remainder of his life. Although he listened to her objections and discussed the topic with her, he simply could not agree. For him, slavery was "a normal part of their lives." Moreover, he felt it helped slaves adjust to life in a civilized society.[17] At this point, Sarah apparently did not reject the institution of slavery entirely, in part because she believed the Bible condoned it.[18] But she could not countenance the brutal treatment slaves routinely received. Her growing repugnance at the institution was part of her eventual decision to leave the South.[19]

Second, in a culture that had clear definitions of gender roles, Sarah was an outlier. She was a curious and intellectually precocious child. Initially, her father, a judge, indulged her thirst for learning. He permitted her to take part in the legal training he provided for his sons, including the debates he encouraged. She excelled at these exercises, prompting him to suggest that, had she been a boy, she "would have been the best jurist in the land."[20] This was no small compliment in a family that produced some notable legal thinkers. Her brother Thomas had a distinguished career as a lawyer and was given an honorary degree by Yale, while her brother Frederick later served on the Ohio Supreme Court.[21] This early introduction to legal thinking and arguments proved valuable to her in her later life.

But Sarah's education was curtailed. During his two years at the College of Charleston, Thomas happily shared his lessons with her.[22] However, when he left to study at Yale, she had no way to further her education and pursue her own dream of becoming a lawyer. In fact, those around her ridiculed her aspirations and her father explicitly prohibited her studying Latin on her own.[23] Much later, she reflected: "Had I received the education I coveted and been bred to the profession of law, a dignity to which I secretly aspired, I might have been a useful member of society, and instead of myself and my property being taken care of I might have been a protector of the helpless and the unfortunate, a pleader for the poor and the dumb."[24] This early thwarting of her educational aspirations initiates a pattern that persisted throughout her life. Repeatedly, society's notion of the proper role of women stymied her desires, ambitions, and even her sense of a divine calling.

Third, in 1805, the birth of Angelina, the fourteenth and final child of the family, began a relationship that profoundly impacted both sisters. For Sarah, her arrival provided a new focus. Thomas's departure for Yale had left her bereft; Angelina's birth opened new possibilities. She was so entranced with this new sister that she begged her parents relentlessly to let her stand as godmother for the baptism, a request they finally granted. Katharine Du Pre Lumpkin reports that, from early childhood, Angelina showed a strong preference for Sarah over their mother and "she sometimes still called Sarah 'mother' as late as her mid-twenties."[25] Sarah took her role in training this baby sister "in the way she should go" quite seriously. Undoubtedly, she influenced Angelina's development significantly as Angelina would later shape her thinking.[26]

Birney opines that Sarah's instantaneous, strong bond with Angelina "foreshadowed the heart and soul sympathy, which notwithstanding the twelve years' difference in their ages, made them one throughout life."[27] Lerner describes their bond as "symbiosis," which was "the blessing of their active days."[28] Both underwent evangelical religious conversion experiences that moved them from the Episcopal Church through Presbyterianism to the Quaker community. In contrast to others in their family, both experienced early disquietude with the abuses of slavery that blossomed into strong abolitionist fervor, and both had a keen sense of their moral agency coupled with a commitment to social action. Their gifts certainly differed: Angelina was a skillful orator; Sarah was shy and inept in public speaking. Perhaps as a heritage from early training with her father and brothers, Sarah showed considerable skill in argument and a talent for biblical hermeneutics. Lerner's joint biography underscores the sisters' interdependence and mutual support. In some respects, their individual accomplishments grew out of their deep relationship.

Sarah's struggle to reconcile her spiritual inclinations with established religion was a fourth formative element in her early life. The Grimké family were stalwart supporters of and regular attendees at St. Philip's Episcopal Church in Charleston. In addition, their mother, Mary, gathered the household for morning prayers and Bible readings.[29] Birney, a friend and early biographer, insists that "Judge Grimké, his family and his connections, were all High-Church Episcopalians, tenacious of every dogma and severe upon the neglect of any religious forms of church or household worship."[30] Du Pre Lumpkin suggests that "it may be that the Grimké home was more rigidly pious than other Charleston homes of similar wealth and station."[31] Sarah was, Birney asserts, "scrupulously exact in her private devotions," although her actions were "done mechanically from habit" rather than from a deep-felt conviction.[32] Sarah recorded in her diaries that, in attending the Episcopal services "her heart was never touched, her soul was never stirred."[33] She was frustrated that religious experiences did not correspond to her notions of deep religious conversion and commitment.

In 1813, a stirring evangelical sermon by the Reverend Henry Kollock, a well-known Presbyterian minister visiting from his church in Savannah, catalyzed her religious interests.[34] For the next few years, she oscillated between a life of frivolity, with the typical parties and focus of young women in her social class, and deep remorse at her behaviors kindled by repeated encounters with Kollock.[35] Only her father's declining health and her decision to accompany him to Philadelphia for treatment provided some relief from her deep internal conflict. Caring for her father moved her focus away from her taxing spiritual and personal struggles. In her words, her father's health was "the merciful interposition of Providence [that] stopped my progress," presumably in her spiritual struggles.[36]

Birney identifies her first sojourn in the North as "the most important event of Sarah's life, for the influences and impressions there received gave some shape to her vague and wayward fancies, and showed her a gleam of the light beyond the tangled path which still stretched before her."[37] Part of that "gleam of light" was undoubtedly her contact with Quaker ideas. In Philadelphia, when she and her father initially lodged with a Quaker family, she encountered both their lifestyle and their beliefs, including their abolitionism. Interestingly, Sarah decided to linger in Philadelphia for two months after her father's death, living among the Quakers before returning to South Carolina. On her return voyage South, she became friends with more Quakers, including Israel Morris, who gave her a copy of the journal of John Woolman, a prominent leader who had been an early staunch supporter of abolitionism.[38]

In South Carolina, during another period of spiritual struggle, she found some short-lived support among a Methodist congregation.[39] After her brother Thomas gifted her with a book of Quaker writings, she began corresponding with Israel Morris about what she was reading. She also returned to Woolman's journal where she found solace in his account of his own spiritual journey. Eventually, Sarah began attending Quaker services in Charleston.[40] As we shall see, this spiritual journey from the Episcopal church through evangelical Presbyterianism into Quakerism profoundly shaped her thinking and prepared her for her work as an abolitionist and an advocate for woman's rights.

Growth of Abolitionist Fervor

Even before Angelina joined her in Philadelphia in 1829, Sarah was dismayed with the racism she perceived within the Quaker community. Although dedicated to the eradication of slavery, some Quakers opposed active participation in abolitionist groups.[41] Moreover, as she discovered, her own meeting practiced racial segregation in their gatherings.[42] Her strengthening commitment to abolitionism intensified her discomfort with both the constraints on political advocacy and the community's racist practices, unsettling her in Quakerism and shaping the arguments she would make in *Letters on the Equality of the Sexes.*

Angelina's arrival, while providing support and companionship, exacerbated her uneasiness because Angelina was far less docile than she and confronted rather than accepted both the criticism they received and the attempts to constrict their activities.[43] Angelina pursued her own course.

In March 1835, Angelina attended her first antislavery lecture, defying her meetings' guidelines.[44] Within a month, she had become a member of the Philadelphia Female Anti-Slavery Society, which Lucretia Mott helped establish.[45] Reacting to increasing resistance to abolitionism in the North and an August 1835 pro-slavery demonstration in Boston, Angelina wrote a private letter of support to William Lloyd Garrison, the editor of *The Liberator*.[46] When he published the letter there without her permission, she immediately became publicly associated with abolitionism. Upset by what they perceived as inappropriate activism, the leaders of the community pressed her to renounce the letter. Even Sarah was dismayed. But Angelina stood her ground.[47] Her abolitionist activities widened the breach between her and the orthodox Quaker leaders of her meeting.[48]

In 1836, the sisters took pen in hand to write two appeals to persons in the South about the cause. Angelina's "An Appeal to the Christian Women of the South" urged her readers, impelled by their "sense of duty as *Christian women*," to read, speak, pray, and act about slavery. She invited them to test her arguments against scripture.[49] For her part, Sarah penned "An Epistle to the Clergy of the Southern States" basing her appeals on a careful reading of scripture.[50] Both were published by the American Anti-Slavery Society and widely circulated in abolitionist circles.

Although their activities violated the guidelines of their orthodox Quaker community against engagement in politics, Sarah tried to maintain ties there. But in later summer 1836, an incident occurred that moved her to sever her connection. Disregarding Quaker meeting rules, Jonathan Evans, a powerful elder in the community, interrupted Sarah's comments, causing her to sit down. Feeling angry and frustrated, she realized that her "bonds had been broken" and that she was free of her loyalty to Quakerism.[51] Many years later, reflecting on the impact of her frustrating experiences as a woman before and after her time among the Quakers, she averred "the poweres [*sic*] of my mind have never been allowed expansion; in childhood they were repressed by the false idea that a girl need not have the education I coveted. In early youth by wrong views of God and religion, then I was fairly ground to powder in the Quaker Society."[52] When Angelina's marriage to Theodore Weld, a non-Quaker, and the sisters' continued activism prompted their meeting to disown them, both had anticipated this action. Their letter back to the meeting insisted "we have committed no offence for which Christ Jesus will disown us as members of the household of faith," before suggesting that the meeting's rules had no basis in scripture. The sisters ended the letter and their sojourn with the Quakers with a small barb: "We are very respectfully, in that love which knows no distinction in color, clime, or creed, your friends."[53]

The sisters subsequently stepped up their involvement in abolitionist advocacy. Determined to draw together female antislavery groups under one umbrella, they helped found a national organization. Because of their first-hand knowledge of slavery, leaders of the American Anti-Slavery Society recruited them to a training session so that they could become agents for the society to women. As the only women at the meeting, their distinctive role was to "meet with Christian women in sewing circles and in private parlors" to discuss slavery and abolitionism.[54] In December 1836, under the aegis of that group, they began to hold "parlor" meetings for women in New York. These gatherings quickly outgrew those confines. Soon men began to attend the gatherings, causing some anguish to Angelina, who only reluctantly transgressed the social barrier that discouraged women from addressing such "promiscuous" audiences.[55]

Then the sisters moved their activities to New England. They anticipated a warm welcome there because leaders of the Boston Female Anti-Slavery Society, including Mary Weston Chapman, Annie Warren Weston, and Mary Parker, enthusiastically supported their efforts.[56] In November, when the women ended their tour, they had visited more than sixty New England towns and lectured to approximately 40,500 people.[57]

Although their tour was exhilarating, it was also exhausting and frustrating. While they attracted large audiences, they also garnered widespread criticism from the pulpit and press because of their topic, their speaking to "promiscuous" audiences of men and women, and their audacity as women in being public advocates.[58] Such criticism of their public speaking on behalf of the abolitionist cause contradicted their strong sense of themselves as simply fulfilling their duties as Christians. The negative response from some quarters to their abolitionist advocacy, including a pastoral letter from a clergy group in Massachusetts, prompted the sisters to respond.

In the summer of 1837, during their lecture tour of New England, irritated by the criticism leveled at them by both ministers and the press, Sarah and Angelina defended their actions publicly. Angelina's protest was a response to an essay by Catharine Beecher, an educator she much admired. In that essay, Beecher contended: "Men are the proper persons to make appeals to the rulers whom they appoint." Women should, Beecher argued, try to influence men into appropriate actions but concluded "they are surely out of their place in attempting to do it [public advocacy] themselves."[59] In her letters to Catharine Beecher, first published in *The Liberator,* Angelina answered Beecher's broad objections to abolitionism, devoting two letters to answering her argument about the proper role of women.[60]

Going in a different direction, Sarah wrote a series of "personal" letters to Mary S. Parker, President of the Boston Female Anti-Slavery Society.[61] After the first two letters, having learned of a Pastoral Letter of the General Association of Congregational Churches in Massachusetts that, in part, took aim at their activities, Sarah determined to respond to their argument in one of her letters. She explained: "When I last addressed thee, I had not seen the Pastoral Letter of the General Association. It has since fallen into my hands, and I must digress from my intention of exhibiting the condition of women in different parts of the world, in order to make some remarks on this extraordinary document."[62] Thus, although the Pastoral Letter was not the catalyst for the project, it reflected the larger social context for Sarah's writing.

Almost certainly, Sarah anticipated that some sympathetic periodical would publish her letters and, indeed, they quickly appeared first in *The New England Spectator* before Garrison reprinted them in *The Liberator.*[63] Later, these groundbreaking *Letters on the Equality of the Sexes* were collected and published by I. Knapp. Her ideas, then, were widely circulated, particularly in female reform groups.

If *Letters on the Equality of the Sexes* was a response to the opposition the two sisters encountered in their advocacy for abolition, it also reflected an extended, sometimes emotionally charged journey of discernment for Sarah. Through a twisting path, she had come to believe that God called her to be an advocate for abolitionism. As she wrote to Henry Wright, a fellow abolitionist and friend of William Lloyd Garrison, in late August 1837: "the Lord knows that we did not come to forward our own interest but in simple obedience to his commands. . . . Brothers [John Greenleaf] Whittier & [Theodore] Weld are anxious we should say nothing on the woman question, but I do not feel as if I could surrender my right to discuss any great moral subject."[64] Sarah had struggled to claim what she saw as her God-given moral agency and she had no intention of relenting.[65]

Religious Grounding of Sarah Grimké's Thought

Although Grimké's journey to Quakerism was circuitous, in truth, her time in both the Episcopal and Presbyterian churches prepared her for the transition and formed her thinking.[66] In particular, her religious experiences undoubtedly help her formulate the feminist hermeneutic that she would deploy so effectively. The Episcopal Church of her childhood embraced reason as a tool for considering both scripture and tradition in determining spiritual truth.[67] Perhaps equally important was the Episcopal Church's attitude toward scripture, which derived from the Articles of Religion of the Church of England. In brief, while the Church held that scripture was divinely inspired, it did not endorse a literalist approach to divine writ. If scripture contained "all things necessary to salvation," Episcopalians were not expected to accept everything contained therein.[68] In contrast to the literalism of some denominations, the Episcopal Church made discernment of the meaning of scripture a process, perhaps led by clergy but open to individuals. Through services in the Episcopal Church and in her mother's Bible study, Sarah was exposed to a range of scriptural readings and was also inculcated with a nonliteralist view of biblical writings. Her mother's Bible study taught her that individuals were free to study scripture for themselves. In that study, individuals could draw on reason to discern the meaning in the writings.

On the other hand, her introduction to Presbyterianism by Reverend Kollock put her in touch with the enthusiasms and spirit of the Great Awakening of the early nineteenth century. Presbyterians had specifically established Princeton, Kollock's alma mater for theological studies, "to train clergymen whose fervent, heartfelt preaching would bring sinners to experience evangelical conversion."[69] And it was there that Kollock's considerable talent as a preacher, which so moved Sarah, had been first acknowledged.[70] Through his ministrations, grounded in his own evangelical zeal and the spirit of the Second Great Awakening, she gained a deep, and what would prove abiding, commitment to the service of others, including reform efforts.[71]

With these formative experiences, Sarah found key elements in Quaker theology and practice congenial. Acknowledging the wide range of Quaker thought, Pink Dandelion, a contemporary historian of Quakerism, argues:

> there are four key theological ideas held in common by Quakers everywhere: 1) the centrality of direct inward encounter with God and revelation and thus forms of worship which allow this to be experienced; 2) a vote-less way of doing church business based on the idea of corporate direct guidance; 3) the spiritual equality of everyone and the idea of "the priesthood of all believers"; 4) based in part on the latter, the preference for peace and pacifism rather than war, and a commitment to other forms of social witness.[72]

The first of these is often captured in the notion of the "inner light," the capacity of any and every individual to receive divine inspiration and revelation. The third tenet essentially disposes of clericalism and empowers individuals to discern and share their insights with others. In fact, that tenet suggests an individual's moral obligation to share perceived spiritual truths. Coming to these ideas with a background that encouraged individual study of scripture, undergirded with reason, and a commitment to social justice from her exposure to evangelicalism, Sarah found both encouragement and empowerment to follow her own spiritual insights.

Implicit in these tenets was an egalitarianism that ideally obliterated notions of class, race, and gender. Anyone could receive direct inspiration from God to be shared with others. Not surprisingly, Quakers were among the first groups to oppose slavery and call for abolition, although they differed in the best way to end the institution itself. In fact, John Woolman, whose diary so impressed Sarah was, in the judgment of one scholar, "the premier Quaker abolitionist" and was influential in igniting the movement among meetings to endorse abolitionism.[73] The Quakers' stance on abolition also reverberated with Sarah.

These tenets also undergirded the Quakers' endorsement of women as ministers. That viewpoint stemmed in large part from the writings of Margaret Fell, who was an early convert and later wife of George Fox, the founder of Quakerism. After conversations with her, he proposed separate meetings for women[74] "to give women their place, their right place, and to stir them up to take it" so that their energies might be liberated for service to God.[75] But from the beginning, controversy swirled around that idea of separate women's meetings. Fell, an inveterate evangelist for her faith both in writing and in person, was well-known in Quaker circles.[76] This controversy provided her with an opportunity to articulate her views on women's appropriate role in religious life, which were shared and endorsed by Fox. In 1666 while she was in prison for her Quaker beliefs, she published "Women's Speaking Justified" to articulate the view she shared with Fox.[77] An extension of her evangelical work for the Quakers, the tract was a thoroughgoing theological rationale for women's full participation in public ministry and religious leadership. This work secured a distinctive place and unusual power for women in Quakerism.

Central to Fell's thinking was the account of the final day of creation in Genesis 1:27–28, which would also become a cornerstone of Sarah's views: "So God created humankind in his image, male and female he created them. God blessed them." After giving the pair dominion over all things, the story concludes with: "And God saw every thing that he had made, and, behold, it was very good." From a Quaker perspective, this account clearly asserts that the divine plan was for equality between the sexes. In their view, the Fall, which is narrated in the second account of creation, disrupted that initial order. Quakers, who came to see themselves as a vanguard working to restore this divine plan, saw women's equality with men as self-evident. As Ruether explains:

> the Quakers, rediscovered and developed the New Testament egalitarian paradigm of redemption. They claimed an egalitarian view of the original creation in the light of which gender subordination was defined as an expression of sin and the Fall, not as the will of God. Emphasizing the first creation story in Genesis which produced a well-ordered, beneficent world, the Quakers saw Redemption in Christ as restoring this original equality in the image of God for women equally with men. The classical Christian theology of subordination was seen as a betrayal of the good news of redemption in Christ for women equally with men.[78]

Although Sarah probably did not have access to Fell's work, she experienced the ramifications of it within the Quaker community. Undoubtedly, her association with Mott, who provided a remarkable role model, influenced her development of a feminist hermeneutic.

Sarah's diverse religious experiences all encouraged individual engagement with scripture and, in the case of the Quakers, a predominant reliance on personal insight. In addition, her early exposure to legal thinking and arguments with her father and brothers equipped her to turn her insights into arguments in support of her views. In essence, when she began to write her letters, she was extraordinarily well-equipped to craft a compelling argument for women's equality.

Evangelistic Fervor and a Spirit of Reform

The larger political and social milieu of the day provided an important part of the context for Sarah's writing. The Second Great Awakening of the early nineteenth century had been "a period of intense revivalism that had spurred hundreds of thousands of believers to reform themselves and their communities in the decades leading up to the Civil War."[79] As the evangelistic spirit prompted efforts for all sorts of reforms, in the 1820s and 1830s a variety of new "denomination-based periodicals," which had a very wide circulation, began to address some of the political issues of the day, among them Indian removal.[80] Perhaps in part stirred by these accounts, historian Mary

Hershberger suggests, many women saw themselves as "moral guardians of the nation's virtue, a duty that required a public presence and public activities."[81] As both Zaeske and Portnoy demonstrate, women who petitioned about Indian removal and abolition confronted the constraints women faced because of gender stereotypes about appropriate female behavior. These women experienced a conflict between the social expectations that they should remain in the domestic sphere and their sense of themselves as moral guardians. In essence, their socially acknowledged moral superiority created a dynamic tension that became a springboard for claiming a voice on certain political topics. From these "various and conflicted discourses," a space for possible dissent emerged.[82]

Not surprisingly, both Angelina and Sarah were caught up in these larger political and social currents. Sarah had twice been challenged and urged to remain silent when seeking to live out her sense of divine calling. Within Quaker circles, her call to ministry was ignored, and on one occasion she had literally been silenced in a Quaker meeting. The leaders of their Quaker meeting had castigated Angelina for her letter to Garrison, trying to compel her to withdraw it. When Sarah and Angelina began their public advocacy for woman's rights as they continued their work for abolitionism, even supporters like Theodore Weld urged them to be silent. Thus, on a deeply personal level, she confronted the tension between social expectations about her role as a female and her strong sense of her responsibility as a Christian. Grimké's response was to juxtapose the "rigidified conventions" about women's submission and silence with the truths and mandates she saw in scripture.

The Dangers Threatening the Female Character

Although Grimké had initiated her project before the Pastoral Letter from the Massachusetts clergy emerged, its tenor and arguments reflect the attitudes she and other women often confronted in their abolitionist activism.[83] On the surface, the letter was not explicitly directed at the Grimké sisters; rather, the ministers who authored it described their meeting as focused on "subjects which at the present time appear to us to have an important bearing upon the cause of Christ."[84] Indeed, only one of the four main topics refers directly to them though without naming them. Most of the letter reflects frustration, irritation, and perhaps even some fear of the erosion of their pastoral power and authority in the face of such unfortunate, disturbing topics as abolitionism and the intrusion of reformers into their churches.

Artfully sandwiched between the concern for the discussion of controversial topics without their permission and the encouragement to attend primarily to one's own spiritual welfare is the implicit criticism of the Grimké sisters' public advocacy. Hoping to draw attention to "the dangers which at present seem to threaten the female character with wide spread and permanent injury," the pastors consider the proper role and conduct of a woman who can have a "mild, dependent, softening influence . . . upon the sternness of man's opinions." Such a woman through "unobtrusive and private" efforts with "unostentatious prayers" and proper involvement "in Sabbath schools, in leading religious inquirers to their pastor for instruction, and in all such associated efforts as becomes the modesty of her sex" can advance "the cause of religion at home and abroad."[85]

For women who forsake the role of a vine "whose strength and beauty is to lean upon the trellis work and half conceal its clusters" and presume "to assume the independence and the overshadowing nature of the elm," they predict a dire future. Such women "will not only cease to bear fruit, but fall in shame and dishonour into the dust."[86] As firm protectors of right-minded women, they "regret the mistaken conduct of those who encourage females to bear an obtrusive and ostentatious part in measures of reform, and countenance any of that sex who so far forget themselves as to itinerate in the character of public lecturers and teachers."[87] Referring almost certainly to discussion of the sexual abuse of enslaved women, they "deplore the intimate acquaintance and promiscuous conversation of females with regard to things 'which ought not to be named'" and may, in due course, open the way for "degeneracy and ruin."[88]

In essence, the pastors perceived women's appropriate role and stance to be docile and dependent, reflecting her "consciousness of that weakness which God has given her for her protection and which keeps her in those departments of life that form the character of individuals and of the nation."[89] When "her softening influence . . . is fully exercised, society feels the effects in a thousand forms."[90] They deplore any public efforts of women, most particularly public advocacy or agitation.

These same arguments had percolated around women's petition drives against both slavery and Indian removal.[91] Being issued after Sarah had penned her first letters, this statement simply affirmed the narrow scope that many deemed appropriate for women. Sarah chose to interrupt the flow of her argument to respond to this letter directly. Convinced that women had a moral obligation to follow their consciences and act in whatever ways they felt God called them and firmly rejecting the narrow visions of those who might agree with the ministers, Sarah undertook not just to write an answer to the prevalent objections, but also to offer a complete rationale for women's role in public discussions of moral issues. In her view, as part of their responsibilities as Christians, women should enter the public arena when moral issues were at stake.

A New Vision Stemming from the Old

Venturing on nearly untrodden ground

—SARAH MOORE GRIMKÉ, *LETTERS ON THE EQUALITY OF THE SEXES*

Letters on the Equality of the Sexes is comprised of fifteen separate, wide-ranging letters, each with a specific topic. In the first letter, Grimké vows to "depend solely on the Bible to discern the sphere of woman,"[92] based on what she will later claim are its "immutable truths."[93] Pointing to "a misconception of the simple truths revealed in Scripture, in consequence of the false translation of many passages of Holy Writ," she abandons "the superstitious reverence which is attached to the English version of the Bible" as translated by men. Further, by rejecting "corrupt public opinion, and . . . the perverted interpretation of Holy Writ," she sets out "in search of truth," she will use "the original as my standard" and judge for herself "the meaning of the inspired writers."[94] Rather than accepting "the views of any man or set of men," she relies on the guidance of the Holy Spirit in her studies.[95] She will, indeed, look at scripture through a woman's eyes. In the ensuing discussions, she draws on her knowledge of both Hebrew and Greek, as well as various commentaries, for the thoughtful consideration of scripture that is, in her view, "the solemn duty of every individual."[96] In her view, only by discerning "the designs of Jehovah in the creation of woman" can women understand and fulfill the role for which they were created.[97] From this starting point, employing a feminist hermeneutic, Grimké presents an alternate analysis of women's sphere as described in scripture. Her subsequent survey of the realities of women's lives across the world reveals how ubiquitous the abrogation of the original divine plan is.

Throughout the letters, Grimké relies on three interrelated rhetorical strategies. First, employing a fully developed feminist hermeneutic, she argues forcefully that God's original divine plan was for the moral equality of males and females. Highlighting passages and examples men often ignored, she finds abundant proof of this throughout the Bible. Second, by grounding her arguments in scripture, she locates her viewpoint as a salubrious realignment of social practices with divine revelation. In the pattern of the

Jewish prophets, she will excoriate contemporary social mores as an abrogation of divine intention. Her perspective is not revolutionary but rather a desirable and even necessary correction to misguided thinking. Adopting this posture of dissent, in and through her language of liberating women from the "bonds of womanhood," she implicitly positions herself and those who follow her as prophetic voices, looking toward the restoration of divine order of equality.[98] Finally, throughout her discussions, she enacts the role of the powerful moral agent she envisions for women, providing an attractive role model for her readers. In short, with considerable adroitness, Grimké seeks not only to gain intellectual assent to her viewpoint, but also to motivate women to become moral agents working for reform of misguided social and political practices.

"Created in perfect equality"

Grimké's careful study of scripture leads to her thesis explicitly stated in her third letter that responds to the Pastoral Letter: that because "Men and women were CREATED EQUAL; they are both moral and accountable beings . . . whatever is *right* for man to do, is *right* for woman."[99] As Bartlett notes, her focus was on the "moral autonomy of women . . . to pursue, discover, and fulfill God's design for them. It was the ability to act on God's purpose."[100]

The first two letters, entitled "The Original Equality of Woman" and "Woman Subject Only to God," develop two interrelated arguments to support her thesis, each grounded in skillful exegesis of scripture, albeit with a feminist viewpoint.[101] First, she highlights the first creation story in Genesis to establish the original equality of men and women. The key passage is in Genesis 1:27, when on the sixth day of creation: "God created humankind in his image, in the image of God he created them, male and female he created them." Then, having blessed them, God gives them both "dominion over the fish of the sea, the birds of the air and over every living thing that moves upon the earth."[102] However, neither was given dominion over the other. Even without access to Fell's work, she echoes her ideas: "Here God joyns them together in his own Image, and makes no such Distinctions and Differences as Men do."[103]

In the second letter, Grimké elaborates this final point. Scripture, she argues, affirms that "woman [is] subject only to God." "Unable to learn from sacred writ when woman was deprived by God of her equality with man," she offers examples that support her argument for the moral equality of men and women. For example, when God renews the covenant with Noah after the flood, God grants Noah dominion over all animals, but not over woman.[104] She refers to Matthew's account of Jesus's response to the third temptation in the desert, the opportunity to rule over all nations, to further substantiate her view: "Worship the Lord your God, and serve only him." In this instance, as many of her readers may have realized, Matthew is quoting Deuteronomy 6:13, part of the Ten Commandments given to the Israelites. "We find," she points out, "the commands of God invariably the same to man and woman; and not the slightest intimation is given in a single passage of the Bible, that God designed to point woman to man as her instructor." Here she concludes with a quote from Isaiah 45:22: "Look unto ME, and ye shall be saved, all the end of the earth, for I am God and there is none else."[105] In her response to the Pastoral Letter, she turns to Matthew 5:14–16, a portion of the Sermon on the Mount. There, Jesus, speaking to a crowd of men and women, urges all his followers to be the light of the world.[106] Drawing on a variety of scriptural passages in both Hebrew and Christian scriptures, she concludes "I find that all his [God's] commands, all his moral laws, are addressed to women as well as to men."[107] In short, Grimké has argued that "God designed woman to be a help meet for man in every good and perfect work."[108] She asserts boldly: "Here I plant myself. God created us equal; — he created us free agents; — he is our Lawgiver, our King and our Judge, and to him alone is woman bound to be in subject, and to him alone is she accountable for the use of those talents which her Heavenly Father entrusted her."

Then she carefully considers the problematic second story of creation in which Eve is created from Adam's rib and eats the forbidden fruit. One verse in that account (Genesis 3:16) was a key text in arguing for women's submission to men: "I will greatly increase your pangs in childbearing; in pain you shall bring forth children, yet your desire shall be for your husband, and he shall rule over you." Her decided feminist analysis subverts traditional interpretations.

God, she observes, created woman explicitly as a helpmeet for man, "a companion *in all respects* his equal; one who was like himself a *free agent*, gifted with intellect and endowed with immortality."[109] This creation of Eve as a helpmeet for Adam is proof of the divine plan of equality. Later, she observes that the command not to eat of a particular fruit tree in the middle of the garden was given to both, further evidence of their initial equality.

Eve's eating of the forbidden fruit disrupts that divine plan. In an intriguing move, Grimké distinguishes Eve's decision to eat the fruit from Adam's, of course to his detriment. In her view, a "satanic intelligence" of which "she was in all probability entirely ignorant" "beguiled" Eve. Her very innocence and naivete made her prey to the snake's sinister manipulation. In contrast, "Adam [was] involved in the same sin, not through the instrumentality of a supernatural agent, but through that of his equal," Eve. "They both fell from innocence, and consequently from happiness, *but not from equality.*"[110] She returns to this theme briefly in her final letter, "Man Equally Guilty with Woman in the Fall." There she points to both Isaiah 43:27 and Romans 5:12 to substantiate her claim.[111] Isaiah declares "Your first ancestor sinned." Paul in Romans writes: "sin came into the world through one man." Both passages highlight Adam's culpability in the fall.

Turning to the consequences of their actions, Grimké focuses more closely on Genesis 3:16. Identifying a perhaps deliberately overlooked linguistic ambiguity, she disputes the usual translation of the last clause in this passage. Her argument centers on the translation of the verb in the phrase "shall rule over you." She points out that the verb form can be translated either "will" in the sense of a prediction or "shall" in the sense of a decree. She insists that translators, who have been accustomed to exercising "lordship over their wives" and see "only through the medium of a perverted judgment, very naturally, though I think not very learnedly or very kindly, translated it *shall* instead of *will,* and thus converted a prediction to Eve to a command to Adam."[112] She notes that the same verb tense is translated as "will" rather than "shall" in God's address to Cain over the slaying of Abel.[113] Just as Yahweh foresees Cain's wandering as an alien as a consequence of his action, so Yahweh predicts (not ordains) that man's dominion over women will follow from the pair's disobedience.[114]

In short, in applying a feminist hermeneutic, Grimké contests centuries of male exegesis. With fresh eyes, she finds in scripture not a mandate for female acquiescence and submissiveness but rather an affirmation of women's status as independent moral agents.

"The first effect of the fall"

In her second argument, which will extend throughout most of the remaining letters, Grimké argues that woman's historical subjugation to man is a deviation from the divine plan that reflects the fallen state of humanity.[115] Feminist theologian Rosemary Radford Ruether observes that this line of argument was commonplace in abolitionism, which held that social systems of domination, like slavery, reflect "sinful departures" from the "original plan of creation."[116] Focusing on women, Grimké later suggests that "the lust of dominion was probably the first effect of the fall; and as there was no other intelligent being over whom to exercise it, woman was the first victim of this unhallowed passion."[117] She supports the first part of that assertion by pointing to two early examples in scripture of individuals seeking dominion over others. Cain, who kills his brother Abel, is the first. The second is Nimrod, whom she titles "a mighty hunter of men" and who is held, in tradition, to have been the first to wage war on others.[118] Grimké also alleges Nimrod is the person responsible for the "Upas of slavery," the ultimate example of the desire for control over others.[119]

Adopting the excoriating stance of a biblical prophet and reflecting on the impact of this "lust of dominion" on women, she claims: "All history attests that man has subjected woman to his will. . . . He has done all he could to debase and enslave her mind; and now he looks triumphantly at the ruin he has wrought, and says, the being he has thus deeply injured is his inferior." To make her point, she reflects on the story of Abraham and Sarah. Although they shared the "same employments," Sarah was relegated to the background when the three visitors appeared in Mamre, to reiterate Yahweh's promise of a son to the barren and aged couple.[120] This pattern of treating women as subordinate persists in the story of Isaac and Rebekah.[121] In that case, the emissary sent to secure a wife for Isaac approaches her not as a "dignified creature, whom he was about to invite to fill an important station in his master's family," but rather by offering incense and jewelry—golden bracelets and a gold nose-ring.[122]

Grimké then scrutinizes the "principal support of the dogma of woman's inferiority, and consequent submission to her husband . . . found in some passages of Paul's epistles." She begins by questioning Paul's credibility. His mind, she argues, "was under the influence of Jewish prejudices respecting women, just as Peter and the apostles were about the uncleanness of Gentiles." For evidence, she points to Paul's insistence that Timothy be circumcised to avoid offending Jewish Christ followers.[123] Paul, thus, inevitably reflects the cultural background from which he came. Further, she insists that the "antiquity of opinions" (former translations and interpretations by males) about Paul's meaning are merely "the opinions of interested judges" who carry no weight with her. Previous commentaries are, in her opinion, neither unbiased nor authoritative.[124]

She also tackles a particularly thorny passage in Paul's first letter to the community at Corinth: "I would have you know that the head of every man is Christ and the head of the woman is the man; and the head of Christ is God," an idea reiterated in Paul's letter to the church in Ephesus: "For the husband is the head of the wife, even as Christ is the head of the Church."[125] In what rhetorical critic Martin Camper refers to as an argument from conflicting passages, Grimké draws on Christian theology to refute this analogy.[126] As he explains, "textual inconsistency presents rhetors with both a problem to be solved and a potentially powerful rhetorical opportunity to reconfigure the logical relations that structure a text's passages in favor of a preferred interpretation."[127] Grimké notes that in John's Gospel, Jesus declares: "I and my Father are one."[128] She contends that in such a divine union "there can be no inferiority where there is no divisibility."[129] In short, Christian theology holds that Jesus and the Father are one being and, thus, co-equal and indivisible. Thus, if the relationship between God and Jesus is the analogy for women's relationship to their husbands, there is no basis of a claim of women's inferiority. By turning to an alternate passage in scripture, she subverts traditional interpretations. A bit later she notes that these passages that urge women to be subject to their husbands are followed immediately by admonitions to men to love and honor their wives "as being heirs together of the grace of life."[130] In her view, these passages support not an inferior position but instead woman's role as a fully equal helpmeet and complement to man.

Following in the pattern of the Jewish prophets, Grimké turns to an assessment of the status of women throughout the world. Quoting extensively from Lydia Maria Child's *Brief History of the Condition of Women, in Various Ages and Nations* albeit without attribution, her fifth letter begins surveying the condition of women around the globe to reveal how ubiquitous and destructive male usurpation of power over women is.[131] In the spirit of Jewish prophets, she proclaims that "men, in the exercise of their usurped dominion over women, have almost invariably done one of two things. They have either made slaves of the creatures whom God designed to be their companions and their coadjutors in every moral and intellectual improvement, or they have dressed them like dolls, and used them as toys to amuse their hours of recreation."[132] Through four chapters, she traces this pattern by exploring the condition of women in different regions.[133]

In this section, continuing with her prophetic excoriation of current practices, Grimké considers how social attitudes toward gender disrupt any possibility of egalitarian interaction between the sexes. In letter four, "Social Intercourse of the Sexes," she contends that all social interactions between men and women are contaminated by the "constant pressure of feeling that we are different sexes; and, instead of regarding each other only the light of immortal creatures, the mind is fettered by the idea which is early and industriously infused into it, that we must never forget the distinction between women and men." This overemphasis on gender consistently leads men to approach women "in the character of a female," an attitude that tends to "destroy the true dignity of woman." Men tend to focus not on the intelligence or abilities of women but to her weakness.[134] "By flattery, by an appeal to her passions, he seeks access to her heart; and when he has gained her affections, he uses her as the instrument of his pleasure—the minister of his temporal comfort. He furnishes himself with a housekeeper, whose chief business is in the kitchen, or the nursery."

The constraints and situations that women confront stem, in no small part, from the laws "which she has had no voice in establishing, and which rob her of some of her *essential rights.*"[135] These laws "have been enacted to destroy her independence, and crush her individuality. A lynchpin of that legal framework is the notion of "coverture" articulated by William Blackstone, a distinguished English jurist, in his *Commentaries on the Laws of England*: "By marriage, the husband and wife are one person in law: that is, the very being or legal existence of the woman is suspended during the marriage, or at least is incorporated and consolidated into that of the husband: under whose wing, protection, and cover, she performs everything."[136] The man-made laws, then, subvert the original divine plan.

Responding to this concept, Grimké bemoans: "Here now, the very being of a woman, like that of a slave, is absorbed in her master."[137] These laws place a woman under her husband's control, depriving her of moral agency and making her largely unable to access protection against his treatment of her. A husband may legally give his wife "moderate correction" and restrain her "by domestic chastisement," even constraining her liberty if he believes it necessary. With marriage, all of a woman's property belongs to her husband and within the marriage her wages go to him as well.[138] The impact of these laws, which are common throughout the United States, leaves women "very little more liberty, or power, in some respects than the slave."[139] This linking of the status of women with that of slaves, although overdrawn, became a commonplace in women's rights discourse because it accentuates the plight of women. She cites Charles Theodore Christian Follen, a professor at Harvard, to support her view: "Woman, though fully possessed of that rational and moral nature which is the foundation of all rights, enjoys amongst us fewer legal rights than under the civil law of continental Europe."[140]

As this discussion reveals, Grimké develops an extended argument for the moral equality of women. At the same time, in typical prophetic fashion, she presents a strong case that current social arrangements, with their focus on the differences between the sexes and their insistence on the inferiority of women, unjustly distort the true nature of women. By subjugating women to men, social conventions run counter to the divine plan. Moreover, in thwarting women's development as responsible beings, men unfairly and callously prevent women from occupying their appropriate role as helpmeets and moral agents. Holding "the reins of *usurped* authority," men have been and are "unwilling to permit us to fill that sphere which God created us to move in."[141] Like all Jewish prophets, she castigates men for preventing women from fulfilling the roles to which God calls them. In moving beyond the confines of domesticity, women will help restore the original divine plan.

"The appropriate duties and influence of women"

Having demonstrated the divine mandate for equality, assuming a visionary prophetic persona, Grimké also suggests the roles she believes women can fill successfully.[142] Throughout her argument for women's equality, she willingly acknowledges some significant differences, such as physical strength, between the sexes. These are, she insists, largely immaterial. Women have the intellect and ability to function effectively as "responsible and immortal beings" in a variety of roles. To prove her point, she points to women's competence and success in various situations.

From her survey of Asia and Africa, she provides examples of women *"filling the throne,* and exercising the functions of royalty" effectively. From the ancient world, she identifies Semiramis of Assyria and Zenobia of Palmyra as women who managed the affairs of state astutely and successfully. Grimké educes three other examples from these areas to demonstrate that women have sometimes performed well as leaders. Nonetheless, legal systems consistently penalize and degrade them, sometimes treating them as impure unholy beings."[143] Although she does not support "woman's holding the reins of government over men," she insists these examples "prove there is no natural inferiority of women" and that "intellect is not sexed."[144]

In her ninth letter, "Heroism of Women—Women in Authority," she considers circumstances "which place them [women] in juxtaposition with men." Although she condemns "the exercise of brute force . . . as contrary to the law of God in men as in women," she admires the effectiveness of both Philippa, the wife of Edward III in England, in bringing victory against the Scots and Joan of Arc, "whose story is too familiar to need repetition." She lauds with fewer reservations an unnamed daughter of Sir John Cochrane who, during the reign of James II, twice disguised herself as a man to rob the mail that was bringing his death warrant.[145] In short, when confronted with challenging situations, women have often risen to the occasion and acquitted themselves well in decidedly unconventional contexts.

Other women, she avers, have "distinguished themselves in a way more consistent with their duties as moral beings." To make this point, she enumerates an array of women, whose stories are more legend than historical fact. For example, she discusses the Sabine women who supposedly intervened with their Roman abductors to broker a truce and Portia, the wife of Brutus, who was reputed to be particularly courageous. She also refers to the sacrifices of women during the Revolutionary War who "were exemplary as the men in various instances of self-denial: they refused every article of decoration for their persons; foreign elegances were laid aside, and they cheerfully abstained from luxuries on their tables."[146] She follows these legendary and unsupported stories with references to successful women rulers such as Catherine the Great, Elizabeth of England, Maria Theresa of Germany, and Isabella of Spain. These examples, she claims, prove that "intellect is not sexed; that strength of mind is not sexed; and that our views about the duties of men and the duties of women, the sphere of man and the sphere of woman, are mere arbitrary opinions, differing in different ages and countries, and dependent solely on the will and judgment of erring mortals."[147]

Although Grimké believes women are perfectly intellectually capable of being leaders and contributing to society in a variety of ways, her primary concern is women's role as moral agents. One venue for that agency is preaching. She begins her fourteenth and longest letter, "Ministry of Women" by declaring:

> According to the principle which I have laid down, that man and woman were created equal, and endowed by their beneficent Creator with the same intellectual powers and the same moral responsibilities, and that, consequently whatever is *morally* right for man to do, is morally right for a woman it do, it follows as a necessary corollary that, if it is the duty of man to preach the unsearchable riches of Christ, it is the duty also of woman. . . . Although among the Quakers, Methodists and Christians, women are permitted to preach the glad tidings of peace and salvation, yet I know of no religious body, who entertain the Scripture doctrine of the perfect equality of man and woman, which is the fundamental principle of my argument in favor of the ministry of women.[148]

A bit later, she is more emphatic about her understanding of women's role as ministers, averring "woman is bound to preach the gospel" precisely because, as a Christian, that is her appropriate role.[149]

In developing this idea, Grimké draws an intriguing distinction between the prophetic and priestly roles in the Judeo-Christian tradition. Pointing to Enoch, who was an antediluvian patriarch and was seen as walking with God, and Noah, who was "a preacher of righteousness," she observes that the prophetic role, which antedated the establishment of the Jewish priesthood, was a completely separate office.[150] One distinction between the roles is that while priests are compensated for their efforts, prophets are not. In addition, the chief responsibility of priests was to offer sacrifices and to read the law to the people; in contrast, prophets were designated to call people to repentance through their declaration of divine truths.[151] She cites Jeremiah 5:31 to substantiate the distinction. In Jeremiah's analysis, one problem among the Israelites is that "The prophets prophesy falsely, and the priests bear rule by their means."[152] This distinction plays into the second phase of her argument.

While the role of priest may have been reserved for men, "that women were called to the prophetic office . . . is universally admitted. Miriam, Deborah, and Huldah were prophetesses."[153] Her last example in the Jewish tradition is Anna, who was on hand when Jesus was presented in the Temple by his parents. Termed a prophet in Luke's Gospel, Anna proclaimed Jesus as Messiah "to all who were looking for the redemption of Jerusalem."[154] In Christian scriptures, Grimké considers Pentecost, when the Holy Spirit descended on the disciples in Jerusalem. In her view, all gathered there received the Holy Spirit, men as well as women. When observers accused the gathered disciples of being drunk, Peter quotes the Jewish prophet Joel who proclaimed: "In the last days it will be, God declares, that I will pour my Spirit upon all flesh, and your sons and your daughters shall prophesy."[155] In her eyes, that proclamation establishes the validity of women filling the prophetic role and exhorting others to righteous action.[156] To bolster her view, she quotes several biblical commentaries reinforcing her interpretation, albeit without full citations.[157] In addition, she highlights examples in Christian scripture of women filling this role: the daughters of Philip as well as Priscilla and Phebe, whom Paul describes as his co-workers in ministry.[158]

The distinction she draws between the prophetic and priestly roles is strategically shrewd. She is not urging the ordination of women. Rather, she is arguing for women to have a voice as moral agents and perhaps, through preaching, as prophetic voices. Her position is, then, not radical or revolutionary. Instead, she seeks restoration of women to a status they enjoyed both in the early church and, more important, in the divine plan.

In her final letter, "Man Equally Guilty with Woman in the Fall," she reiterates some of her arguments and underscores her view that women have a moral imperative to assume the role God intends for them. Mentioning the custom of Jewish women's lighting the Sabbath candle, she suggests that act was to remind them of "their original mother, who first extinguished the lamp of righteousness,—and to remind them of their obligation to re-kindle it." If women are responsible for the Fall, as popular opinion held, Grimké reasons they have a powerful reason "to labor with double diligence, for the regeneration of that world she has been instrumental in ruining."[159] Woman, who is "charged with all the sin that exists in the world" has, she suggests, "a solemn duty to labor for its extinction." In the present circumstance, women are permitted to offer religious instruction and guidance in Sunday school and to proclaim the good news through singing under the guidance of men. In addition, they have frequently labored to support the education of young men for ministry. Breaking out of the false constraints imposed upon them, they must, in the current crisis, "prepare themselves for more extensive usefulness by making use of those religious and literary privileges and advantages that are within their reach, if they will only stretch out their hands and possess them."[160] Women must rise to the occasion to address the wrongs of the current day. "In contemplating the great moral reformations of the day, and the part which they are bound to take in them, instead of puzzling themselves with the harassing, because unnecessary inquiry, how far they may go without overstepping the bounds of propriety, which separate male and female duties, they will only inquire, 'Lord, what wilt thou have us to do?'"[161]

A Prophetic Rhetoric of Dissent

In arguing for the moral equality of women and their divinely conferred status as moral agents, Grimké urges women to live into their identity as Christians. Women, she insists, must be accountable to God "for the use of those talents with which her Heavenly Father has entrusted her."[162] To enable women to do so, rather than completely abandoning contemporary gender stereotypes, she wants to loosen the inappropriate, oppressive "bonds" that constrict women's activities to a narrowly conceived domestic sphere. Hers was what modern scholars term a rhetoric of dissent, "the balancing point between stability and change."[163] She accomplishes this delicate balancing act by drawing on scripture to warrant women's political activism as she affirms some elements of contemporary gender stereotypes.

In her consideration of gender stereotypes in the nineteenth century, historian Barbara Welter explains: "Religion or piety was the core of woman's virtue, the source of her strength."[164] In this view, women's innate religiosity made them more open to divine inspiration and invited them to work in cooperation with the divine to improve the world.[165] This widely held stereotype provides Grimké with an opening to suggest, not abandoning this stance, but embracing it more fully. In essence, by affirming and then extending gender stereotypes, she opens a space for pious women, as women, to become advocates for others. She does not dispute the idea that piety is key to a woman's identity. Instead, she firmly dissents from the understanding of female piety that limits it to the domestic sphere. With strong conviction, she avers: "To perform our duties, we must comprehend our rights and responsibilities; and it is because we do not understand, that we now fall so far short in the discharge of our obligations . . . we have rested satisfied with the sphere marked out for us by man, never detecting the fallacy of that reasoning which forbids woman to exercise some of her noblest faculties, and stamps with the reproach of indelicacy those actions by which women were formerly dignified and exalted in the church."[166] In her interpretation, women's identity as moral beings compels them to be the light of the world and, consequently, to enter the fray of politics. Women should not, she insists, simply urge men to take up the "great moral reformations" of the age. They should, instead, recognize "it is the Lord's work" that they themselves must advance with or without the aid of men.[167]

From this perspective, Grimké criticizes women's obsession with dress and frivolities, an interest supported and encouraged by men. Women's often keen interest in these matters reflects men's seeking to divert them from their true natures by appealing to their basest instincts. As she puts in her fifth letter, men have refused to treat them as equals, instead encouraging their frivolity.[168] Adam Clarke, an Irish Wesleyan cleric, author of an important biblical commentary, substantiates her claim: "woman has been invidiously defined, *an animal of dress.* How long will they permit themselves to be thus degraded?"[169] As her discussion indicates, Grimké believes that women were made for grander, greater, more important things than obsession with dress.

In her personal life, to reinforce this idea, she invariably wore simple Quaker attire, a strategic move that enabled her to hold onto the "rhetorical advantage and safe social image that such dress" afforded her.[170] Her attire, in other words, both demonstrated her rejection of an unhealthy fixation on finery and located her squarely in appropriately decorous femininity. In addition, as Mattingly observes, both sisters' dress "lessened the masculine perception associated with their public speaking" advocacy and augmented their rhetorical effectiveness.[171]

Grimké's choice of genre reflects her honoring and concomitantly subverting gender stereotypes. In writing private letters that she intends for a public audience, she adapts and modifies a form with deep roots in Christian history: the pastoral epistle. Of the twenty-seven books in Christian scripture, twenty-one are epistles, many of which Paul wrote to early Christian communities with advice and theological explanations. Her earlier effort, "An Epistle to the Clergy of the Southern States," followed the Pauline model. Kristin Vonnegut argues that an epistle in such a Pauline mode implied a particular relationship between the author and its intended recipients: "that of superior to an inferior." Moreover, such an epistle "was considered a public, rather than a domestic, activity and, consequently, inappropriate for women."[172] Vonnegut suggests that Grimké learned from that experience both the value of the epistolary form and its risks when employed by a woman. In effect, a public epistle might alienate some members of her likely audience.

Consequently, for this effort Grimké ostensibly chose a personal letter, which suggests discretion and restraint, although her topic is controversial. As Karlyn Kohrs Campbell and E. Claire Jerry observe, women must be careful to find a role and format that "affirms her femininity," rather than risk appearing masculine.[173] The writing of an ostensibly private letter, in contrast to public speaking or even public letters, lay within the boundaries of female decorum. As Jean Wasko notes, letter writing perfectly fit the social construction of femininity during the era.[174] Moreover, just as petitions about political issues became an acceptable form of public action, while public speaking was controversial, the letter was a venue that was far less aggressive than a magazine article or a newspaper column. Vonnegut opines: "Apparently, Grimké chose the letter form for its elasticity. By writing letters, she remained within woman's sphere yet addressed public issues."[175]

Her choice of a correspondent for the letters was also telling and strategic. Mary S. Parker was President of the Boston Female Anti-Slavery Society and had supported the sisters' earlier lecture tour. Thus, Grimké could address her as "Dear Friend" throughout the text and close with "Thine in the bonds of womanhood." This approach gave her letters a personal flavor, although they were certainly directed toward a larger audience.

Her private letters quickly became public. The initial publishing periodical was perfect for her format. *The New England Spectator* was a short-lived (late 1824–1838) periodical whose motto was "A family newspaper, designed to promote the study of the Bible, family religion, active piety, the abolition of war, slavery, licentiousness, & c, and the circulation of useful intelligence."[176] Her third letter, which was her response to the Pastoral Letter, was published on the front page of *The Liberator* on October 6, 1837, and the entire series appeared there in early 1838.[177] Clearly, a primary focus for Grimké is women and men within reform circles. Many readers of the publications that printed her letters were veterans of the petition drives both for abolition and Indian removal. Thus, as Zaeske and Portnoy argue, these readers already conceived of themselves as fully engaged citizens. In many ways, Grimké's ideas affirmed their new identity as political agents around and for pressing moral issues. At the same time, the letter format preserved at least the allusion of her speaking from the domestic sphere and practicing appropriate female decorum.

Her allegedly "personal" letters to a friend and her grounding of her appeals for a change in women's status in scripture enabled her to perform the "balancing act" between stability and change that Ivie describes as typical of dissent. Rather than rejecting gender stereotypes outright, she was able to expand them. Indeed, in her purview, women's activism was a natural extension of their roles as Christian women. She did not question the domestic sphere as women's special province; rather she saw women as capable of enlarging that role. In her work on women's education, she urged: "let her fulfill in the circle of home all the obligations that rest upon her, but let her not waste her powers on inferior objects when higher and holier responsibilities demand her attention."[178]

Grimké's decision to approach her project as dissent rather than explicit confrontation reflects both her personal views and her background. Her entire view of women's proper sphere derived from scripture. Not surprisingly, she relied on that resource to make her argument. Furthermore, although she supported women's education and advocated for their opportunity to find their own path, she perceived their role as complementary to men's, not identical. Although some of her ideas seemed radical to her contemporaries, in truth, she insisted that she was simply trying to free women from artificial bonds so they could be better wives, mothers, and Christians.

Rhetorical dissent is inherently prophetic. Dissent always affirms ideas or principles that are embraced and even revered by a community as it calls for corrective measures. In making her argument, Grimké dons the prophetic mantle. She carefully limns the contemporary status of women, castigating males for oppressing and marginalizing them much as the Jewish prophets criticized religious leaders for misleading followers. When women are freed from the "bonds of womanhood," they will be able to join with men in bringing the kingdom of God to fruition in this world. Like the Hebrew prophets, Grimké foresees restoration and new life after the long Babylonian exile of male control and usurpation.

Grimké's rhetorical posture of dissent was especially forceful and appealing to her target audience. She called her audience to return to first principles as established in scripture, to claim their divine identity as moral agents bound to work for the purification and reform of social injustices. Those who heed her call join her as prophetic voices, not only advocating for significant reforms, but also, in so doing, building God's kingdom in the world.

The genre and medium she chose, the grounding of her argument in scripture, and her affirming but gently correcting contemporary conceptions of gender roles were ideally suited for women interested in the moral reform issues of the day. In some sense, she was "preaching to the choir" of women who had confronted constraints in their efforts to advocate on behalf of the downtrodden and disprivileged. Her approach justified and dignified their work.

Enactment

Perform your duties as moral beings.

—SARAH MOORE GRIMKÉ, *LETTERS ON THE EQUALITY OF THE SEXES*

Certainly, with and through a feminist hermeneutic, Grimké makes a compelling argument for her view of women's appropriate role as moral agents. Her situating that role as a corrective to contemporary gender stereotypes rather than an abrogation of them is also appealing. Her final move is to craft a compelling persona that reflects the competent, morally engaged, and empowered role she envisions for women. In seeking not only to persuade her readers, but also to empower and embolden them, she reveals herself as the model of a moral agent scripture outlines.

First, in making her arguments Grimké demonstrates significant skill in biblical exegesis. As she looks at scripture through a feminist lens, revealing a deep familiarity with biblical texts as well as commentaries, she demonstrates an ability to find new meanings in familiar texts and to rescue some passages from obscurity. Repeatedly, she suggests to her readers that the interpretations they have received from ministers and religious leaders reflect a biased, limited, male view. Her alternative translation for a key verb in the passage in Genesis, which male commentators typically construed to mandate women's submission to their husband, begins this approach. Within the Christian scriptures, she points to a woman involved in Paul's ministry. In standard translations, Phoebe (she refers to her as Phebe) is called a "servant of the church at Cenchreae." However, in reference to Tychicus in Ephesians, the same Greek word, *diakonos,* is translated as "minister."[179] Lucretia Mott, quite possibly following Grimké, will use this same example to expose the bias in male translators. Frances Willard and Elizabeth Cady Stanton, who also knew Grimké's work, will later reiterate, as she argues, that "almost all that has been written on this subject [the proper sphere of woman] has been the result of a misconception of the simple truths revealed in Scriptures, in consequence of false translation of many passages of Holy Writ."[180] Those translations are the work of men.

She strengthens her arguments by drawing on external sources, most often written by men. Throughout her letters, she quotes contemporary biblical commentaries to support her views. In her letter on women in the ministry, she cites no fewer than nine commentaries written by men that support her ideas. The diverse and intriguing list includes: Thomas Scott, an Anglican clergyman and one of the founders of the Church Missionary Society; Adam Clarke, an influential member of the Methodist Wesleyan Conference; Joseph John Gurney, a Quaker minister and abolitionist; and Matthew Henry, a nineteenth century nonconformist minister who produced a verse-by-verse commentary on scripture. Using such sources demonstrates that, although her ideas may be fresh and challenging to her readers, they are not outside the ken of more open-minded male experts. In proving her point, she also cites two men, who, initially opposed the preaching of women, changed their opinions when they heard women preach.[181]

In making her arguments, Grimké shows a willingness to debate with men, from the ministers who penned the Pastoral Letter to the authors of standard biblical commentaries. She directly indicts men for their role in the subjugation and oppression of women. In her second letter, she has insisted that men have deliberately debased and enslaved women's minds.[182] Here she pleads: "All I ask of our brethren is, that they will take their feet from off our necks, and permit us to stand upright on that ground which God designed us to occupy."[183] Grimké softens her attack somewhat by identifying males who support her views. Nonetheless, her willingness to go toe-to-toe with men whom she perceives to be the oppressors of women suggests significant strength and resolve, two characteristics not typically attributed to women of her time.

Second, throughout her letters Grimké evinces a deep concern for women's spiritual integrity in being permitted to follow their sense of God's call to them. She clearly responds to the claim in the Pastoral Letter that the New Testament suggests "the appropriate duties and influences of women" and affirms that "no one can desire more earnestly than I do, that woman may move exactly in the sphere which her Creator has assigned her." She explains that "the Lord Jesus defines the duties of his followers in his Sermon on the Mount" where he calls on all his followers, men and women, to be the light of the world: "Let your light so shine before men, that they may see your good works, and glorify you Father, which is in heaven."[184] By connecting her perspective to that call, Grimké suggests that her ultimate concern is the spiritual welfare and well-being of women.

Explicitly confronting the portion of the Pastoral Letter, where the ministers castigate women advocating for social reform and assert that such work makes their character "unnatural," Grimké responds with strong moral fervor:

> The motto of woman, when she is engaged in the great work of public reformation should be, — "The Lord is my light and my salvation, whom shall I fear? The Lord is the strength of my life; of whom shall I be afraid?" [Psalm 27:1] She must feel, if she feels rightly, that she is fulfilling one of the most important duties laid upon her as an accountable being, and that her character, instead of being "unnatural," is in exact accordance with the will of Him to whom and to no other, she is responsible for the talents and gifts confined to her.[185]

As Christians, women have a responsibility to address the political issues of their day that have moral entailments. With real passion, she exclaims:

> It is not my intention, or indeed do I think it is in my power, to point out the precise duties of women. To him who still teacheth by his Holy Spirit as never man taught, I refer my beloved sisters. There is a vast field of usefulness before them. The signs of the time give portentous evidence, that a day of deep trial is approaching; and I urge them, by every consideration of a Savior's dying love, by the millions of heathen in our midst, by the sufferings of women in almost every portion of the world, by the fearful ravages which slavery, intemperance, licentiousness and other iniquities are making of the happiness of our fellow creatures, to come to the rescue of a ruined world, and to be co-workers with Jesus Christ.[186]

By adopting this prophetic tone, Grimké is appealing to women to become agents for others, to work not for their own aggrandizement but instead for the protection and support of other human beings. Such a role accords perfectly with the widespread belief that one of women's prime virtues was her piety, her natural inclination toward morality.

Although we have no evidence that Grimké knew or formally studied classical rhetoric except possibly in her brief informal legal studies with her father and brothers, her *Letters on the Equality of the Sexes* reveals a firm understanding of basic principles of persuasion. If Aristotle is accurate in asserting that "rhetoric is the faculty of observing in any given case the available means of persuasion," then Grimké is a master of that art. Indeed, her letters provide almost a textbook case study of the skillful deployment of the three forms of proof he and other classical theorists embrace: logos, pathos, and ethos.[187] As we have seen, she constructs a careful argument for women's moral equality. At the same time, by employing the strategy of dissent, she crafts a rhetorical space for her followers to embrace their moral agency within the framework of prevailing gender stereotypes. In so doing, they become prophetic voices in their society, calling others to help reform and improve their society. Finally, through the persona she constructs, she reveals herself to be a person of good will, good sense, and good moral character, the key components of ethos.[188]

To appreciate Grimké's accomplishment, we must also recall her specific focus. In this work, she is not, as others will do, arguing for the broad spectrum of women's rights. Rather, she seeks to liberate women to discern and engage the roles and activities to which God calls them. Although her focus is narrow, as we have seen, her persuasive appeal is substantial.

Treading New Ground

I do not feel as if I could surrender my right to discuss
any great moral subject.

—SARAH AND ANGELINA GRIMKÉ, *LETTER TO WRIGHT*

Grimké's letters did, indeed, venture into "nearly untrodden ground." Emerging ten years before the Seneca Falls meeting, Grimké's *Letters on the Equality of the Sexes* played a critical role in what might be called a "pregenesis" stage of the movement for woman's rights.[189] As Gring-Pemble argues, before the movement for woman's rights crystallized into organization, potential members had to develop a "feminist consciousness" that enabled them to explore their identity as women, to share experiences, and to identify shared challenges.[190] For many, Grimké's feminist hermeneutic opened new perspectives on what scripture said and meant. Her deft exposure of male's biased translations and interpretations support her idea of how males usurp power over women. If Miriam, Deborah, and Huldah could be prophets and if Phoebe could stand alongside Tychicus as a minister, then clearly God intended women to be instruments of bringing light into the world. While the world might criticize their activities and castigate them as unfeminine, Grimké offered an alternate identity: moral agents commissioned by God to be prophetic voices in the world. Fortified and empowered by her work, Christian middle-class women could see themselves in a new way and claim their place in movements for social reform. Her arguments provided them abundant fodder not only to answer opposition but also to vindicate their actions. Within the frame she provided, they could and should be in the vanguard of perfecting American society and calling it to a nobler vision.

Later scholars have also acknowledged the enduring importance of her ideas. Lerner observed her "feminist thought had leaped far ahead of her generation" and secured her position as a "major feminist thinker."[191] She also notes that Sarah "offered the best and most coherent Bible argument for women's equality yet written by a woman."[192] In *Mothers of Feminism,* a survey of Quaker women's role in nineteenth reform efforts, Margaret Hope Bacon indicates her letters "served as a clarion call to the coming struggle."[193] But Grimké did more than simply summon women to a fuller role as moral agents—she provided them with an arsenal of arguments to support their advocacy.

These well-deserved accolades do not mean, however, that her views were warmly embraced in all quarters. Grimké's idea of women's proper role as moral agents was radical for her day. Within male abolitionist circles, the issue of women's involvement produced a split.[194] While William Lloyd Garrison remained a staunch supporter of women's efforts, including their speaking to promiscuous audiences, even supporters like Theodore Weld and the Reverend Amos Phelps had reservations and urged restraints.[195] Some leaders like the poet John Greenleaf Whittier and the Tappan brothers "feared that the sisters endangered the cause of abolition by mixing in a new issue, women's rights."[196] In a letter to a friend in August 1837, Angelina expressed her support of her sister even as she acknowledged the tensions they produced: "I am still glad of Sisters Letters & believe they are doing *great* good. Some nobleminded *women* cheer her on, & she feels encouraged to persevere, the brethren notwithstanding. I tell them that this is part of the great doctrine of Human rights & can no more be separated from

Emancipation than the light from the heat of the sun; the rights of the slave & woman blend like the colors of the rainbow."[197]

Just three years later, the 1840 World Anti-Slavery Conference's refusal to seat Lucretia Mott as a representative of Philadelphia Female Anti-Slavery Society proved the sisters right about the need to advocate for women's rights. That experience prompted Lucretia Mott and Elizabeth Cady Stanton along with others to found a separate movement for women's rights, in part to allow women to follow their consciences and divine calling.[198] Since both women knew and admired Grimké's work, there can be little doubt that her arguments undergirded that critical decision.

The trajectory of Sarah and Angelina's public careers was nothing less than meteoric. When Garrison published what he termed a "soul-thrilling epistle" without Angelina's permission in the *Liberator* on September 19, 1835, he catapulted her into the mainstream of abolitionist activism.[199] By the next year, Sarah Grimké had penned "An Epistle to the Clergy of the Southern States," a decidedly public piece of activism. In the fall of that year, she and Angelina began meeting with women's groups in New York about the evils of slavery and in favor of abolitionism. Their work and the reaction to it made clear the need for women to begin advocating for themselves. After the publication of *Letters on the Equality of the Sexes* in 1838, Grimké largely left the public arena although she remained active in organizations. However, in a career that lasted just three years, she exerted an immense influence on both abolitionism and women's rights. She eloquently articulated arguments that grounded the work of women who followed her. At the same time, she offered a role model for them in their own advocacy.

Despite their prominence in the early abolitionist and woman's rights movements, Angelina and Sarah Grimké quickly disappeared from the public consciousness. In the early 1960s when feminist historian Gerda Lerner became interested, "Sarah and Angelina Grimké were virtually unknown to the American reading public."[200] Her joint biography introduced the sisters to contemporary audiences and stimulated a number of volumes devoted to their work as abolitionists and women's rights advocates. Now, more than 150 years after her death, it is clear that, for all her reserve and modesty, Sarah Grimké was, indeed, a prophetic foremother of American feminism.

FOUR

Lucretia Coffin Mott's "Discourse on Woman"

Woman as God Meant Her to Be

There is nothing of greater importance to the well-being of society at large—of man as well as woman—than the true and proper position of woman.

—LUCRETIA COFFIN MOTT, "DISCOURSE ON WOMAN"

When Lucretia Coffin Mott turned her attention to the "woman question" in Philadelphia in 1849, she was already well-known within both Quaker and abolitionist circles for her strong views on that topic.[1] But she did not seek out the opportunity to explore that subject. Rather, at the invitation and insistence of friends, she accepted the challenge to respond to a talk by Richard Henry Dana Sr., a popular lecturer, who had argued strongly and apparently persuasively for women's traditional role as a retiring helpmeet to men and whose proper sphere was the home.[2] In her response, "Discourse on Woman," Mott offers a strikingly different picture of women, their roles, and their responsibilities in the world.

Becoming an Advocate for Women's Rights

In the speech, she acknowledges that the subject of the "woman question" had "claimed my earnest interest for many years."[3] In fact, William H. Johnson, a fellow abolitionist, opined that "as early as 1825 she was generally known to have a peculiar testimony on this subject [female elevation]."[4] She was almost certainly familiar with and may have read Margaret Fell's "Women's Speaking Justified," which provided the theological framework for her own ministry as a Quaker woman.[5] Moreover, writing to Caroline H. Dall in August 1867, Mott reports forty years earlier she had read Mary Wollstonecraft's *Vindication of the Rights of Woman,* which offered both a natural

: 83 :

rights argument for women's having political voice and a stinging critique of contemporary practices of acculturation for women. That work had since been "a centre table book," which she had circulated wherever she could find readers. She notes that Sarah Grimké had also read the book sometime around 1835.[6] By the time of her "Discourse on Woman" speech, she had read Grimké's *Letters on the Equality of the Sexes,* which she called "the most important work" since Wollstonecraft.[7] In essence, when Mott responded to Dana she had both a long history of reflecting on women's rights and a solid arsenal of arguments.

Lucretia Mott's Quakerism and Nine Partner Schools

Mott's views on abolition and women had their roots in her Quakerism and, throughout her life, the two issues were intertwined. A birthright Quaker, she was born on Nantucket Island on January 3, 1793, as the second daughter of Anna Folger Coffin and Thomas Coffin Jr. Quaker historian Margaret Hope Bacon contends that "the life of the island" gave "women a great deal of responsibility" while their husbands were at sea as whalers. Furthermore, Quakerism, the dominant religion there, acknowledged the spiritual equality of men and women and "created a climate in which a woman could find her way."[8] Her mother modelled independence and self-reliance in running a small store and managing a family during her husband's long absences. From her, Mott derived a view of women as empowered and competent. She was apparently proud of these Nantucket roots and frequently referred to them. As one biographer observes, "the island of her birth shaped her and gave her a sense of herself that she carried with her all her life."[9]

While she was still in Nantucket, she learned also about the horrors of slavery. One of her school readers, *Mental Improvement,* contained a rather strong (for school age children) critique of the slave trade. In that account "natives of Africa were snatched from their own country, friends, and connections by the hand of violence and power" to be transported by British ships to the West Indies where they were "sold in an open market like cattle, and afterwards employed in the most laborious and servile occupations," and would "pass the rest of their lives in involuntary and wretched slavery." The Europeans involved in the trade induced cooperation from some Africans in procuring slaves "by bribes of rum and other spiritous liquors, of which they are immoderately fond."[10] Apparently, her teacher also had a copy of British abolitionist "Thomas Clarkson's diagram of the ship Brookes, which showed almost five hundred African captives being transported to slavery in

Jamaica."[11] Thus, Mott's childhood upbringing and experiences introduced her to two subjects that became central concerns in her adult life.

Her enrollment at age thirteen in Nine Partners School in Dutchess County, New York deepened and profoundly shaped her understanding of Quakerism and her opposition to slavery. The New York Yearly Meeting founded Nine Partners in 1796 to provide both "'useful and necessary learning' and immersion in the religious culture of the Society of friends." In the hopes of grounding children in Quaker principles and preventing their succumbing to the lures of the larger society, the school "sought to discourage materialism" and inculcate the Quaker doctrines of "obedience to the inward Principle of Light & Truth," as well as "Silence & Attention."[12] Arriving at Nine Partners as a boarding student in 1806, she "enjoyed an extraordinary education, giving her skills superior to those of most men at the time." At this co-educational institution, "male and female students received the same education in reading, writing, math, accounts, and grammar," although "business and domestic training were implicitly segregated by sex." Bacon suggests that "Quaker academies were the first to attempt co-education. . . . As a result Quaker girls as a group were among the first to receive any sort of higher education in this United States."[13] This approach reflected the Quaker view of "entirely distinct spheres for men and women as unnatural."[14] In addition to traditional academic subjects, the school "exposed her to the tensions between Quaker simplicity and prosperity, their antislavery testimony and the slave economy, their peculiarity and their connections to the larger society."[15]

At Nine Partners, Mott learned still more about slavery and its horrors.[16] Elias Hicks, who "felt led to shake his beloved Society of Friends awake to its present duty in regard to slavery," was one of the founders of the school and on the school committee. Hicks was known for his "fiery denunciation of the sin of slavery, of spilled blood and human degradation and defilements."[17] James Mott Sr., the superintendent of the school and the father of Lucretia's future husband, was "a determined abolitionist and often spoke against slavery in Meeting."[18] There she first read "An Essay on Slavery" by Thomas Clarkson, whose diagram of a slave ship had hung on the walls of her Nantucket classroom. His accounts outraged her. Even as the instructors acknowledged that some Quakers continued to use the products of slave labor, they attributed this to the "bias of custom" and insisted on "the immorality of slave products."[19] In a lesson that would characterize Mott's reform efforts, students were encouraged to believe that "zeal and perseverance, in a right cause, seldom fail of success."[20] Implicitly, then, students, including Mott, were encouraged to develop such qualities in seeking to eliminate slavery.

Mott studied the Bible. But she also encountered the differing views among Quakers about the relative weight of scripture and the inner light in discernment. Some Quakers, like many early nineteenth century Protestants in the grip of the Great Awakening, placed an emphasis on scripture. "Other Quakers, however, believed that Scriptures were subordinate to inner light." James Mott Sr. urged students to "consult the Scriptures more than the systems of men; but attend still more to that divine principle in your own hearts . . . it is by submitting to the teachings of this inward monitor, that we both learn, and are enabled to fulfill our duty to God and to one another."[21] His emphasis on the inner light aligned with Hicks; that viewpoint would be a key element in the schism that soon positioned Hicksite Quakers against Orthodox Quakers. Clearly, the "commitment to the inner light and individual moral authority" that characterized Mott's later ministry had deep roots in these Nine Partner years.[22]

In time, when she moved into the role of teacher, Mott also received an important early lesson in gender inequities. Her future husband, James, was an assistant teacher who made far more than Deborah Rogers, the head female teacher. Mott herself worked for room and board but without pay. Four years later, the inequity had grown. According to biographer Margaret Hope Bacon, the injustice of the situation "outraged Lucretia," who "resolved to claim for myself all that an impartial Creator had bestowed."[23]

Mott's parents sent her to Nine Partners for a "religiously guarded education" that would protect her from "contamination with 'the world's people.'"[24] The school had certainly provided that. In that "protective politically and theologically liberal community" she blossomed, coming to appreciate her own talents: "a quick, retentive memory; a probing brilliant mind; an ability to reason logically."[25] There she also memorized William Cowper's "The Task," which she would draw on throughout her life, in part because it reflected her attitudes toward the prevailing views of both women and abolition.[26] A few lines of that poem, which she quotes in her speech, summarized her attitude toward Dana's position:

> Such dupes are men to custom, and so prone
> To reverence what is ancient, and can plead
> A course of long observance for its use,
> That even servitude, the worst of ills,

Because delivered down from sire to son,
Is kept and guarded as a sacred thing.

Quaker Minister and Abolitionist

In 1811, at age 18, Lucretia married James during a regular Quaker meeting, where, as was the custom, they made their vows to each other without a presiding minister and with no mention of obedience. She noted that in Quaker marriages, there was no "assumed authority or admitted inferiority; no *promise of obedience.*" Rather between the partners, "independence is equal, their dependence mutual, and their obligations reciprocal."[27]

When she and James settled in Philadelphia and began to raise a family, they were active in the Twelfth Street Monthly Meeting. However, Lucretia did not emerge as a leader in that group until 1818, a year after the death of her son Thomas.[28] When she rose to speak, after acknowledging that "all our efforts to resist temptation and overcome the world prove fruitless unless aided by the Holy Spirit," she prayed for God to preserve them from evil "that we may be wholly devoted to Thee and Thy glorious cause." Some members of the community recognized her words as "an appearance in the ministry." Impressed by "her sweet, clear voice and her earnestness" and "stirred by the spiritual power behind her simple words," they encouraged her to speak again when she was moved to do so.[29] Gradually, as she discovered her own abilities, the community perceived a "genuine gift" and in 1821 they formally recognized her as a minister.[30]

Almost immediately, she excited criticism. In one presentation, some members took exception to her suggesting that persons should be judged more by their "likeness to Christ" rather than their "notions of Christ." When two women elders visited her to offer a gentle corrective, she silenced them by pointing out she was simply quoting William Penn, the early American Quaker leader. Moreover, from time to time, she challenged some actions by the community, believing them to be unfair. She rather quickly developed a reputation as controversial, a charge that would recur throughout her life and which she sometimes embraced.[31] She also became known for introducing the subject of women's appropriate role both in "social circles and in her public communications." Since this was more than two decades before the Seneca Falls meeting, advocates for women's rights were rare. Faulkner opines that "Lucretia's focus on the female sex suggested her transformation over the course of the decade from a respectable Quaker minister, wife, and mother to a controversial dissenter, social critic, and activist."[32]

During these years, as the Mott family grew, "the Hicksite controversy split the Society of Friends in America." Hicks criticized Quaker leaders in Philadelphia, including Jonathan Evans who had interrupted Sarah Grimké, for silencing those who disagreed, for emphasizing the Bible rather than the inner light in discernment, and for continuing their financial connections to slavery. Finally, in 1827, these disagreements produced a rupture in that meeting that quickly spread throughout the Society. The Motts, who had known Hicks since their Nine Partners days and had hosted him in their home, agreed with his views. Ejected from the Twelfth Street meeting they had attended, the Motts began joining the Hicksites in worship.[33] For her part, Lucretia spent the next few years defending and working for the Hicksites.

In the 1830s, the Motts met William Lloyd Garrison, a young radical who had worked for fellow Hicksite Quaker Benjamin Lundy on the *Genius of Universal Emancipation*. At his request, they arranged a public meeting for him there in Philadelphia, after which Lucretia offered him some coaching on his public speaking.[34] This meeting proved fateful for both; the Motts became sympathetic to Garrison's call for immediate emancipation, which echoed Hicks's views, and he gained powerful supporters. Mott admitted her admiration for Garrison: "there are few of my contemporaries whose characters I more revere." In a letter to his wife, Garrison described her as a "bold and fearless thinker," later observing that she had helped him banish "the theological dogmas which I once regarded as essential."[35]

Having begun publishing *The Liberator* in 1831, Garrison, along with Arthur Tappan, moved abolitionism further into the spotlight by gathering abolitionists in Philadelphia to organize the American Anti-Slavery Society. Not surprisingly, as in most antislavery groups, many were Hicksite Quakers.[36] From the balcony of that organizational meeting, Mott, one of seven women attending, was permitted to offer some ideas, but not participate fully in the discussion. But her contribution was significant. At her suggestion, the meeting's proposed statement, the "Declaration of Sentiments,"[37] connected its view first to the Declaration of Independence and then to "Divine Revelation: "With entire confidence in the over-ruling justice of God, we plant ourselves upon the Declaration of our Independence and the truths of Divine Revelation as upon the EVERLASTING ROCK."[38] After hearing her comments, one delegate remarked: "I have never before heard a woman speak at a public meeting. She said but a few words but they were spoken so modestly, in such sweet tones, and yet withal so decisively, that no one could fail to be pleased."[39]

Because one resolution from the meeting urged women to organize their own antislavery societies, just three days later Mott and others organized the Philadelphia Female Anti-Slavery Society.[40] Many, including Mott, had been and were involved in antislavery petition drives and were eager to further their work.[41] Their organization was distinctive because of its rather unusual biracial membership.[42] Later she recalled she had "no idea of the meaning of preambles and resolutions and votings."[43] The preamble to their constitution declared slavery was "contrary to the laws of God and of our far-famed Declaration of Independence." The women pledged themselves "as professing Christians" to publicize their views about the "flagrant injustice and deep Sin of slavery" and to work for its eradication so that slaves could enjoy their inalienable rights" delineated in the Declaration of Independence.[44] Over time, the group engaged in all sorts of activities to support abolitionism, including hosting antislavery fairs and gathering signatures for petitions to Congress.[45] One modern critic contends the organization was also a "cradle of feminism."[46]

As committed as these women were to eradicating slavery, their public efforts were often unwelcome. Responding to the opposition Angelina Grimké's speaking to promiscuous audiences aroused, the 1836 annual report of the Philadelphia Female Anti-Slavery Society echoed Sarah Grimké's call for women to be guided by God's direction rather than human rules: "We would never overstep the boundaries of propriety, we would not needlessly provoke the frown of anyone, but when our brethren and sisters lie crushed and bleeding under the arm of tyranny, we must do with our might what our hands find to do for their deliverance, pausing only to inquire 'What is right?' and not 'What will be universally approved?'"[47]

In 1840, as a delegate from Philadelphia Female Anti-Slavery Society, Mott and her husband, also a delegate, traveled to the World Anti-Slavery Convention in London. Among their traveling companions were Elizabeth Cady Stanton and her husband, Henry, also a delegate.[48] After a lively debate, the convention declined to seat the women delegates, consigning them to seats in the balcony if those were not required by recognized delegates.[49] One record of the meeting reported the women's disappointment with the decision "to exclude women from a seat in the convention, as co-equals in the advocacy of Universal Liberty."[50] At that point, Stanton and Mott agreed that women needed to organize and advocate for their own rights. But Stanton's growing family delayed their action for eight years. Then in 1848, they summoned the Seneca Falls meeting, which James Mott agreed to chair since the women did not feel comfortable in that role.[51]

Empowered and guided by Quaker theology and the denomination's commitment to abolition, Mott and women like the Grimké sisters were willing to risk public opprobrium by advocating publicly for what they saw as a moral imperative. Like Sarah and Angelina Grimké, Mott "received harsh criticism, even from fellow antislavery advocates, for speaking to 'promiscuous' audiences. Among proslavery forces she was denounced as a racial 'amalgamator' and more than once was threatened by unruly, violent mobs."[52] However, Mott embraced the controversy she attracted, arguing that "it was the obligation of reformers 'to stand out in our heresy'" in defying both social norms and unjust laws.[53] Her sense of moral agency and responsibility moved her forward. Richard Dana's lecture opened a welcome opportunity to air her views.

Richard Dana's "Sentiments" About Women

Humanity being made of two Sexes

—RICHARD DANA, "WOMAN"

As women moved to advocate for their role in public life, Dana, a well-known critic, poet, and co-founder of the *North American Review,* lectured extensively on Shakespeare's plays. A contemporary account described his work as showing "great skill in discrimination, guided by a certain logic of the heart and life, and not by mere artificial dialectics."[54] His lecture entitled "Woman," which a report in the New York *Literary World* of March 9, 1850 suggested was well-received, precipitated Mott's response. Sympathetic to Dana's viewpoint, the author of the account observed: "Mr. Dana is not at all of the modern school, who affect to make Woman what she is not, never has been, and never can be, man and woman both, or perhaps we should rather say, simply man for the unsexing philosophy ignores the woman altogether."[55] Although the author acknowledged that "there has been some cavil at Mr. Dana's lecture, as it has been delivered on other occasions, we are convinced that the heart of every woman present responded to its beauty and truth; its harmonious position of woman in the scale of creation, not the inferior of man, but his divinely constituted complement, the other half of a perfect whole."[56]

With its traditional view of women's role, Dana's lecture reflected the "romantic idealism" of traditional gender stereotypes as had the Pastoral Letter more than ten years earlier.[57] Endorsing the view of True Womanhood, Dana's talk both reflected the social context for Mott's speech and catalyzed her response. Thus, a consideration of it can illumine her effort.

As the epithet for his lecture, Dana chose lines from a 1641 poem from by William Cartwright that honored a royal marriage:

[Then you will know what Bliss
Angels both have and miss;]
How souls do mix and take fresh growth,
In neither whole, and whole in both.[58]

Echoing these sentiments, Dana insists that, because humanity is "made up of two Sexes, to understand it as a whole we must know its two parts, and to know these truly, we must look at such not respect to itself alone, but relatively to the other,—not simply in its resemblances, but especially in its distinctive attributes."[59] The sexes are, in their essence, complementary.

To understand "woman," Dana insists we must acknowledge that "the essential difference between man and woman," is "grounded" in "a law" which cannot be broken without materially impairing them,—a law and not an accident which has come about through peculiar circumstances, nor as something arbitrarily instituted by man."[60] The source of that law is divine plan. "The increate God alone is independent and complete in himself. Creatures are dependent and incomplete;—dependent upon God absolutely, and reciprocally upon each other; partially to be sure, in the latter case, yet partially in every part."[61] For humans, God has established the institution of marriage, ordaining: "that man and wife are one; and that by the two one perfect being is realized."[62]

Within this context, woman's nature, proper role, and essential characteristics are, in Dana's view, easy to discern. A woman, he avers, may "love with a passion as deep as his, but it must be of a stiller surface, made, as it were, to reflect his love in all its varying forms and hues;—in its utmost ardor, touched with somewhat of a beautiful passiveness." This love must display "her spirit of happy dependence, passiveness, retiring delicacy." If a woman wishes to "be blessed with companionship, sympathy and union," she must "cultivate her mind, her affections, her whole womanly nature, in the spirit of a woman, with all its modest unobtrusiveness, its gentler action, and its quiet retirements."[63] Rather than seeking the man's "strength, authority, command" of power, a woman will find her path to influence in "persuasion, beseeching, gentleness." Rather than man's "stern aspect" of courage, woman should display hers in "patient endurance."[64] The realm where she is most likely to receive the love she seeks and exercise her peculiar form of love is the home. Dana reasoned that rather than seeking the public fray "to act most effectually upon the world, then, and to permanent good, woman must act mediately, rather than directly."[65] Within the home, her influence can shape the man who, in turn, will work in the world.

Dana contends that "the infidel spirit," which seeks to claim "political rights for women in common with men" demands that the "distinctions made between the sexes in the affairs of life, are . . . barriers raised in days of ignorance and tyranny, which must be broken down."[66] Similarly, cries for equality suppose "a sameness of condition, alike regardless of adaptedness in the individual, of that principle of particular diversities and contrarieties, balances, repulsions, and affinities, through which discords and varieties combine, and result in a beautiful and grand harmonic whole."[67] Believing such calls for equality and rights are wrong-headed, he warns of dire consequences if these agitations go unchecked. As he imagines: "It would be fearful to look upon. Crowded by her at the ballot-box, jostled by her in the market-place, out-talked by her in the legislative hall, out-wrangled by her at the bar, and posed by her, if you will, in the professional chair, the very idea of Woman—of the sex feminine would be lost! . . . The change in the world would be monstrous, monstrous!"[68]

Dana cautions women attracted to these new ideas to think instead of "her country's good and the elevation of the public at which she aims" and to consider the profound importance and influence of their role as nurturing mothers in the home.[69] He pleads earnestly with women: "Come not with us, then, into the dust, and toil and strife of outer life."[70] Rather woman should create a haven for the weary man, a place of solace and refreshment from his struggles in the world.

Although his approach may seem antiquated and unpersuasive to most modern ears, it embodies what Aileen Kraditor identifies as a perspective "close to the heart of all antisuffragist orators . . . a sentimental vision of Home and Mother, equal in sanctity to God and the Constitution."[71] Disputing this vision involved challenging "theology, biology, and sociology" because his argument drew loosely on each of these sources for support. For Dana, in the divine plan God established the relationships between males and females as complementary, man and wife, the public figure and the domestic angel. He does not develop the theological argument, but instead takes it as a given, with only slight references to the scripture.[72] In line with that divine plan, woman's biology—her small frame, her perceived physical inferiority, her "gentle" voice—unsuited her for work in the public arena, even the act of voting. As Dana noted, her impetuosity, often labelled elsewhere as "emotionalism" or "illogicality," made woman ill-equipped for the exercise of the franchise.[73] The current social arrangement, he explains, derives from biological and theological truths. He argues that the sociological construction of gender reflects a "separate but equal doctrine of the respective spheres of man and woman."[74] In his view, the entire social order was organized around the home, in which gender relationships were clear and fixed. From this viewpoint, the family enshrined in the home is the primary and critical social unit.[75] Although the lives of women slaves and working women belied these characterizations, these stereotypes were pervasive and persuasive. And, as we shall see, Mott implicitly confirms this view, but also sees an important role for women beyond the domestic realm.

When Mott rose to respond to Dana, she faced a daunting rhetorical challenge. By assuming the public platform, she risked proving his predictions about the results of trespassing gender roles. If she were too aggressively argumentative, she would prove herself to be the "mannish" woman he and many others deplored. On the other hand, if she were too self-effacing and gentle, she would demonstrate his point about the unfitness of women for the public fray. His theological argument, although not well-developed, was especially problematic since his interpretations aligned with well-known and widely accepted views of scriptural passages. What was required of Mott was a firm yet deft rhetorical approach, treading carefully to avoid resembling the unfeminine woman Dana had foretold.

Mott's "Discourse on Woman"

More exalted views upon the subject
—LUCRETIA COFFIN MOTT, "DISCOURSE ON WOMAN"

Although well prepared for this topic, Mott faced a popular and distinguished male lecturer who grounded his position in what he alleged to be God's plan for humanity. Rising to the challenge, she adopts three rhetorical strategies. First, she adroitly assumes the persona of a gentle but prophetic pastor, who guides her audience to see the errors in Dana's position as she gently undermines his authority. Second, employing a brief but clear feminist biblical hermeneutic, she provides an alternate view of God's plan for women, which she carefully grounds in scripture. Unlike Grimké, whose focus is the exegesis, Mott uses exegesis to support and enhance a larger argument. Finally, with examples, both biblical and real life, she demonstrates how women can fill the societally useful role for which God destined them without sacrificing their femininity.[76] Their doing so furthers God's plan of restoring humanity. She is, then, a prophet, pointing society to a path that leads to a fuller realization of God's kingdom on earth. Through and with these strategies, she skillfully invites her audience into a "free discussion" of this important topic that will lead to a fuller understanding and to moderate reforms.[77]

The Gentle Prophetic Pastor

Cognizant of Dana's depiction of women who "talk of privileges and rights in common with man" as having "quitted the better part of womanhood," Mott makes three significant moves in her introduction to create a compelling persona that belies his predictions of "mannishness" while at the same time directly engaging his arguments. First, eschewing a confrontative stance, she positions herself as an interested, admiring, but concerned observer. As Hogan and Solomon note, because "the true and proper position of women" is a topic of great concern for both men and women, she expresses disappointment in Dana's presentation: "It was with great regret, therefore, that I listened a few days ago to a lecture upon this subject, which, . . . was yet fraught with sentiments calculated to retard the progress of woman to the high elevation destined by her Creator."[78] She compliments him fulsomely, suggesting that his speech was "replete with intellectual beauty," contained "much that was true and excellent," and was "presented with such intellectual vigor and beauty." But she does so tactfully, within the context of regret and disappointment. With her compliments and gentle disappointment, Mott both commends and chides Dana. He has not, she indicates, lived up to his potential. Avowing her intent "to point out the fallacy of its reasoning," she concludes that "the speaker . . . did not profess to offer anything like an argument, but rather a sentiment."[79]

Second, in contrast to Dana, she deftly positions herself as forward looking and progressive.[80] Thus, her "regret" about his persuasive comments is not simply personal: she is concerned that "these sentiments . . . would likely ensnare the young."[81] Looking toward the future, she sees youth whose minds are "more open to the reception of more exalted views upon this subject." Additionally, the cultural shift, evidenced by "the increasing attention to female education" and "the improvement in the literature of the age, especially in what is called the 'Ladies' Department,'" signals "a higher estimate of woman in society at large."[82] These things, she hopes, are preparing "the intellectual and the intelligent . . . for the discussion of this question in a manner, which shall tend to ennoble woman and dignify man."[83] Having complimented Dana for his skills, in her introduction, she adroitly places him in the benighted past, not yet open to the winds of progress. This contrast reflects her theological orientation as a Quaker: she is in the prophetic vanguard trying to lead the as-yet unenlightened toward the Light.[84]

Third, in a related vein, Mott also locates the purpose for her talk as in the interest of the common good. She does not "come here with a view to answering any particular parts of the lecture alluded to, in order to point out the fallacy of its reasoning." In her case, the lecture has prompted her not to prepare a formal address but instead "to offer some views for your consideration, though in a desultory manner, which may lead to such reflection and discussion as will present the subject in a true light."[85] In her depiction, she is not there to mount a refutation, although she will do that, but rather to invite conversation and open discussion. With her audience, she is seeking to discern the truth about a vital topic. Her views will test Dana's position, encouraging the audience to decide for themselves where truth lies.

In essence, within a short space, Mott "avoided egregious violations of taboos against female rhetorical aggressiveness, especially avoiding any appearance of debating; she invited audience participation by addressing her listeners as peers capable of sensible deliberation."[86] Simultaneously, she diminished Dana's status. Her acknowledgment of his skillfulness, her orientation of her work as toward the future and for the young, and her depiction of herself as stimulating discussion rather than engaging in argument all build her image as an intelligent and competent pastor. At the same time, she has suggested implicitly that Dana is backward-looking, unfortunately using his considerable skills to prevent what should be a lively and open discussion. With her measured approach, Mott embodies the new woman for whom she will advocate.[87] Moreover, her persona is prophetic: holding current practices up against eternal truths. As we shall see, she positions her ideas as a restoration of the female to her original role in the divine plan and is evidence of the gradual unfolding of God's kingdom on earth.

A Feminist Hermeneutic Uncovers Women's Role in the Divine Plan

Although she labels her presentation as being "desultory," Mott situates her view in the contest of a progressive salvific trajectory.[88] For Quakers, in some senses, Christianity is "a religion of waiting . . . founded on the promise of the second coming of Christ and the end of the world."[89] In that context, Quakers saw themselves as having a particular role to play and a special responsibility to fulfill. Believing that through a profound experience of Christ all people could be brought into a state of "perfection," a forerunner of the second coming, Quakers regarded themselves as a "vanguard elect" whose role was to help others reach that pinnacle.[90] Thus, their role as Christians is to work to usher in God's new creation by working to restore humankind to the original divine plan.[91]

Drawing on the Quaker theology of the second coming, Mott shifts the frame for considering the role of women from the sociological status quo to the trajectory of God's salvific work with humankind. Part of that work is returning women to their divinely ordained sphere. As she traces that salvific arc in and through scripture, with an optimistic, progressive view of the world, Mott delineates the challenge of the present day as letting go of the past, of abandoning outworn traditions so that God's new creation can emerge.[92] Dana's focus is the world as it has been and is; Mott situates the issue of women's role in the context of a world becoming God's kingdom realized on earth.[93]

Throughout his presentation, Dana referred to traditional gender roles as "a law" rather than something "arbitrarily instituted by man."[94] The source of that law is, of course, God, who differentiated the sexes as part of the creative process. To refute his vague theological argument, Mott employs a feminist hermeneutic and relies on specific examples and citations from scripture to disparage his analysis. To begin the body of her remarks, Mott directly denies Dana's claim without mentioning him. Like Sarah Grimké, she turns to the first creation story in Genesis: "In the beginning, man and woman were created equal."[95] "Male and female he created them, and blessed them, and called their name Adam."[96] In contrast to Dana who had simply alluded to God's plan or law for humanity, Mott warrants her views with a direct quotation from scripture.

Strategically, Mott does not dwell on the second account of creation in Genesis in which woman is created from man's rib.[97] She does, however, respond to one portion of that account that seemingly undergirded Dana's position: "To the woman he [God] said, 'I will greatly increase your pangs in childbearing; in pain you shall bring forth children, yet your desire shall be for your husband, and *he shall rule over you.*'"[98] Apparently referring to the portion in italics, Mott insists, as had Grimké, that "The cause of the subjection of woman to man, was early ascribed to disobedience to the command of God. This would seem to show that she was then regarded as *not* occupying her true and rightful position in society."[99] Rather than being God's plan for humankind, as Dana had insisted, male's domination of women was a consequence of the Fall. The social arrangement Dana embraced was a disruption of God's plan, not the divine plan itself. In highlighting the tension between this account and the first story of creation, Mott resolves the contradiction by reinterpreting the traditional male exegesis. Although she does not follow Grimké's explanation of the translation issue, her conclusion is the same: the subjugation of women was a predictable outcome of the Fall and a departure from the divine plan.

Through a feminist hermeneutic, in Hebrew scriptures Mott finds, not the subjugation of women that Dana has seen as God's plan, but instead divine egalitarianism and empowerment of women. Her biblical exegesis here is selective, not exhaustive. As Grimké had done and others will do, she observes that "The laws given on Mount Sinai for the government of man and women are equal, the precepts of Jesus make no distinction."[100] Although she limits this discussion to one sentence before going on to offer examples of women leaders among the Israelites, this point is telling. The Ten Commandments were the basis for the social organization amongst the Israelites, through which God lays the same moral obligations on men and women, not distinguishing their roles in any way. Her insights about the gender neutrality implicit in the Ten Commandments strengthens her argument about the equality implicit in God's plan for humanity. The reference to Jesus's teaching as also being gender neutral adds force to this argument. As Grimké had argued in setting forth guidance for human lives, Mott avers that God has consistently ignored gender differences, holding men and women to the same moral standards.

To support her notion that the divine plan intended a more significant role for women, she uses examples of God's empowerment of women: Miriam, the sister of Moses; Deborah, one of the Judges; and Huldah, a prophetess, all of whom later women would highlight.[101] Alluding to the fuller stories of Deborah and Miriam, Mott offers a pointed, forceful depiction of these two women: they "enlisted themselves on the side which they regarded the right, unitedly going up to their battles, and singing their songs of victory."[102] That the women were moral agents and that they led victory celebrations highlights God's endorsement and encouragement of women's participation in public life. For Deborah, Mott adds details of her participation in a military campaign, an involvement that emerged because the army commander Barak would not move forward without her.[103] Admitting that the story of Deborah's co-worker Jael is "revolting" because they were a "semi-barbarous people," she quotes Deborah's account of Jael's killing Sisera, the most extensive scriptural passage she employs. Her point may be that, although Jael's brutality is unattractive, her dramatic action shows a woman acting as a moral agent at a critical point. For Mott, the facts that Deborah served as a judge for "many years" and that Jael slayed the military commander of the enemy clearly indicate that God calls women beyond the domestic sphere to involvement in the affairs of their day.

Before moving to Jesus's ministry, Mott highlights Deborah along with Huldah "and other honorable women" who were "looked up to and consulted in times of exigency, and their counsel was received."[104] Deborah was probably familiar to many in her audience. If perhaps less known, Huldah's role was, however, equally important. During the renovation of the Temple in Jerusalem as part of a reform prior to the Babylonian conquest, King Josiah called on her to verify that the document they had rediscovered was, indeed, legitimate, an important authentication for their future.[105] In both cases, their male companions acknowledged the power and authority of these women, recognizing them as ordained by God. That these women acted outside the domestic arena at decisive junctures not only refutes Dana's view, but also implicitly ratifies women's involvement in the public sphere in such critical reform causes as abolitionism.

Within the context of Christian scriptures, Mott briefly mentions a number of women, beginning with Anna who recognizes Jesus as the Messiah when Mary and Joseph present him as an infant in the Temple and including women like Tryphena and Tryphosa who were "co-workers with the apostles in their mission."[106] Because her references are only snippets, she relies heavily on her audience to supply the missing details and the fuller stories. God's use of these women to advance the work of Jesus in the world indicates not only a positive attitude toward women but also the value of their contributions to the church in its earliest phase.

Mott uses the case of Phoebe (whom she identifies as Phebe) to suggest how male translators sometimes obscure women's leadership. She observes that the Greek word *diakonos* is used to refer to Phoebe in Romans 16:1 and Tychicus, a male companion of Paul, in Ephesians 6:21 and Colossians 4:7.[107] In the King James version, the translation for female is "servant," while for the male it is "minister."[108] Like Grimké, Mott's interpretation indicates that both Phoebe and Tychicus fulfilled the role of "minister," working to advance God's work in the world.

Without citing the reference, Mott contests another translation issue regarding "professing" versus "preaching." Her allusion is apparently to I Timothy 2:10: "also that the women should dress themselves modestly and decently in suitable clothing, not with their hair braided, or with gold, pearls, or expensive clothes, but with good works, as is proper for women who profess reverence for God."[109] Part of a series of instructions first to men and then to women about how to pray, this passage immediately precedes a section frequently used to silence women: "Let a woman learn in silence with full submission. I permit no woman to teach or to have authority over a man; she is to keep silent."[110] To counter the traditional interpretation, Mott disputes the translation of the Greek word *epangellomenais* as "profess" rather than "preach," the latter of which she believes is more accurate. Although she gives no indication of the source for her translation, her biblical knowledge is sound. The authoritative *Strong's Concordance* translates *epangellomenais* as "to announce upon" and indicates it is used reflexively; the root is *aggelos,* meaning "to bring tidings."[111] Although Mott's translation as "preach" seems a bit tendentious, the word apparently can carry a notion of public proclamation. In identifying this ambiguity, she reconstrues the meaning of the passage. Further, if this passage indicates how women are to dress to profess (or "preach" as her translation suggests), then, she reasons, the subsequent instructions about remaining silent are not universal.[112]

Focusing on the feast of Pentecost when the Holy Spirit descended on the disciples gathered in an upper room in Jerusalem, she notes, as both Lee and Grimké had, the first announcement was "the fulfillment of ancient prophecy, that God's spirit should be poured out upon daughters as well as sons and they should prophesy."[113] In the passage alluded to (Acts 2:17), Peter, defending the ebullient disciples against charges of inebriation, quotes Joel 2:28, the passage with that prophecy. Women were certainly part of that group. Building on her earlier arguments that all the Mosaic commandments as well as the precepts given by Jesus apply equally to men and women, Mott indicates that the Holy Spirit, which motivates human beings to good actions, is also sent to both sexes without distinction, a point Peter affirms with his quotation of Joel. In the new community being formed, both men and women will "prophesy," a clear indication that God intends women's full participation in the life of the early church.

With this background, Mott turns to a troublesome passage from I Corinthians 14:34 that instructs that "women should be silent in the churches, for they are not permitted to speak, but should be subordinate as the law also says." In contrast to Fell who provided a well-developed argument around this passage, Mott simply points to a later passage which offers instructions about how women are to appear when they prophesy. The passage she seems to be referring to is I Corinthians 11:5: "but any woman who prays or prophesies with her head unveiled disgraces her head [husband]." Considering this passage, she urges: "Judge then whether this admonition, relative to *speaking* and asking questions, in that excited state of that church, should be regarded as a standing injunction on woman's *preaching,* when that word was not used by the apostle."[114] Then, turning in another direction, with a deft touch, she questions: "Where is the Scripture authority for the advice given to the early church, under peculiar circumstances, being binding on the church of the present day? Ecclesiastical history informs us, that for two or three hundred years, female ministers suffered martyrdom, in the company with their brethren."[115]

She finishes her refutation of Dana's vague and poorly supported theological argument with this claim: "These things are too much lost sight of. They should be known, in order that we may be prepared to meet the assertion, so often made that woman is stepping out of her appropriate sphere, when she shall attempt to instruct public assemblies."[116] Women must, she concludes, be able to "know the ground whereon you stand" so that they may proceed to be co-workers with men in the important work—"to reform the inebriate and the degraded, to relieve the oppressed and the suffering. . . . The blessing to the merciful, to the peacemaker [Matthew 5:7, 5:9] is equal to man and to woman."[117] Women must be free of human-made constraints so that they can become the moral agents they are called to be and participate in God's salvific work.

Significantly, in her refutation of Dana's theological argument Mott does not choose to offer a complete inventory of all the scriptural warrants for women's greater scope within religious communities and the larger world. Through her feminist lens, she judiciously chooses particular women for her examples, omitting, for example, Mary Magdalene in the New Testament and Tamar and Rahab from the Hebrew scriptures.[118] Her goal is not to offer every example possible but instead to provide strong evidence of God's empowerment and employment of women in the salvific history that began in Eden, continued with the Israelites, was intensified with Christ's ministry, and now moves forward through the church, the priesthood of all believers. She supports her view with abundant scriptural evidence, often requiring her audience to supply details of the stories she treats enthymematically. In contrast to Dana's rhapsodic, vague discussion of the allegedly God-given "law" that consigns women to secondary roles, Mott has developed a thoughtful, persuasive demonstration of how God has empowered women for public ministry.

Revealing the True and Proper Position of Women

With the scriptural arguments in place, Mott challenges her audience (and Dana) with a rhetorical question: "Why should woman not seek to be a reformer?" and simply eschew that role out of "fear to exercise her reason, and her noblest powers, lest she should be thought 'to attempt to act like a man' and 'not acknowledge his supremacy.'" Accepting the "narrow sphere assigned her by man" is a "mournful prospect for woman." The thrust of this argument, though unstated, is clear: women are given talents by God to be used for reform and on behalf of others, regardless of what church officials contend. "It is our duty to develop these natural powers by suitable exercise, so that they may be strengthened by 'reason of use.'"[119] In essence, as Grimké had contended, Mott argues that women have a moral responsibility to develop their talents so that they can participate in the vital work of reform, the progress toward restoring the original divine plan.

Here Mott inserts a long quotation from Catharine Beecher's *Suggestions Respecting Improvements in Education* (1829) to describe a bright future prospect. Looking to a coming time when women will awaken to the need and possibly of acknowledging "her nobler powers, . . . her highest destinies and holiest hopes," Beecher predicts we will find woman "with the delighted glow of benevolence, seeking for immortal minds, whereon she may fasten durable and holy impressions, that shall never be effaced or wear away."[120] Significantly, for Beecher as for Mott, the removing of obstacles and barriers to women's fuller development is not just about personal development. Rather the improvement of the status of women is to facilitate the benevolent, constructive work they should be doing.

Moving to answer Dana's dire predictions about women who move beyond the domestic sphere, as Willard will do, Mott offers counter examples of women who have done important work in the world without losing their "feminine character" even when they displayed great courage.[121] In the argumentative move known as denying the consequence, she offers two women reformers, Elizabeth Fry, who worked for improved conditions in prisons, and Dorothea Dix, who also worked in prison reform particularly for the mentally ill. For Fry, she notes that "having performed the duties of a mother to a large family" she felt "that she owed a labor of love to the poor prisoner, she was empowered by Him who sent her forth, to go to kings and crowned heads of the earth. . . . Did she lose the delicacy of woman by her acts? No."[122] She asks of Dorothea Dix, is she "throwing off her womanly nature and appearance in the course she is pursuing? . . . Is not a beautiful mind and a retiring modesty still conspicuous in her?"[123] These examples disprove Dana's conjectures about the impact of women's involvement in public life.

To refute Dana's claims that the courage of women is "patient endurance" rather than an "active" trait, she offers the examples of Grace Darling, a young English girl, who displayed great courage in rescuing shipwrecked mariners, and Joan of Arc, as evincing equal bravery that has elicited public admiration.[124] Clinching this argument, Mott educes two male reformers, Horace Mann and William Emery Channing, who display the same appealing "modesty" that Fry and Dix have conveyed, virtues that are not specific to men or women and that call "forth our admiration wherever manifested."[125] Mott argues, then, that participation in reform or even courageous deeds does not, *ipso facto,* undermine the character of women or men.

To this point, Mott has been the Quaker minister, elucidating her view of truth to her listeners, encouraging them to engage with her in testing Dana's ideas in light of the interpretations she offers. In a passage that highlights her prophetic role, she challenges her audience:

> The question is often asked, "What does woman want, more than she enjoys?" What is she seeking to obtain? Of what rights is she deprived? What privileges are withheld from her? I answer she asks nothing as favor, but as right, she wants to be acknowledged [as] a moral, responsible being. She is seeking not to be governed by laws, in the making of which she had no voice. She is deprived of almost every right in civil society, and is a cypher in the nation, except in the rights of petition. In religious society her disabilities, as already pointed out, have greatly retarded her progress. Her exclusion from the pulpit or ministry—her duties marked out for her by her equal brother man, subject to creeds, rules, and disciplines made for her by him—this is unworthy of her true dignity. In marriage, there is assumed superiority, on the part of the husband, and admitted inferiority, with a promise of obedience, on the part of the wife. This subject calls loudly for examination, in order that the wrong may be redressed.[126]

Her depiction of women's calls for their rights as enabling them to be "moral, responsible" beings here is critical. In Mott's theology, all are called to work for God's kingdom; depriving women of the opportunity to exercise that role is to interfere with their ability to act on their moral commitments as Christians. By extension, silencing women empowered and called by God would also interfere with God's plan.

Rather than being treated as morally responsible individuals, women have been, she avers, severely restricted and confined with disastrous effects. As Grimké had done, donning her prophetic mantle, Mott asserts: "She has so long been subject to the disabilities and restrictions, with which her progress has been embarrassed, that she has become enervated, her mind to some extent paralyzed; and, like those more degraded by personal bondage, she hugs her chains."[127] In the spirit of the Hebrew prophets, she condemns current practices as repudiating God's plan. Linking the situation of women to the condition of slaves highlights the urgency of her cause, even as she acknowledges that some women like some slaves "may be so degraded by the crushing influences around them, that they may not be sensible of the blessing of freedom."[128]

Drawing her presentation to a close, Mott becomes more impassioned and prophetic. As she acknowledges the growing list of accomplishments of women—entering the medical profession and serving as editors—she urges women forward: "Let women then go on—not asking as a favor, but claiming as a right, the removal of all hindrances to her elevation in the scale of being—let her receive encouragement for the proper cultivation of all her powers, so that she may enter profitably the active business of life."[129] Although she evinces strong concern for equality in marriages, she aspires for women to "occupy such walks in society, as will befit her true dignity in all the relations of life."[130] In so doing, woman should not fear losing her "female delicacy" because "true modesty will be as fully preserved in acting out those important vocations to which she may be called, as in the nursery or at the fireside, ministering to man's self-indulgence."[131] Quoting the playwright, author and journalist Nathaniel Parker, she concludes: "Credit not the old fashioned absurdity, that woman's is a secondary lot, ministering to the necessities of her lord and master! It is a higher destiny I would award you. If your immortality is as complete, and your gift of mind as capable as ours, of increase and elevation, I would put no wisdom of mine against God's divine allotment."[132] With this flourish, Mott ends her presentation. She has risen to the occasion, delivering a withering response to Dana' lecture.

The Prophetic Voice in Movement Leadership

Those important vocations to which she may be called

—LUCRETIA COFFIN MOTT, "DISCOURSE ON WOMAN"

Mott's speech did not put to rest the use of scripture to argue against women's rights. If resistance to women's public advocacy abated over time, countless other men and women still turned to particular passages in scripture to argue for women's role as secondary to men and as focused on domesticity. No matter how careful and compelling her hermeneutical skills, Mott could not erase the challenging passages in I Timothy and I Corinthians; those passages continued to buttress established social patriarchal patterns.

We do not know the contemporary impact of this speech. Those who had invited her to speak and many of her Quaker friends probably found it compelling and authoritative while her enemies saw it as presumptuous and inappropriate. Whatever the reaction, Mott continued her advocacy undaunted, and many hearers found her a strong voice for causes of reform. Writing to his wife about hearing Mott on another occasion in January 1843, Ralph Waldo Emerson reported: "it was like the rumble of an earthquake—the sensation that attended the speech, and no man would have done so much and come away alive."[133] She was admired and respected in her community before this speech and, until her death in 1880, she continued her work for the rights of freed slaves and women.[134] Certainly, at the Seneca Falls Convention of 1848 and at subsequent meetings of women, she encouraged other women as she helped shape the course of the agitation for woman's rights. History has judged her "one of the foremost figures in the woman's rights movement."[135]

A Feminist Hermeneutic on the Public Platform

Throughout her response to Dana, viewing scripture through a feminist lens, Mott reinterprets familiar biblical passages, recovers previously overlooked stories about women, and refutes other passages traditionally used to circumscribe women's activities.[136] Her command of scripture is one trait that modern women's studies and rhetorical scholars have come to admire. For example, rhetorical critic Malcolm Sillars calls the speech a "*tour de force* of detailed argument about Biblical history, authority, evidence, and experience."[137] Karlyn Kohrs Campbell opines that, with "sophisticated and original responses, both direct and indirect, to arguments based on Scripture against woman's rights," Mott demonstrated a hermeneutic that both honored sacred writ and adapted its interpretation to modern issues. In doing this, she "developed convincing arguments, took strong stands, and blithely accused her male opponent of both sentimentality and a lack of logic."[138] With those efforts, Campbell concludes, Mott becomes "the proof, along with the examples she presented, that women could move into the public sphere and retain their moral character and their commitment to humane values."[139]

Mott's ability to deploy her hermeneutical skills and those of her predecessors in the public sphere is evidenced by her fingerprints on the 1848 Declaration of Sentiments, for which she was the first signatory. Although that document is modelled on both the Declaration of Independence and the 1833 Declaration of Sentiments for the American Anti-Slavery Society, it also bore the influence of Mott's ideas, which in turn were influenced by Grimké. That document adapts the language of the Declaration of Independence to claim that "all men and women are created equal," a clear allusion to the first story of creation. It further asserts that men have made women "morally irresponsible" beings because they can commit certain crimes with impunity. Further, it suggests: "He has usurped the prerogative of Jehovah himself, claiming it as his right to assign for her a sphere of action, when that belongs to her conscience and her God." Drawing on many of the same examples and explanations as Grimké employed, Mott moves those ideas from the pages of abolitionist newspaper to the public platform. In so doing, Mott carries many of the arguments circulating in abolitionist circles into the emerging nineteenth century woman's rights movement.

Dissent through a Feminist Hermeneutic

Through her feminist hermeneutic, Mott grounds her views in scripture, a source central to the lives of many of her listeners. By appealing to principles of equality and founding documents like the Declaration of Independence, Mott skillfully connects her views to widely shared values and sacrosanct political documents. Although she disputes current socially constructed beliefs about women's proper sphere, her view is progressive, not radical. Indeed, her vision of women's expanded roles corresponds more fully with widely professed principles and ideals. Moreover, her feminist hermeneutic draws on scripture to expose weaknesses in Dana's "sentiments." With a carefully calibrated rebuttal, as she demolishes Dana's viewpoint, she grounds her views in established political principles and, more importantly, biblical truth.

As impressive and progressive as Mott's call for a new conception of women's role was, we should not misconstrue what she is advocating. Like Grimké and later Willard, she did not intend to upend gendered social stereotypes. Indeed, she saw separate roles for men and women, but equally important ones. "We would admit all the difference, that our great and beneficent Creator has made, in the relation of man and woman, nor would we seek to disturb this relation; but we deny that the present position of woman, is her true sphere of usefulness."[140] This approach of dissent is clever; she does not deny the existence of difference but rather how men have perverted those differences in ways that compromise women's God-given moral status.[141] Like Grimké, she simply sought to break the bonds of man-made constraints and barriers that constrict women's ability to develop their divinely bestowed talents and to function as moral agents. To cap her argument, with specific examples she proves how valuable women's contributions are and can be for the general good. Grace Darling, Harriet Martineau, Elizabeth Gurney Fry, Dorothea Lynde Dix, and Maria Mitchell are all women whose work contributed to the welfare of others. Mott's call is not for freedom to develop one's talents for self-aggrandizement; women's freedom is for a commitment to constructive social action, which is, implicitly at least, in full alignment with her natural piety.

Further, Mott endorses the primacy of the marital relationship and even the preservation of distinctive female traits. Women are to be the equals of men in marriage, but the family remains the primary social organizational unit. So, for example, she notes that Fry only moved into reform work after "she performed the duties of a mother to a large family." Similarly, Dix did not abandon her "womanly nature and appearance" in her work.[142] When women are liberated, "true modesty" will be preserved and there need be "no fear that she will transcend the proper limits of female delicacy."[143] Mott calls for the "elevation" of women, not their complete freedom from all gendered expectations. In this respect, Mott stops short of rejecting the traditional gendered stereotypes of her day. Instead, she insists that women can remain feminine and womanly even as they move into the public sphere. Her entire presentation substantiates that point.

To complement her arguments, Mott carefully manages her public presentation, demeanor, and dress to conform to societal standards. Even as she engages in brisk argument from the public platform, she remains a decorous female. As Carol Mattingly concludes in her study of dress among nineteenth century women: "women speakers used appearance to negotiate expectations restricting them to limited locations in order to challenge and reconstruct the power hierarchy."[144] As long-time friend and ally Elizabeth Cady Stanton observed about Mott: "she always dressed in quaker costume," a style of dress that reinforced her piety and femininity.[145] Mott's decidedly feminine appearance suggests her commitment to certain gender stereotypes even as she embodies and argues for an expanded role for women in the public sphere, one that allows women to develop fully as moral agents.

Mott is clearly adept at embedding her progressive views into traditional values, a prime example of the power of rhetorical dissent. Quaker attitudes toward abolition and women's roles clash with constrictive gendered stereotypes. This "moment of conflict in which the taken-for-granted rules, topics, and norms of public deliberation are contested, opposed, or transgressed" provided Mott the rhetorical space to challenge discourse rules.[146]

Artfully crafted, Mott's response to Dana allows her to maintain her womanly decorum and affirm socially sanctioned viewpoints, even as she marshals a compelling rebuttal of the biblical passages that constrict women's roles.

Prophetic Vision, Moral Agency, and a New Model of Womanhood

In directly taking on Dana's eloquent advocacy for the status quo, Mott became a prophetic voice. In her view, the elevation of women was a key step both in social progress and in restoration of the divine plan. Her "Discourse on Woman" outlines a progressive salvific trajectory: the divine plan corrupted by the Fall with its restoration begun in Christ and continuing among and through true believers. In so doing, she is also able to enact the model of a woman as a moral agent that Grimké envisioned. In essence, she becomes a public face for a new model of womanhood.

Operating outside the artificial constraints imposed by men but within the boundaries of biblical truth and social decorum, she argues for the full participation of women and reveals the value of their contributions. As one scholar observed: "While Quakers obviously did not claim secular equality for women, the opportunities it offered its female members and the dignity it accorded them could nurture such a claim. In the mind of Mott, the long-standing belief in female spiritual equality transformed into a full-blown claim for their secular equality as well."[147] She makes that claim with skill, fervor, and confidence. She does this while preserving an appealing femininity, delicately balancing authority and decorum. Both in her text and in her public demeanor, she enacts the new vision of womanhood that emerges from reaffirming God's original plan for humankind.

Mott provides an early model for all social movement leaders who ground at least some of their appeals in the Judeo-Christian scriptures. Exploiting moments of social unrest or perceiving currents of change, such leaders assume a prophetic role to diagnose social ills and to advocate a corrective. They depict the change they urge as a restoration of and step toward realization of God's divine plan for humankind.

Lucretia Mott's Lasting Influence

Lucretia Mott's influence in the nascent nineteenth century woman's rights movement is well-documented. She argued fearlessly and fervently for the "true and proper position of woman," seeking to bring women to "a more elevated position than that which custom for ages has allotted to her."[148] Deeply committed to the cause of the downtrodden and marginalized, she devoted her considerable energies to proclaiming a nobler vision. In the end, she was, in the words of one Quaker historian, "a great minister, a deeply spiritual woman, an enemy of humbug of all kinds."[149]

The timing of Mott's speech is also fortuitous. Coming just a year and a half after the Seneca Falls Convention and its issuing of the Declaration of Sentiments, her speech offered an avenue for even traditional women to support the nascent woman's rights movement. Together, her arguments and her demeanor modeled a distinctive yet important public role for women. In joining the movement for woman's rights, Mott's contemporaries could see themselves as part of a rich tradition of divinely sanctioned women's activism. Thanks to Mott, participation in the movement meant that women were simply enacting their role and fulfilling their responsibilities as Christians.

Mott's text also reveals the inextricable link between a strategy of dissent and a prophetic ethos. Prophets always return to the foundational texts of a society to diagnose and suggest correctives for present ills. In a sense, prophets locate themselves as a bridge between the key values of the past, the present deviations from those values, and a future where those ideals are fully realized. Through her reliance on scripture, seen afresh through women's eyes, as revealing their true roles, and with an artful affirmation of elements of prevalent gender roles, Mott demonstrates the power of dissent to help followers conceive of progressive change as a realization of eternal truths.

FIVE

Frances Willard's *Woman in the Pulpit*

Awakening Women to the Possibilities of True Womanhood

Do Everything.

—FRANCES WILLARD, *DO EVERYTHING:*
A HANDBOOK FOR THE WORLD'S WHITE RIBBONERS

In her autobiography *Glimpses of Fifty: The Autobiography of an American Woman,* Frances Willard reflected: "All my life I have been devoted to the advancement of women in education and opportunity. I firmly believe God has work for them to do as evangelists, as bearers of Christ's message to the ungospeled, to the prayer-meeting, to the church generally and the world at large, such as most people have not dreamed. It is therefore my dearest wish to help break down the barriers of prejudice that keep them silent."[1] Focusing on this issue, *Woman in the Pulpit,* her "most ambitious work," a "magnum opus," attempted to dismantle the arguments that prevented women from preaching and participating fully in the life of the church. At the end of chapter 2, "The Spirit Giveth Life," she issues a bold challenge to women who feel called to preach and to all Christians: "Let me, as a loyal daughter of the church, urge upon younger women who feel a call, as I once did, to preach the unsearchable riches of Christ, their duty to seek admission to the doors that would hardly close against them now, in any theological seminary . . . and let me pleadingly beseech all Christian people. . . . to encourage every true and capable woman, whose heart God has touched, in her wistful purpose of entering upon that blessed Gospel ministry."[2] This "well-researched and tightly reasoned little volume" not only shows "considerable mastery of church history and biblical texts,"[3] it also provides "a feminist theological resolution to the separate spheres ideological debate of the nineteenth century."[4]

: 109 :

In Willard's account, *Woman in the Pulpit* grew out "of an article prepared by me in compliance with the request of my good friends the Editors of *The Homiletic Monthly.*"[5] Biographer Christopher Evans reports that she wrote a series of articles for the magazine during early 1888, which would eventually be published as *Woman in the Pulpit.*[6] Indeed, *Woman in the Pulpit* takes on what Willard and other women believed was the single greatest obstacle to women's being able to preach and be leaders within their denominations: scripture seen through male eyes.

By the time Willard published this text, she had achieved nearly iconic status. Called "God's best gift to the American women of the nineteenth century,"[7] "America's best known woman,"[8] and "next to Queen Victoria, the most influential woman of the age,"[9] she was "widely hailed in the nineteenth century as America's 'heroine.'"[10] "No woman in America was better known, none was more universally loved."[11] Her status stemmed from her advocacy for many social reforms. In her biography of Willard, Ruth Bordin observes: "The causes to which she made lasting contributions—for example, the vote for women, the public kindergarten, separate correctional institutions for women, Protestant ecumenicism—became part of the permanent fabric of American life."[12] But "beyond and above all these," notes Edward J. Wheeler, editor of the *Literary Digest,* in his eulogizing remarks, Willard "was an awakener of women to the possibilities of true womanhood and she has probably done more than any other person who ever lived to bring to those of her own sex the world over, an adequate realization of their own powers."[13]

Throughout her personal and professional life, Willard confronted obstacles and frustrations that made her keenly aware of the societal barriers women faced both in their attempts to live into their professional ambitions and their desire to live out their commitment as Christians. Enmeshed in her own struggles with the Methodist Church and painfully cognizant of the efforts of other women to find a home in that denomination, she exerted the full force of her considerable public ethos to breach one particularly salient and seemingly intractable stronghold of male privilege: the pulpit. Written at the pinnacle of Willard's career and influence, *Woman in the Pulpit* was, in some ways, the culmination of a lifelong struggle to reconcile her views on women with her strong Methodist faith.

At this point, Willard chose to address a controversial issue that was polarizing her beloved Methodism and exciting debate in many Protestant denominations.[14] Although, strictly speaking, women's preaching was unconnected to temperance work, she drew on her Woman's Christian Temperance Union (WCTU) position and ethos to publish this provocative argument. In a real sense, this work is a response to her living her life in a strongly gendered society where, from her earliest years and throughout her professional life, she was frustrated and thwarted by social norms derived from male exegesis of scripture.

The Frustrations of Living a Gendered Life

Willard was born September 28, 1839, in New York into a close-knit family. Encouraged by her mother to take pride in being a woman and to develop her intellect and talents, she enjoyed great freedom in her early childhood. "If my dear mother did me one crowning kindness," Willard wrote, "it was in making me believe that next to being an angel, the greatest bestowment of God is to make one a woman."[15] Like Grimké, Willard, who was known as "Frank," took a keen interest in her brother's activities. She most enjoyed playing with Oliver, "walking on stilts, climbing trees, tossing quoits, and shooting cross guns."[16] With him and their sister Mary, she explored her creativity and her interests in history, the sciences, and literature, some-times oblivious to the male privilege her brother enjoyed.[17] For example, the three created Fort City, an imaginary town, which had its own *Fort City Tribune* and bylaws that outlined the roles and responsibilities of the mayor, secretary, treasurer, tax gatherer, and postmaster. Uninhibited by the larger society, the three took turns assuming the various positions.[18]

Youthful Vexations

Not surprisingly, Willard eschewed many female tasks such as housework and cooking. Eventually, however, she was forced to submit to societal expectations. In her autobiography, she reports: "No girl went through a harder experience than I, when my free, out-of-door life had to cease. . . . I always believed that if I had been let alone and allowed as a woman, what I had had as a girl, a free life in the country, where a human being might grow, body, and soul, as a tree grows, I would have been 'ten times more of a person,' every way. . . . I cried long and loud when I found I could never again race and range about with freedom."[19] She also chaffed at beauty standards such as uncomfortable hairstyles and constrictive dresses.[20] Her journal recalls that "[my] hair is twisted up like a corkscrew; I carry eighteen hair-pins; my head aches miserably; my feet are entangled in the skirt of my hateful new gown. I can never jump over a fence again, so long as I live. . . . I recognize the fact that my 'occupation's' gone."[21] Willard was slowly realizing the limitations and restrictions that her gender entailed. Future experiences provided more painful evidence.[22]

As Jean Miller Schmidt suggests, although the Wisconsin frontier where Willard spent much of her childhood allowed her to "escape many of the limitations of prescribed roles for young women . . . she early envied her brother's rights to an education, the vote, and a ministerial career."[23] Bordin argues that Willard's "tomboy ways" and "her eagerness to participate in her brother's games and chores" foreshadow the difficulty she would face in conforming to "the established gender patterns of the mid-nineteenth century."[24]

At 17, Willard confronted the political realities of her gender. From a window, she and Mary watched their brother travel with their father so Oliver could cast his first ballot. Willard recalls: "Somehow I felt a lump in my throat and then I couldn't see their wagon any more, things got so blurred. . . . I said, 'Wouldn't you like to vote as well as Oliver? Don't you and I love the country just as well as he, and doesn't the country need our ballots?' " Her sister responded with a warning " 'course we do and 'course we ought, —but don't you go ahead and say so, for then we would be called strong-minded."[25] Later Willard would lament: "I . . . only wished, although I dared not say it, that I had been born to a boy's chances in the world."[26]

Although her father had a strong sense that women's proper sphere was the home, both parents believed in the value of an education. Willard, an excellent student, was keen to pursue her studies.[27] She and her sister Mary attended Milwaukee Normal Institute, which Catharine Beecher founded. Later when they attended North Western Female College (NWFC) in Evanston, Illinois, she became the "editor of the College paper, and leader of all the intellectual forces among the students."[28] Admired for her "enthusiasm of knowledge and excellence," she was, her close friend and later sister-in-law Mary Bannister recalled, "wild with the girls and doesn't care a snap for the boys."[29] Although NWFC was not on par with Northwestern, it did provide women like Willard with a strong foundation in the liberal arts.[30]

There Willard excelled academically, graduating first in her class.[31] Still, during her studies from 1858 until her graduation in June 1859, she struggled to understand women's place in society. Her aspirations to cultivate her mind and achieve her full potential made the rigid, socially circumscribed role for women unattractive.[32] She lamented in her journal that "I shall be twenty years old in September, & I have as yet, been of no use in the world." She resolved: "I will earn my own living—'pay my own way'—& try to be of use in the world."[33]

At the end of her time at NWFC, Willard underwent a transformative religious experience. Her parents and sister had all undergone conversion experiences, "the mystical feeling of received grace that the Methodist Church taught was essential to salvation."[34] To the shock of her college friends, Willard who had not been baptized, openly admitted that she questioned her faith. One friend declared that Frances "won't confess that she knows or believes anything. She says she doesn't know whether there is a God, and she doesn't know whether the Bible is true;—she is trying to find out."[35] In her autobiography, she vividly recounts that pivotal spiritual awakening.

> It was one night in June, 1859. I was nineteen years old and was lying on my bed . . . with typhoid fever. . . . My whole soul was intent, as two voices seemed to speak within me, one of them saying, "My child, give me thy heart. I called thee long by joy, I call thee now by chastisement; but I have called thee always and only because I love thee with an everlasting love." The other said, "Surely you who are so resolute and strong will not break down now because of physical feebleness. You are a reasoner, and never yet were you convinced of the reasonableness of Christianity. Hold out now and you will feel when you get well just as you used to feel." One presence was to me warm, sunny, safe, with an impression as of snowy wings; the other cold, dismal, dark, with the flutter of a bat. . . . But at last, solemnly, and with my whole heart, I said not in spoken words but in the deeper language of consciousness, "If God lets me get well, I'll try to be a Christian girl."[36]

Realizing this silent "resolve did not bring peace," she heard the inward voice call her to declare her resolution aloud. "After a hard battle, in which I lifted up my soul to God for strength, I faintly called her from the next room, and said, 'Mother, I wish to tell you that if God lets me get well, I'll try to be a Christian girl.' She took my hand, knelt beside my bed and softly wept, and prayed. I then turned my face to the wall and sweetly slept."[37] Finally, in January 1860, six months after this experience, Willard proclaimed herself a member of the Methodist Church to which she remained fiercely devoted until her death. That affiliation with Methodism, despite the frustrations and disappointments, would dramatically impact the course of her life.[38]

In truth, Willard, like Jarena Lee and Sarah Grimké, aspired to be a preacher. She reflected: "The deepest thought and desire of my life would have been met, if my dear old Mother Church [the Methodist Church] had permitted me to be a minister. The wandering life of an evangelist or a reformer comes nearest to it, but cannot fill, the ideal which I early cherished, but did not expect ever publicly to confess."[39] Unlike Lee, however, Willard, who did not feel a clear inward call, "was too timid to go without a call." She wrote: "while my unconstrained preference would long ago have led me to the pastorate, I have failed of it."[40] Of course, even if she had received a call, Willard also recognized that her "dear old mother-church did not call women to her altars."[41]

Facing reality, Willard realized that women of her social class had only two options after they completed their education: become a wife or a teacher.[42] For Willard, marriage was an unattractive option. As she wrote in her diary: "If I truly believed that the fifth chapter of Ephesians (twenty-second to twenty-fourth verses) was to be understood literally and applied to *me,* if ever I'm any man's wife I should think the evidence sufficient that God was unjust, unreasonable, a *tyrant.*"[43] Still, undoubtedly feeling pressure to settle down, she accepted a marriage proposal from Charles Fowler, a promising young Methodist seminarian.[44] Rather than experiencing joy and expectation, she felt conflicted.[45] She recalls "for three-quarters of a year, I wore a ring and acknowledged an allegiance based on the supposition that an intellectual comradeship was sure to deepen into unity of heart. How grieved I was over the discovery of my mistake the journals from that epoch could reveal."[46] Finally, after several months, in February 1862, she broke off the engagement.

The death of her beloved sister Mary soon after she ended her relationship with Fowler and the marriage a few weeks later of her brother to her best friend and great admirer Mary left her feeling "unbefriended and alone."[47] As Evans writes, "Willard still faced the prospect of a future with few options outside of teaching."[48] Seizing that career path, she took various positions including, at her alma mater, NWFC, and the Grove School in Evanston.[49] In 1863, Willard became a teacher at the Pittsburgh Female College. Later, she held different posts including that of preceptress of Genesee Wesleyan Seminary in Lima, New York.[50]

A Thwarted Educational Innovator

As Willard's reputation as a teacher grew, a new and promising possibility arose in 1869. Aware that the NWFC was not as advanced as other colleges, a group of Evanston women, including her friend and now Oliver's wife, Mary Willard, "petitioned the city for a donation of land on which to build" what would become the Evanston Ladies College.[51] The initial vision was that the women students could take classes and attain degrees at Northwestern, but be housed in a separate administrative unit. At this point, women in institutions of higher education were a novelty. In her history of women's education, Barbara Miller Solomon notes that "between the 1850s and the 1870s several models developed: the private women's college, the religiously oriented coeducational college, the private coordinate women's college, the secular coeducational institution, both public and private, and the public single-sexed vocational institution."[52] Gradually, state institutions admitted women: the University of Iowa in 1858, Wisconsin in 1863, and Michigan in 1870. By the early 1860s a handful of "ladies colleges" existed. Most universities did not provide their female students with housing or a ladies college curriculum in "manners and morals" as did Evanston Ladies College and some other women-only institutions.[53]

In 1869 when Northwestern University selected Erastus O. Haven as President, he accepted on the condition that women be admitted.[54] "The decision [to accept women] was not without contention. At least one faculty member expressed concern about the additional supervision women would need to keep them out of mischief. Faculty knew how to educate women, but not how to manage them in close proximity to men. In the end, the Board chose to leave the details of coeducation to Haven."[55] Haven's vision, however, "was not of one campus where the two sexes commingled, but something closer to the "coordinate model"—a sister school, considered a "department" of the university. Under this plan, women would be situated in a separate building, under separate supervision by women faculty. "In this way," Haven said in his inaugural speech, "the inconvenience and evils which many dread may be avoided."[56]

In 1871, when Willard accepted the presidency of the Evanston Ladies College, she became "the first woman college president in America to confer degrees." There she could implement her ideas about education.[57] As Evans explains, Willard "held in tension two themes in her approach to her students: women's independence and the need for her students to conform to predominant models of Protestant womanhood." The result was an educational philosophy she dubbed "moral horticulture," which "revolved around the shaping of women's moral character."[58] She had a distinctive vision for the Ladies College, which paralleled Haven's ideas: "Our pupils of the Evanston College for Ladies were to have all the school privileges of the University at the regular tuition rates; they were to take music, art, and several other studies at our own college building, and were to be under our care exclusively as to morals and manners."[59] To that end, she instituted a system of governance with a "Roll of Honor" that recognized the students who adhered to her exacting standards of appropriate female behavior.[60] This moral oversight, coupled with access to university courses with men, would, she trusted, produce a new kind of woman suited for work in the world but evincing appropriate female gentility.

When Haven accepted another position, the Board of Trustees appointed Willard's former fiancé, Charles Fowler, as president in 1872. Soon, despite her enthusiastic efforts, financial challenges overwhelmed the small school. Finally, in 1873, the Ladies College merged into Northwestern University. Willard relinquished her presidential title, becoming the dean of the Woman's College.

This new role proved difficult. A female professor instructing males was still a novelty. Not surprisingly, Willard confronted pranks by male students: writing belittling comments on the blackboard, sabotaging her lectures, locking a "howling cat" in her desk, and arriving late to class separately as they slowly opened and closed the squeaky door.[61] Although one friendly student used a bar of soap to end the squeaking, the challenges remained.

More important, Willard disagreed with Fowler's approach to higher education for women. In her autobiography, she recounts her struggles with him. Her "bone of contention," was about who should have oversight of the Women's College. Unlike his predecessor, Fowler "held that the University faculty of men was the final authority in everything pertaining to those who received instruction there." That approach subverted Willard's power, undercutting her ability to execute her vision for the college.[62] Recognizing the "utter uselessness of making an issue with the president," she resigned in June 1874, resolving that "the world was wide and I would not waste my life in friction when it could be turned into momentum."[63] Once again her dreams for advancing the cause of women and making a difference in the world were thwarted. But fate intervened and another promising opportunity beckoned.

Working for the Good within the Woman's Christian Temperance Union (WCTU)

Assessing her future, Willard was drawn to a "less conventional course" within the WCTU, which was attracting more and more women to the cause. Her commitment to temperance stretched back to her childhood. Her father had been a member of the Washington Society, an organization founded by alcoholics to offer support and help to others on an individual basis.[64] On the wall in their home was a picture that showed "a bright, happy temperance home with a sweet woman at the center" juxtaposed with "a dismal, squalid house with a drunken man staggering in, bottle in hand."[65] Inspired by the picture, Willard copied a poem from *Youth's Cabinet,* a popular young person's periodical, and pasted it in the family Bible. The poem concluded with a pledge of "perpetual hate to all that can intoxicate." She insisted every member of the family sign it. She reported: "It is still there, thus signed, and represents the first bit of temperance work I ever did. Its object was simply to enshrine in the most sacred place our home afforded a pledge that I considered uniquely sacred."[66]

In late 1873, a spontaneous uprising of women that began in Ohio and spread quickly captured Willard's attention. Inspired by Dr. Diocletian Lewis's lecture on "The Duty of Christian Women in the Cause of Temperance" in Hillsboro, Ohio, local women sprang into action. Led by Eliza Jane Thompson, women began approaching "the various dispensers of alcoholic beverages—druggists, grocers, physicians, innkeepers and saloon owners—to sign pledges they would cease to sell." Prayer and song services followed in the establishments of those who refused.[67]

Willard called these events "that wonderful Christmas gift to the world." She reported that "All through that famous battle winter of Home *versus* Saloon, I read every word I could get about the movement. . . . Meanwhile it occurred to me, strange to say, for the *first time,* that I ought to work for the good cause *just where I* was—that everybody ought."[68] As she thought about how to support the cause in light of her financial responsibilities (supporting herself and her mother), she "opened the Bible lying on the hotel bureau and lighted on this memorable verse: Psalm 37:3, *'Trust in the Lord, and do good; so shalt thou dwell in the land, and verily thou shalt be fed.'* That was a turning point for me. Great spiritual illumination unequaled in all my history before, had been vouchsafed me in the sorrowful last days at Evanston, but here came clinching faith for what was to me the most difficult emergency."[69] From this point forward, temperance would be her life's work.

As she was pondering her future, she received an offer to become president of the Chicago women's temperance group, a paying position. Committed to this new course, she refused an offer from an "elegant school for young women, adjoining Central Park" with a handsome salary. She reported: "Here was my 'open door' all unknown and unsought—a place prepared for me in one true temperance woman's heart and a chance to work for the cause that had in so short a time become so dear to me."[70]

In the early days of her work for temperance, Willard got an opportunity to try a career path she thought was closed. While she was the corresponding secretary of the national WCTU, she met Dwight Moody, a Chicago businessman, turned preacher. Moody and his partner, singer and organist Ira Sankey, gained considerable renown as "superb showmen and spellbinding lay preachers."[71] They held revival meetings in the British Isles, "attended by an estimated 2,530,000 people" and returned to the United States with a "ready-made audience for their message."[72] Moody invited Willard to "lead in prayer a Sunday service attended by 9,000 women."[73] Interested in exploring a career as an evangelist, she enthusiastically accepted and subsequently conducted prayer meetings, delivered "informal" homilies, and was "thrilled" by the size of the audiences and the prospect for national fame.[74] But she and Moody disagreed over several issues, one of which was Willard's taking offense to "Moody's sexist approach to saving souls" in insisting on separate meetings for women and men.[75] Another issue was Willard's belief that religious activity and political activity were inseparable.[76] The conflict resulted in the dissolution of their partnership; Willard's dream for a career as an evangelist ended. As a result, she was able to throw herself wholeheartedly into her work for temperance and other social reforms.

National Leadership Versus Methodist Politics

As Willard's work with the WCTU prospered, her beloved Methodism was engaged in a prolonged controversy over women's proper role in the Church. Somewhat surprisingly, her leadership of the WCTU would lead her into the very center of that fray and catalyze her into action.

As Willard well knew, Methodism was then, and always had been, deeply ambivalent about the roles women should play. Despite his Anglican roots, Wesley embraced the idea of some women having "an extraordinary call" and supported their evangelistic efforts, although always with reservations. Empowered both by Methodism's emphasis on the spirit as the force behind preaching and the fervor of the Second Great Awakening, "between 1784 and 1845, at least twenty-two women preached for the Methodists and the African Methodists."[77] Brekus suggests that "Methodists' acceptance of female evangelism made them virtually unique in the late eighteenth and early nineteenth centuries."[78] By the 1830s, the quest for "Methodist gentrification" diminished opportunities for women preachers.[79]

However, in and from her home in New York City, Phoebe Palmer charted her own course, in what became known as the "holiness movement" within Methodism. She not only represented the challenges that male Methodist leaders confronted in controlling women moved by the spirit; she also was an inspiration for other women, including Willard. Each week she attracted large crowds who came "to sing, pray, enjoy the company of other Christians and, most important, to seek holiness or entire sanctification," a particular hallmark of Methodist spirituality.[80] In time, "by adhering ostentatiously to as many aspects of the Cult of True Womanhood as would also allow her to speak in public" and assiduously avoiding formal sermonizing, she became "the most famous Methodist woman preacher in nineteenth-century America, and, indeed, one of the leading Methodist theologians of the period."[81] In truth, Palmer was a challenge to male domination of Methodism, but her popularity and success made her an almost unassailable target as well as a compelling role model.

At the same time, according to Mark Chaves, "the rise of a broader women's movement changed the meaning of women's ordination. Largely because of the secular women's movement, women's ordination came to be understood as an issue of gender equality in a way that it was not in the absence of this social movement."[82] Indeed several other women began to bring direct pressure on the Methodist Episcopal Church (MEC) to expand roles for women in the church.[83] Mary Oliver, who graduated from the Boston University School of Theology in 1876 and received a local preacher's license from the Jamaica Plain Quarterly Conference in Boston, established a reputation as an effective pastor at various churches. With Anna Howard Shaw, a seminary classmate who also had a license to preach, she approached the New England Annual Conference to press for ordination.[84] Although the "Conference Examination Committee could find no reason to deny their candidacy for ordination," the presiding bishop, Edward Andrews refused to accept their nominations.[85] He told them "bluntly that there was no place for women in the ministry of the Methodist Episcopal Church, and that they should leave the church if they persisted in their dream."[86] Shaw moved to the Methodist Protestant Church where she was ordained in 1880; however, just four years later that group deemed her ordination "out of order."[87] Oliver chose to fight the bishop's decision. As she pressed her case, Lorenzo Thayer, the presiding elder of the Boston district, appealed Andrew's ruling. Ultimately the General Conference not only sustained the bishop's decision, but also, in a manner Chilcote terms "punitive," rescinded all local preacher's licenses granted from 1869 onward.[88] At the same time, they ruled that "women could be members of a Quarterly Conference (the local church governing body) by virtue of their positions as Sunday School Superintendents, Class Leaders, and Stewards (offices in local church government)." This ruling meant that "women who held local church offices could legitimately participate in the electoral process for GC [General Conference] delegates."[89]

In 1879, the WCTU appointed Willard, their new president, to attend the national gatherings of several Protestant churches, a natural affirmation of their deeply Christian roots.[90] Her credentials along with those of Methodist laywoman Jennie Duty were sent to the conference officials for the 1880 General Conference. The conference quickly determined that only "ecclesiastical visitors would be seated."[91] Although a male friend who was a delegate pressed the matter, requesting that she be allowed to share greetings from the WCTU, a fierce debate ensued because "it became clear that the General Conference was really addressing itself to the 'Woman Question.'"[92] Although the tone of the debate was "acrimonious," the final vote was 238–138 to allow her to speak for ten minutes. James M. Buckley, a delegate and editor of the influential *Christian Advocate,* was "so angry at the result that he secured an adjournment of the assembly for the rest of the day." Under pressure from her friends who were sensitive to the further "obstructionist tactics" Buckley might deploy, she declined the opportunity.[93]

The debate over women's rights in the Church then turned to considering women's rights as laity. In 1888, five annual regional conferences carefully selected well-known women leaders in the Church to serve as lay delegates to the General Conference, Willard being one.[94] The key question was "would the General Conference seat them?"[95] As De Swarte Gifford observes: "By the time the GC convened on May 1, 1888, at the Metropolitan Opera House in New York City, the MEC was in an uproar. The galleries of the opera house were packed with spectators, and the secular newspapers were reporting the event on their front pages."[96] The "Woman Question" divided the Methodists.

Opposition to Willard and her supporters was fierce. Despite her various maneuvers behind the scenes, before the formal seating of delegates could begin, the bishops announced that the five women could not be seated "because their eligibility as delegates had not been properly determined according to the constitution of the MEC."[97] Charles Fowler, her former fiancé and opponent at Northwestern, was one of the presiding bishops.[98] After five days of sometimes acrimonious debate, by a majority of 39 (of 435 votes), the conference determined that the word "laymen" referred exclusively to men.[99] Women had no rights in the Church, even as lay members.

Later that year, at her annual address at the 1888 WCTU New York Convention, Willard was defiant:

By a strange and grievous paradox, the Church of Christ, although first to recognize and nurture woman's spiritual powers, is one of the most difficult centers to reach with the sense of justice toward her. . . . I love my mother-church so well . . . I would fain give her a little time in which to deal justly by the great household of her loving, loyal, and devoted daughters. . . . The time will come, however, and not many years from now, when, if representation is still denied us, it will be our solemn duty to raise once more the cry, 'Here I stand, I can do no other,' and step out into the larger liberty of a religious movement where majorities and not minorities shall determine the fitness of women as delegates, and where the laying on of hands in consecration, as was undoubtedly done in the early church, shall be decreed on a basis of 'gifts, graces and usefulness,' irrespective of sex.[100]

Willard's quote from Luther, "Here I stand, I can do no other," underscores the depth and intensity of her feeling.

Evans reports that she wrote inside one of her books on Methodist history: "As a loyal 'Methodist Sister' I choose to know something of that grand old Mother Church whose ministry I would gladly have entered in my early prime if she had understood Christ's gospel well enough to call me!" With a heavy heart, Willard realized that "the denomination's doors were shut to her leadership potential."[101] But she took pen in hand to fight the battle on another front.

Woman in the Pulpit

The church that silences the woman is shorn of half its power.

—FRANCES WILLARD, *GLIMPSES OF FIFTY YEARS*

Seeing the Methodist Church's exclusion of women from leadership roles as linked to the restrictions on women in other areas of life and thwarted in every battle with the male Methodist hierarchy, Willard had reached a critical juncture.[102] She was "deeply distressed by her peremptory treatment from the very churchmen who had welcomed her to church halls and auditoriums as a popular lecturer and who had professed great admiration for the work she was doing as a temperance advocate."[103] The response to the WCTU's overtures to the Presbyterian and Methodist conventions frustrated and angered her. "This demeaning treatment of women by Protestant religious leaders and ecclesiastical governing bodies led Willard to examine critically and aggressively the overall position of women in the Protestant church. *Women in the Pulpit* was the result of this examination."[104] David Hempton concludes: "The discriminatory attitudes of male Protestant clergy, supported by the hierarchical bureaucracies of their churches radicalized Willard and pointed her toward a more critical biblical exegesis."[105] Moreover, during this period, "Willard increasingly identified with emerging themes of theological liberalism. Many church leaders, theologians, and biblical scholars were accepting the 'New Theology' which used historical-critical methods of scriptural study and challenged literal interpretations of long-cherished texts."[106] She would draw on this approach in making her case.

Willard knew well the struggles of other women in gaining ground in public life. The WCTU's newspaper, *The Union Signal,* frequently mentioned both Mott and Grimké. For example, a July 2, 1885, *Union Signal* article announced that on July 3 or "Foremothers Day," the program would include "fit memorials to the noted women of our history who toiled and sacrificed for their country. Such names as those of Abigail Adams, Martha Washington, Lucretia Mott . . . and others will occur to every woman who loves to honor the brave and true womanhood, the loving and the daring."[107] A May 20, 1886, article observed that "woman is assuming greater social and political prominence in this country" as a result of "the work of Christianity" and people like George Fox who "planted his foot on the rock when he proclaimed her spiritual equality" and women like Sarah and Angelina Grimké who were the "first women who addressed mixed audiences of men and women on the slavery question." The Grimké sisters, the article goes on to note, "opened the way for woman to the public platform, to lecture and make addresses on suffrage, politics, temperance or any other public interests . . . this woman movement . . . is a new and ever increasing influence in politics aside from the question of suffrage, for they are and ever will be agitating moral questions, and thus stimulating legislation."[108]

Because the efforts of these foremothers resulted in "improved legal status" and "intellectual opportunities," Willard's focus was necessarily much narrower than her predecessors. The concern of previous women had been the broad scope of women's rights. In the ensuing years many inroads they sought had been achieved. For example, women had gained access to higher education, some could control their own property, and some, like Willard herself, had entered professions. Thus, although Willard's text draws on the thread of biblical argument and feminist hermeneutical strategies other women had developed and used, it mounts a formidable argument against one of the most problematic issues women continued to face—access to the pulpit. Like Lee, Willard undoubtedly hoped *Woman in the Pulpit* would influence the ongoing struggle within Methodism.

In making a case for women's preaching, Willard makes three strategic moves that enable her to connect her views with widely shared values and, simultaneously, adopt a prophetic stance. First, she employs an organizational structure that positions her arguments as an explanation of and support for expert testimony, much of it from males. This enables her both to avoid seeming too directly confrontational and to locate her arguments within a larger arena of progressive thought. Second, employing a feminist hermeneutic in conjunction with the Methodist theological practice of applying reason and experience to interpret scripture, she develops a devastating attack on masculine literalist exegesis that has privileged some passages and ignored others. Scripture, so often used against women, was her touchstone. Finally, she grounds her calls for progressive change within traditional values, most particularly notions of women's moral superiority. In essence, in supporting women's preaching she is arguing for the full realization of women's moral agency. With these strategies, she becomes the prophetic voice, honoring the fuller truth of scripture as she enables women to live into their identity as Christians.

A Strategic Structure

The unusual and decidedly strategic structure of *Woman in the Pulpit* enhances the strength of Willard's argument. The book consists of a preface, introduction, and seven chapters with a closing quote from Nathaniel Hawthorne. Willard authors only one-third of the book, the short preface and three chapters. Her first two chapters, "The Letter Killeth" and "The Spirit Giveth Life," provide the exegetical argument. The third, "The Earth-Born Argument," deals with arguments that preaching is unwomanly and impossible for a woman with children. She strategically sandwiches her arguments between testimonials, letters, and a debate about the role of women in the pastorate, almost all authored by men. As Donawerth observes, Willard constructs "her argument not straightforwardly, but interwoven with refutation and what Aristotle calls 'inartistic proofs'—testimony from witnesses."[109] This testimony will both precede and follow her own arguments, effectively framing and then affirming them.

Even before the Preface, Willard begins her argument. As an epithet, she chooses Galatians 3:28 from the new revised translation: "There can be no male and female: for ye are one man in Christ Jesus." As we shall see, her argument will be that God can and does empower both men and women to preach. Her scriptural epithet, then, foreshadows the substance of her views.

Her dedication is both touching and strategic: "To The Sacred Memory of my only and beloved brother, Revered Oliver Atherton Willard." Willard had a close relationship with her brother from childhood; later in adult life, she supported him as he dealt with alcoholism and financial woes. In dedicating the work to his "sacred memory," she was simultaneously acknowledging his importance in her life and positioning herself as a devoted sister. In a society that saw women's primary status as familial, Willard was, in modern parlance, "virtue signaling" to soften her thoroughgoing professional image.

In the Preface, Willard reports that she sought an assessment of her work before publishing it: "Wishing to learn the opinion of three ministers than whom none living are more devout, gifted or renowned, I wrote asking their opinion of 'Woman in the Pulpit.'" Their replies will, she opines, "be of interest to their millions of readers in all lands." Positioning herself as an obsequious, thoroughly demure woman, she continues: "I count myself fortunate to be able to introduce this little book with the approving and brotherly words of these great men, and I beg a patient and unprejudiced attention, not only to *their* words, but to the words of *all* the witnesses that follow them."[110] This approach is both decorously feminine and strategically shrewd. Rather than launching into her argument, which she knows will be somewhat controversial, she frames her ideas with supportive comments by well-known men. In essence, she is predisposing her readers to look favorably on her work.

Her choice of letters is also artful because they vary in tone and approach. Thomas De Witt Talmadge, a popular and prolific preacher, after describing her letter as a "great glow of sunshine" on his table, avers: "I do not think the story of the Gospel will be fully told until Christian women all round the world tell it. There is a tenderness and a pathos and a power in woman's voice, when she commends pardon and sympathy, which the masculine voice can never reach."[111] This notion of the complementarity of male and female insights and skills will be a key element in Willard's argument. A bit later, and somewhat off topic, he indicates his support for woman suffrage.

Joseph Cook, a Methodist friend and head of the Australian Labor Party, provides what he terms "a single, unembarrassing example, fairly typical of thousands of cases occurring in both Christian and pagan fields of efforts" of a young woman of "distinctively feminine refinement and sensitiveness, conjoined with remarkable intellectual and spiritual endowments" who, in her teaching and missionary work, labors side by side with men. He insists that "no proof texts" would convince him that "this young lady had not a divine call to be a preacher as well as a teacher."[112] He concludes: "Undoubtedly, the home is woman's chief sphere; but if spiritual and intellectual gifts indicate a divine call to any woman to be an author, a lecturer or even a preacher, how is she to find excuse for disobedience to such indications of Providence?"[113] Women must not hide their lights under a barrel. With a poetic flourish, he ends: "Hand in hand, man and woman build the home; hand in hand they ought to build the state and the church. Hand in hand they left an earthly Paradise Lost; hand in hand, they are likely to enter, if at all, an earthly Paradise regained."[114] Significantly, foreshadowing the ideas Willard will offer in her third chapter, Cook affirms traditional notions of women's roles while simultaneously acknowledging the validity of Wesley's notion of an extraordinary call.

Finally, praising Willard as a "peaceful warrior" whose reasoning is unassailable, Joseph Parker, a congregational minister from London, declares: "Miss Willard holds an invincible position, scriptural and experimental upon this subject, and it will be much difficult to answer her argument than to sneer at it."[115] He continues that society has not fully embraced the great work that women are called to do, and he admits that women can be "divinely qualified" to engage in higher callings. Parker's observation about the strength of Willard's argument enhances her ethos as it also provides a positive frame for the discussion to follow.

As different as these statements are in substance and tenor, all three affirm Willard's central argument of women's value in the pulpit. Moreover, their diverse backgrounds and approach suggest widespread support for her ideas. These letters by male religious leaders make Willard's arguments, developed over three chapters, explanatory and supportive of their conclusions. They also locate her ideas in a larger, progressive cultural milieu, making her a prophetic voice in Methodism.

The chapters that follow Willard's three chapters of argument are letters from men and women who support women's preaching. Her descriptions of the male leaders are telling: "a prominent pastor in a large city," "the leading pastor of his denomination in New England," and a professor, who has "more students in New Testament Greek than any other."[116] She includes a good sampling of Methodist clergy, but the majority seem to be from other denominations, indicating that other groups are more progressive than her own beloved Methodism. Her closing citation is from the son of Gilbert

Haven, a distinguished Methodist bishop. Although he apologizes for being able to find in print any expression of his father's views, he avers that his father thought and frequently stated "that women whom God calls to preach should be licensed and ordained by the church."[117] As a group, Willard labels these male leaders "the progressives who are multiplying among the clergy" and who are as "dissatisfied" as women with the current situation.[118] She asserts that they represent "the consensus of opinion among ministers who belong to the progressive school of exegesis."[119]

In the chapter "Testimony of Women Preachers," Willard cites the religious denominations that have ordained women, listing among them the Methodists. Then she includes a sampling of views from the 500 women who work as evangelists. Although her list includes friends and a leader in the WCTU, she also quotes Catherine Booth, a co-founder and joint-Chief of the Salvation Army and Phebe [sic] Palmer "of sainted memory."[120] These women offer testimony about their own experience and success, respond to arguments against women's preaching, and agree wholeheartedly with a Quaker minister who insists: "The prophecy of Joel ii; 26–28 settles the question."[121] If these letters from women perhaps have less force than those from more prominent men, they do provide evidence of women's efficacy in ministry.

The final two chapters feature a debate about women's preaching between Henry J. Van Dyke Jr., a distinguished Presbyterian clergyman, friend of Woodrow Wilson, and later ambassador to Luxembourg, and L. T. Townsend, a Methodist minister and Boston University School of Theology professor. These two adversaries provide a clear exposition of the arguments on both sides and permit Willard to escape charges of appearing too argumentative or unfeminine.

Van Dyke attacks Willard's argument, which he acknowledges is "the best argument that has been or can be made on the affirmative side."[122] He claims that women are not qualified for the ministry and that God prohibits their role as preachers, offering many biblical passages to support his claims. Meeting fire with fire, Townsend responds with an incisive point by point refutation, citing different passages to support his position. Their debate coalesces around a key point in Willard's argument: the resolution of conflicting passages.[123] Van Dyke draws on the passages that suggest that women should not teach or preach and Townsend counters with different interpretations of those same passages and references to other scripture that warrant women's right to speak. In his discussion of this exchange in *Arguing Over Texts: The Rhetoric of Interpretation,* Martin Camper explains how Townsend uses the argumentative strategy of conflicting passages to his advantage: "Townsend uses the threat of the Bible contradicting itself, in a context where the Bible cannot be understood to contradict itself, to put those biblical passages that seem to prohibit women from speaking in church in relationship with other passages that seem to permit and authorize this activity. The relationships that Townsend constructs between these two sets of passages unsurprisingly support his position that women have the right to preach."[124] In the end, Townsend crafts a solid argument that resolves the tension between the passages that he and Van Dyke cite in favor of women's preaching.[125]

Willard's decision to place this debate after her own arguments is rhetorically astute. The person opposing her views compliments the strength of her argument, while the response refutes his. The book concludes, then, with an affirmation of her position delivered by a distinguished male.

The last page quotes Miles Coverdale, a character in Nathaniel Hawthorne's *Blithedale Romance*: "Oh, in the better order of things, Heaven grant that the ministry of souls may be left in charge of women! The gates of the blessed City will be thronged with the multitude that enter in, when that day comes! The task belongs to woman. God meant it for her. He has endowed her with the religious sentiment in its utmost depth and purity, refined from that gross, intellectual alloy, with which every masculine theologist—save only One, who merely veiled Himself in mortal and masculine shape, but was, in truth, divine-—has been prone to mingle it."[126] This citation is wonderfully apt. Not only does it affirm Willard's central argument that God intends women to be involved in ministry, but it also reinforces gender stereotypes of women as particularly pious. Since Willard worked assiduously to locate her advocacy as the natural extension of women's traditional roles, this independent testimony, albeit from a fictional character, is an appropriate ending.

"A Pinch of Common Sense" through a Feminist Hermeneutic

Careful biblical exegesis is central to Willard's arguments because, as Hempton observes, she "explicitly made the connection between biblical hermeneutics and power."[127] Recognizing that the "trail of equal rights for women, whether in church or society, or both, ended with the Bible and its exegesis," Willard draws on the feminist hermeneutic developed by earlier women to offer her own carefully reasoned exegesis to provide a compelling case for women's ministry.[128] Because her focus is on claiming women's voice in churches, she will pay special attention to passages invoked to silence and marginalize women.

In her argument, Willard melds a feminist hermeneutical with the exegetical approach derived from Methodist doctrine. As we have seen, Wesley firmly believed that Christians should bring experience as well as reason to bear in interpreting scripture. If scripture was the primary source of Christian theology, "'Christian antiquity'[tradition], critical reason, and an existential appeal to the 'Christian experience of grace'" could help individuals discern scriptural meaning. In Wesley's view, "private judgement was a keystone of the Protestant Reformation."[129] Skillfully blending the feminist hermeneutic with the application of reason and experience, Willard questions the legitimacy of existing, largely male, interpretations that focus on a few carefully selected passages while ignoring both other individual passages and the larger spirit of Jesus's teachings.[130]

Beginning her argument against a literal reading of scripture, in her first chapter, "The Letter Killeth," Willard draws on a *reductio ad absurdum.* She gently mocks a church in New Jersey that permitted only men to sing in the choir because the Church adhered to a strict literal interpretation of Paul's commandment for women to keep silent.[131] To reinforce her argument, she notes that both Martin Luther and George Washington must have risked divine wrath for resisting established powers because Romans 13:1 clearly demands: "Let everyone be subject to the governing authorities, for there is no authority except that which God has established. The authorities that exist have been established by God." Moving still further into an area more salient for her audience, she reminds readers that Ephesians 6:5 adjures: "Slaves, obey your earthly masters with respect and fear, and with sincerity of heart, just as you would obey Christ."[132] A literalist approach to scripture would, then, fault Luther for confronting the Roman ecclesial authority, condemn Washington for fighting the British government, and consign slaves to obedience.

She then accuses those who would argue for a strict interpretation of the Bible with being willing to slant translation when it serves their purpose. She disparages one explicit male exegetical practice: "Side by side with the method of exegesis which would enforce this literal view, and promulgated by the same class of exegetes, is another, which may be called the method of playing fast and loose."[133] For example, echoing Grimké, Willard points out how masculine exegesis has offered two contrasting interpretations of the same phrase when it is applied to a man and then to a woman: "In Genesis, the Lord says to Cain, the elder brother, speaking to him of Abel, 'Unto thee shall be his desire, and thou shalt rule over him.'" She observes that "our exegetes do not find here divine authorization of an elder brother's supremacy, and yet they construe the same expression when the Lord speaks to Eve, as the assertion, for all time, of a woman's subjection to her husband."[134] Moreover, she notes that in making that move, male interpreters completely ignore God's "explicit declaration 'Let *us* make man in *our* image, after *our* likeness . . . so God created man in his own image, in the image of God he created him, *male* and *female* he created *them*.'"[135]

She exposes how male interpretations of pieces of biblical texts skew the work's broader meaning. But even as she points out the errors of interpretation from a literal perspective or a "fast and loose" approach, she also acknowledges that she does not "impugn the good intention of the good men who have been our exegetes" and she "bow[s] humbly in the presence of their scholarship."[136] But later, she opines that these various examples indicate that "exegesis, thus conducted, is one of the most time-consuming and man-made of all sciences, and one of the most misleading of all arts."[137] In typical Methodist fashion, she proclaims: "A pinch of common sense forms an excellent ingredient in that complicated dish called biblical interpretation, wherever it is set forth at the feast of reason."[138]

In a persuasive demonstration of the problems both with literal interpretation and the bias of male exegesis, Willard inserts a chart that displays conflicting passages that clearly stand in tension. Below is a portion of a chart (Table 5.1) that contrasts every problematic injunction from Paul with another citation from him as well as an additional scriptural passage. This visual presentation of contrasting paragraphs reflects the critical approach developed and used by nineteenth-century biblical scholars and is, indeed, a "pinch of common sense."

Although other women had pointed out the tensions between some passages, particularly in Paul's epistles, Willard's chart is innovative. As Lisa Zimmerelli observes, "What is unique about Willard's text is her presentation." She notes that the "table format was commonly used in scientific works of the period to demonstrate classification and systematic cataloging."[139] In making visual what others had argued verbally, she deals a devastating critique of male exegesis. Her presentation makes especially clear that prohibitions on women's preaching reflect male control, not divine mandate. With a flourish, she appends a lengthy footnote to the passage from 1 Timothy that observes women constitute the majority of Sunday school teachers.[140] Clearly, when convenient, the Church ignores its own male exegesis.

Table 5.1. Contrasting Passages

PAUL	OTHER SCRIPTURES	PAUL
1 Timothy 2:11 But I permit not woman to teach nor to have dominion over a man, but to be in quietness	Judges 4:4–5 Now Deborah, a prophetess, wife of Lappidoth, she judged Israel at the time. was judging Israel . . . And the children of Israel come up to her for judgment.	Galatians 3:28 There can be no male and female; for you are all one man in Christ Jesus.
1 Corinthians 14:34 Let women keep silence in the churches for it is not permitted unto them to speak.	Joel 2:28–29 And it shall come to pass afterward . . . that . . . your daughters shall prophesy . . . and upon the handmaids will I pour out my spirit.	1 Corinthians 11:5 But every woman praying or prophesying with her head unveiled dishonoreth her head.
1 Timothy 2:11 Let a woman learn in quietness with all subjection.	Acts 17:26 Apollos . . . began to speak boldly in the synagogue. But when Priscilla and Aquila heard him they took him unto them and expounded unto him the way of God more clearly.	Romans 16:3–4 Salute Priscilla and Aquila, my fellow workers in Christ Jesus, unto whom I not only give thanks but also the churches of the Gentiles.

NOTE. From *Woman in the Pulpit,* 24–25. Abbreviated table.

Because exegesis of only selected passages can be so misleading, Willard sets another standard for establishing the appropriate role for women. "Christ," she avers, "not Paul, is the source of all churchly authority and power."[141] This emphasis on a divine call was a commonplace throughout many of her published works. In *How to Win: A Book for Girls,* Willard writes: "God has given us each 'a call' to some peculiar work."[142] Later, she continues: "Ours is a high and sacred calling. . . . so shall we be Christ's disciples, and so shall we safely follow on to know the work whereunto we have been called."[143] In "A White Life for Two," she declares that "Woman

Frances Willard's *Woman in the Pulpit* : 131

is becoming what God meant her to be and Christ's Gospel necessitates her being, the companion and counsellor not the incumbrance and toy of man. To meet this new creation, how grandly men themselves are growing; . . . It doth not yet appear what they shall be, or we either, for that matter, but in many a home presided over by a Temperance voter and a White Ribbon worker, I have thought the Heavenly Vision was really coming down to terra firma."[144] For Willard, as with Lee and Grimké, the greatest argument for woman preaching is that God calls her to this work. When women heed God's call, they are helping realize the original divine plan on earth.

Offering additional evidence of God's call, Willard reasons that Christ's relationship with women, how he spoke about them, and how he interacted with them provides the strongest evidence of women's appropriate roles in the Bible. Echoing earlier women, in the first and second chapters of *Woman in the Pulpit* she offers a litany of women who served as prophets, judges, and leaders. She speaks of "Miriam, the first prophetess and Deborah, the first judge; of Hannah, whose answered prayer brought Samuel to be the hope and stay of a dejected nation; of Esther, the deliverer of her people; of Judith, their avenger; of the gracious group of Marys that clustered around her who was blessed among women; . . . of Lois and Eunice who trained Timothy for the ministerial office. . . . Suffice it to say that these all stand forth the equal stewards with their brethren of God's manifold grace."[145] She notes that "there are thirty or forty passages in favor of woman's public work for Christ, and only two against it, and these not really so when rightly understood."[146] In effect, she presents a compelling case that women are called by divine authority to preach the Gospel.

Her decision to title one chapter "The Letter Killeth" before the chapter entitled "The Spirit Giveth Life," highlights another of her argument strategies that Camper refers to as "letter versus spirit" or "pitting the exact wording of a text against its spirit."[147] As outlined above, in "The Letter Killeth," Willard demonstrates how literal interpretations of scripture can become absurd if taken to their logical extension. In contrast, in "The Spirit Giveth Life" she offers interpretations of passages that follow the spirit of scripture. For example, she addresses a common objection that Christ had no female disciples. Willard acknowledges that Jesus "did not designate women as his followers," but she also notes that "from their sex he had his human origin; with the immeasurable dignities of his incarnation and his birth, only God and woman were concerned; no utterance of his marks woman as ineligible to any position in the church he came to found; but his gracious words and deeds, his impartation of his purposes and plans to women, his stern reproofs to men who did them wrong, his chosen companionships, and the tenor of his whole life and teaching, all point out precisely the opposite conclusion."[148]

In contrast to narrow literalist interpretation of scripture, she provides substantial evidence that the spirit of Christ's actions and words suggests he had women followers. For example, she notes that Christ "drew from Martha the same testimony that he required of his Apostles."[149] Like many women rhetors have done, she points to the empowerment of Mary Magdalene to proclaim the resurrection. She provides substantial evidence that the spirit of Christ's actions and words suggests he intends women to be full participants in his new kingdom. In another passage, she discusses Jesus's interaction with the disciples after his resurrection. Quoting the words that Jesus said to his disciples and "*them* that were with them," she asks rather pointedly, "Does any reasonable person suppose that His mother was not there, or that the other Marys were not? Or the great company of women that had ministered to Him?"[150] "But we are not left in doubt," Willard continues, directing her reader to Acts 1:13–14. Drawing on this text, she observes that the disciples "returned unto Jerusalem, and when they were come in, they went up into an upper room where abode both Peter and James and John. . . . These all continued with one accord in prayer and supplication *with the women,* and Mary, the mother of Jesus. . . . And they were *all* with one accord in one place. . . . . And they were *all* filled with the Holy Ghost. . . . Then Peter said 'This is that which was spoken by the prophet Joel, I will pour out my Spirit upon *all* flesh, and your sons and *your daughters* shall prophesy, and on my servants and on my *handmaids,* I will pour out my Spirit, and *they shall prophesy.*"[151] The spirit of scripture, she argues, indicates that women as well as men followed Jesus, witnessed his resurrection, and received the Holy Spirit at Pentecost. She pursues this argument by quoting more scripture that affirms women's roles as witnesses, followers, and preachers. She concludes: "'Behold, I make all things new;' 'the letter killeth, the spirit giveth life.' These are his words, who spake not as a man speaketh; and how the letter killeth to-day, let the sectarianism, the sacerdotalism, and the woman-silencing of the church bear witness."[152]

Although the organizational structure of the text has diminished the appearance of Willard as aggressively argumentative, her exegesis has been devastating. While her application of a feminist hermeneutic has been more limited than Grimké's, she has gained analytical power and persuasive appeal by drawing on the Methodist emphasis on reason and experience. Further, in offering her analysis as an antidote and corrective to male exegesis, she speaks prophetically, calling her beloved Methodism to account for its deviations from, and distortions of, sacred writ.

"She is a woman first of all."

Willard draws on woman's essential nature to argue for what might be perceived as a radical change.[153] Throughout her career, she had a keen ability to meet her audience where they were to advocate for progressive change. As Karlyn Kohrs Campbell notes, she "framed her demands for change so that they appeared to reinforce traditional gender roles."[154] One central tenet of *Woman in the Pulpit* is that woman's nature is ideally suited to preaching. "Religion," proclaims Willard "is an affair of the heart" and "a Christian woman's heart enshrines that holy Guest more surely than many a 'consecrated' pulpit."[155] Elsewhere she argues that "if the purest should be called to the purest ministries, then women, by the men's own showing, outrank them in actual fitness for the pulpit, and the fact is that woman's holiness and wholesomeness of life, her clean hands and pure heart, specially authorize her to be a minister of God."[156] She effectively draws on the values expressed in the Cult of True Womanhood to warrant women's aptitude and fitness for preaching.

To that end, Willard incorporates metaphors and descriptions of the female nature that reinforce women's traditional gender roles. She speaks of the "mother-heart," "loyal daughter," and "home-force." Considering woman's role in the home, she lists women's qualities: "gentle," "compassionate," and "earnest-hearted." A "sweet Madonna's halo" reveals a woman's purity.[157] She also speaks of the "tender Gospel of the New Testament, so suited to be the proclamation of a woman's lips."[158] She implicitly links feminine qualities to God such as when she asserts that the "mother-heart of God will never be known to the world until translated into terms of speech by mother-hearted women."[159] She cites scripture that evokes God's feminine qualities such as when she quotes Isaiah 66:13: "As one whom his mother comforteth, so will I comfort you."[160] As Zimmerelli stresses, Willard is "careful not to suggest a feminine divine nature but rather to identify the feminine in the divine."[161] Her argument is that both feminine and masculine qualities are present in the divine and both male and female interpretations of scripture are essential to understanding the full truth of the Bible.

Drawing on woman's morality and purview over the home, Willard suggests that motherhood requires women to teach the word of God to their children. To neglect woman's sacred duty as a minister in her home, she argues, "is to deprive the children of one of life's most sacred ministries—that of their mother's voice in prayer and in the giving of thanks for daily food."[162] In essence, she suggests that in their roles as Christian wives and mothers, women are necessarily interpreting scripture and preaching the Gospel.

Willard powerfully attacks those who claim that motherhood and ministry are mutually exclusive. In her chapter "The Earth-Born Argument," she begins by citing examples of many women who excelled at motherhood as well as other professions such as medical providers in the Civil War. Her contention is that the ministry is much more conducive to motherhood than any of the other professions she cites. She then declares: "The influence of the two most exalted possible—that of a mother and a minister—combined in one personality ought, by the law of heredity and pre-natal influence, immeasurably to spiritualize and exalt the nature of her children."[163] Drawing on women's experience in childbirth, she avers that only a mother could testify to the miracle of God made flesh. She concludes that "our holy faith can have no human ally so invincible as she who, with strong crying and tears, has learned the sublime secrets of pain and pathos that only mothers' hearts can know."[164] Once again, she reiterates women's distinct nature as a warrant for her calling to preach.

Throughout *Woman in the Pulpit,* Willard responds to arguments that when women venture into the public sphere, they "disrupt the home."[165] She makes clear that woman's nature will not be tarnished when she follows her divine calling: "The mother-heart will never change. Woman enters the arena of literature, art, business, what you will, becomes a teacher, a physician, a philanthropist, but she is a woman first of all, and cannot deny herself. In all these great vocations she has still been 'true to the kindred points of heaven and home;' and everybody knows that, beyond almost any other, the minister is one who lives at home."[166]

Including women in ordained ministry, argues Willard, ultimately benefits both men and women. Echoing Talmadge, she avers "We need women commentators to bring out the women's side of the book," a bold assertion that an exegesis is incomplete without both male and female perspectives.[167] She claims that the "equipping of women for the pulpit" will result in increasing "men's hopes of heaven."[168] Donning a prophetic mantle, she insists that when women enter the ministry, they "will give humanity just twice the probability of strengthening and comforting speech, for women have at least as much sympathy, reverence, and spirituality as men, and they have at least equal felicity of manner and of utterance. Why then, should the pulpit be shorn of half its power?"[169]

Unfortunately, the answer to her question was long in coming and emerged well after her death. Not until 1920 did the Methodist Church restore the possibility of local licensing of women preachers; only later in 1922 did it permit women as delegates to the General Conference.[170] Willard was, indeed, a prophetic voice and, as was often the case for the Jewish prophets, her immediate audience ignored her.

Willard's Rhetorical Accomplishment

An Earnest Prayer that Christ's Blessed Kingdom in the Earth May be Advanced a Little

—FRANCES WILLARD, *WOMAN IN THE PULPIT*

Following in the footsteps of many other women, including Lee, Grimké, and Mott, Willard foregrounds arguments that had been percolating in abolitionist and women's rights discourse for more than fifty years. With and through the skillful application of a feminist hermeneutic, Willard's *Woman in the Pulpit* provides a compelling, if not immediately successful, repudiation of the scriptural arguments that limited women's participation. In one sense, her text is the culmination of the ongoing conversation about women's moral agency that began with Grimké's argument for women's rights. In another way, *Woman in the Pulpit,* in tandem with her many other books and articles, creates a transition from women's reliance on their moral agency to warrant their participation in public life to the argument from expedience, which will dominate the woman's movement at the end of the century. Willard assumes and reasserts women's moral agency as a starting point for her insistence on the beneficial impact of their public engagement on American life.

A Strategy of Dissent

Key to Willard's success was her skill at connecting arguments for dramatic change to strong prevailing values, a classic use of the strategy of dissent.[171] Even as she offers her incisive critique of scripture, for example, Willard is deferential toward the religious community to which she belongs, attributing the incorrect interpretation of scripture to the natural human tendency to err. As Hempton observes, her "beef was not so much with patriarchy in the Scriptures as with the interpretation of those Scriptures by the male leadership of the church in the nineteenth century."[172] This distinction is important. Willard is willing and, indeed, wants to work within the Methodist Church and at the same time, challenge prevailing interpretations of scripture.[173]

She also co-opted traditionally accepted understandings of women's nature to argue for an expansion of women's roles in the public sphere. As she challenged the religious and social proscriptions that circumscribed women's roles, she conformed to and embraced key elements in the traditional images of womanhood. In so doing, she "directly confronted the issue with which nineteenth-century American women struggled: the binding force of the American religious-cultural tradition whose institutions interlocked to uphold the image of the ideal woman as pious, pure, domestic, and submissive, shut up in the private sphere of the home and its extension the church."[174] Under her construal of True Womanhood, women could preserve their femininity as they assumed activist roles. As one newspaper explained, she made it clear that "the grace of womanhood need not be sacrificed in order to accomplish beneficent results in world activities."[175] In making her argument for progressive reforms such as women's preaching and voting, she "relabel[ed] and reframe[ed] proposals in ways that transformed them from demands for social change into reaffirmations of traditional arrangements and values."[176] She referred to petitioning and participating in political activities as "gospel politics," to women's activism as a "calling," and to God with language like "mother-heart," all phrases and images that coupled feminine behaviors with political action.[177]

Willard's rallying cry of "home protection" is a quintessential example of her strategic co-optation of traditional values. She was keenly aware that women could not exceed their "proper" place, either because of societal prohibitions or because they believed doing so was unacceptable. As Bordin explains: "Women felt comfortable with activism and protest only if it was based in the private sphere, if it took as its starting point women's position with the home."[178] Willard gave women a reason to move outside of their home, pointing out how social ills like drunkenness made homes unsafe. Linking public action to the home as well as other traditional conceptions of women, she made a compelling case for suffrage. The vote was the essential tool that women needed to protect their homes and to fulfill their role as women. Thus, "Willard remade the public space of the platform into an extension of the home."[179]

Willard's carefully cultivated and scrupulously maintained public persona enhanced this argument. Not only did she cloak her radical reforms with religious and domestic euphemisms, she also embodied femininity in public. She worked to project an image consonant with social expectations even as she challenged constraints on women. Whenever she spoke, she dressed in modest clothes, used feminine gestures, and created a "'womanly' atmosphere" with "patriotic and religious tones," which "made reserved women comfortable without offending more liberal women."[180] She, an unmarried professional woman, was, as *The Christian Advocate* reported the "perfect specimen of womanliness,"[181] "the embodiment of American womanhood."[182] Because "the vast majority of women were interested in just two things—their home and their church," Nancy Hardesty praises Willard for being the only woman leader of the time who had the prescience to see that a successful movement must relate to these two institutions.[183] Willard did this in her rhetoric and in her public image.

Willard's ability to manipulate existing stereotypes and values to accomplish her strategic agenda makes her unique brand of feminism difficult to classify. Bordin points out the inherent tensions in her public image: "Willard instinctively became the womanly rebel, the pious iconoclast, the feminine feminist."[184] Assigning her an ideological label is difficult: "Her activism does not fit neatly into twenty-first-century understandings of terms such as 'progressive,' 'feminist,' or 'conservative,' although aspects of her career reflect iterations of each of those."[185] Slagell accurately notes she was the "embodiment of the oxymoronic womanly public speaker."[186] Her skill in navigating the contradictions and different social, political, religious, and geographical differences is testament to her strategic use of dissent. Willard was able to participate in the transformation of existing power and knowledge structures across many domains and challenge prevailing social views in ways that enlarged the woman's movement audience.

Because of her rhetorical astuteness and her masterful adaptation of a posture of dissent, she was able to gain a "hearing with white, middle class, Protestant, conservative audiences, which the more revolutionary women's suffragists could not get."[187] Radical reformers, like "Elizabeth Cady Stanton and Susan B. Anthony, failed to evoke images of woman that appealed to the majority of mainstream Evangelical Protestant women who were more timid and loath to challenge the status quo than Stanton and Anthony."[188] She also could maintain strong friendships with those radical reformers like Anthony even as she appealed to more conservative women who were reluctant to act as moral agents. Her widespread appeal and skill in strategic mass organization helped to spread arguments for social reform and woman's rights into new arenas. In and through her rhetoric, Willard altered the self-perception of her audience so that they were able to see themselves as Christian moral agents who needed the right to vote to advance causes near to their hearts.[189] By organizing large groups of women into the WCTU with opportunities for meetings, rhetorical training, and leadership positions, Willard created consciousness-raising enclaves where women could share their views and experiences. This consciousness-raising element was essential to women seeing themselves as agents of change in the political realm and learning the rhetorical tools to advocate for their rights.

Further, in broadening support for women's rights, she played a major role in women's gaining the right to vote; she mobilized tens of thousands of women in support of enfranchisement, helping to amass the numbers of supporters necessary for ultimately instigating legislative action.[190] In doing so, she accomplished a critical goal for this social movement by attracting unprecedent numbers of movement followers. Slagell observes: "It is not implausible to suggest that the success of the woman suffrage movement was dependent upon masters of incremental persuasion such as Willard."[191]

Willard as Prophetic Voice

Willard, like many women before her, drew on socially accepted perceptions of women to argue for a new future that more closely approximated God's plan. In effect, she adopted the persona of a prophet. As Evans avers: "Often casting herself in the role of a prophet from the Hebrew Scriptures, Willard took on the prophet's mantle of a visionary leader who sought to lead her army of women."[192] She urged each woman to "set herself free from the standards of this present time, and to fashion herself by the standard of the Higher Life."[193] In her 1887 President's Annual Address at the National Woman's Christian Temperance Union, Willard clearly articulates her prophetic vision:

> In the world as He created it first, by whose word the worlds were made, man and woman dwelt together, and to *them* He gave dominion over every living thing. After the fall, they began to drift apart, he into the realm of force and she into that of seclusion; but in Christ's kingdom, . . . man and woman have been steadily traveling back to Eden—that is, they have been slowly learning that they were created to live in one world—not two. . . . Under the blessing, man and woman go hand in hand wherever they are called to go . . . man and woman have one and the same standard, . . . Under the curse, man has mapped out the state as his largest sphere, and the home as woman's largest. [U]nder the blessing, man and woman shall map out home as the one true state, and

she who . . . has learned to govern there, shall help man make the great, cold, heartless state a warm, kind and protecting home. The White Ribbon women are tired of this unnatural two worlds in one, where men and women dwell apart; they would invade the solitude of the masculine intellect; break in upon the stereotyped routine of the masculine hierarchy in church and state; and ring out in clear but gentle voices the oft-repeated declaration of the Master whom they serve: "Behold, I make all things new."[194]

This future that Willard envisions for men and women is a "new combined entity, one that does not *erase* the separate identities of male and female but rather *encourages* their dual contributions to theology and society."[195] Willard's vision, then, is for husbands and wives to engage in the "Christian method of dual headship" as they together lead their households.[196] This new world order, she contends, is one that offers the promise of a return to Eden and a world in accordance with the divine plan. As Willard frequently prophesied: "Indeed, if I were asked the mission of the ideal woman, I would reply: It is to make the whole world homelike. . . . home is woman's climate, her vital breath, her native air. A true woman carries home with her everywhere. Its atmosphere surrounds her. . . . But 'home's not merely four square walls.' . . . For woman will make homelike every place she enters, and she will enter every place on this round earth. . . . All gospel civilization is radiant with the demonstration of this truth: 'It is not good for man to be alone.' . . . the home, embodied and impersonated in womanhood, shall go forth into the world."[197] She clearly foresaw a bold and expansive future for women where they could be called to achieve their fullest potential in every realm throughout the globe.

Interestingly, some did understand her call. *Methodist Magazine and Review* referred to her as a "true Deborah of our spiritual Israel." A few years earlier, an article in *The Presbyterian Messenger* compares Willard to Jesus: "Nearly nineteen hundred years ago, at Calvary, the world learned the lesson of the highest Philanthropy, in this fact, 'HE GAVE HIMSELF.' The pressing needs of this age, call for the same spirit, and years ago, Frances Willard laid her life, her God-given powers, her all, herself, on the altar of humanity, . . .—till through her efforts the world has been made 'broader for woman, and brighter for mankind.'"[198] A February 26, 1898 article in *The Outlook* likened Willard to a biblical prophet: "greatness is shown perhaps in nothing more than in a clear perception of a great providential tendency in the midst of which one is living. . . . To perceive such a tendency, to avail one's self of it, and to guide it in novel and right directions, is the function of the prophet; such a prophet we count Miss Willard."[199]

Indeed, her prophetic voice underscores an interesting blending of two streams of argument in her work. Like the other texts profiled in this volume, *Woman in the Pulpit* reinforces traditional notions of Christian women as moral forces inside their homes. But as Christians, they also had an important obligation to bring their moral insights into the larger world in working for needed reforms. This argument from moral agency was critical in the early woman's movement as women struggled to find their way to balance their responsibilities as Christians with their identity as women. Like Willard's larger body of work, however, this text moves toward what Kraditor labels the argument from expediency.[200] If women have an obligation to honor their call to preach, that preaching will balance out and complement male preaching. Moreover, it will bring a distinctive and valuable angle of vision currently missing when only the male voice is heard. So as Willard calls women to bring the full weight of their more innate deep morality into all facets of the public realm, she insists their efforts will have a salubrious impact. In becoming moral agents in the political arena, they will reshape and improve American society. Her *Woman in the Pulpit* helps create and popularize the argument from expediency that Kraditor delineates. Willard insists that empowered wives and mothers have the power to help realize the creation of God's kingdom in a modern world.

Willard's Legacy

With her death on February 17, 1898, at age 58, Willard left a powerful, lasting, and complicated legacy. Her influence in the nineteenth century is indisputable. Although she faced public criticism for her stance on some issues, she has been remembered as an extraordinary woman with a gift for mass organization around major social issues.[201] More than 20,000 people gathered to bid this "Woman of the Century" farewell.[202] Her death prompted sometimes ally and other times antagonist, Elizabeth Cady Stanton, to write to editors of the *Woman's Journal* where she expressed her deep admiration for Willard and reflected upon the many conversations they shared. "When the morning papers announced the death of Willard, I felt the loss to womankind . . . one of the greatest women of this generation has passed away . . . no other woman has ever been so honored and adored."[203] Indeed, with her womanly feminism, Willard blazed a new path for American women.

Conclusion

I would wish that every woman might read the Gospel and
the Epistles of St. Paul and would to God they were translated into
the tongues of all men.

—DESIDERIUS ERASMUS, *ON THE NEW TESTAMENT*

Power is the ability to take one's place in whatever discourse is
essential to action and to have one's part matter.

—CAROLYN G. HEILBRUN, *WRITING A WOMAN'S LIFE*

Martin Luther's posting of his ninety-five theses on the doors of the church
in Wittenberg set in motion forces that would transform western society.[1]
Refusing to recant his views at Worms in April 1521 unless scripture and
reason convinced him to, Luther not only repudiated the Church's control
over biblical interpretation, but also suggested "that any man or woman
possessed on the open Bible could be his or her own theologian."[2] Luther's
surmise has proved true. As biographer Derek Wilson observes: "Making
the Bible available to all in vernacular languages was Luther's most enduring legacy, a legacy that was both rich and powerful. The open Bible was a
revolutionary document."[3] The hermeneutical power Luther unlocked was
critical to the nineteenth-century woman's movement in the United States
in women's quest to gain a voice in the pulpit, on the platform, and in the
public arena.

As we have seen, at the beginning of the century, both the public platform and the pulpit were largely the province of men. Women's proscription
from those arenas was grounded in scripture, albeit scripture as interpreted
by males in religious hierarchies dominated by men. Thus, a central challenge in the struggle for women's rights was to contest the discursive rules

that dictated, in Foucaultian terms, who could speak about what and under what conditions.

In contrast to other studies of the nineteenth-century woman's movement, this work has traced a stream of argument, derived from the application of a feminist hermeneutic to scripture, that enabled a nascent movement for woman's rights to contest discursive rules and, in so doing, gain legitimacy and attract followers. Arising in different contexts and responding to distinct challenges, the texts studied in this volume all participated in and influenced an ongoing conversation about the implications of women's identity as Christians in a society that marginalized and silenced females. Over time, doing their own scriptural exegesis, women claimed their roles as preachers, moral agents empowered to advocate for change, full participants in the affairs of their day, and eventually political activists working to perfect American culture. For the authors of these texts, these new roles were, in truth, merely a fuller realization of their true identity as Christian women.

As we have explored these texts, we have also elucidated how the argument they derived with a feminist hermeneutic allowed them, as moral agents, both to assume a rhetorical posture of dissent and to adopt a prophetic persona. Together those rhetorical strategies invited possible followers into a comfortable subject position of being committed and responsible Christian women working to reform American society. What we learn from these texts also has important implications for the study of other social movements, particularly those seeking to reform the practices and outlooks in their communities.

A Brief Review of the Sociopolitical Context

Chapter 1 reviewed the important sociopolitical currents of the 1820s and 1830s that catalyzed women's efforts. First, the American Revolution had disrupted many social hierarchies. Founding documents like the Declaration of Independence reinforced a commitment to equality, freedom, and individual liberty. As the population soared, cities grew and so too did social and economic opportunities. The spirit of the age imbued citizens, including women, with a stronger sense of their self-worth and ability to think for themselves.

Second, the Second Great Awakening, stirring evangelical zeal throughout the country, "inspired numerous religious and moral reform efforts. As revivalist ministers empowered listeners by explaining salvation was in their own hands, they also emphasized humankind's ability to evangelize the world, remedy social problems, and Christianize their culture through the activities of voluntary organizations."[4] Susan Zaeske observes: "Most evangelicals believed they were charged with a duty not only to cultivate personal morality but to employ their energies to safeguard the morality of the community. . . . The evangelical impulse also gave rise to organizations aimed at reforming a variety of social ills by altering public opinion through pamphleteering, lecturing, and petitioning."[5] To fulfill what they saw as their responsibilities as Christians, women formed benevolent societies, moral reform groups, and, later, when barred from men's groups, female antislavery organizations.

Third, issues around the racial environment in American society galvanized many women. The Constitution, which had been ratified just twelve years before the beginning of the century, had implicitly endorsed slavery with the 3/5th provision.[6] That same provision also established Indigenous people, not as citizens of the United States, but as independent political entities, whose relationship to the American government would be determined by treaties and agreements. In the early years of the nineteenth century, ignoring or abrogating treaties, various states sought to seize lands of Indigenous people and move the inhabitants into new areas. This precipitated the crisis of "Indian removal."[7] Almost simultaneously, calls for the abolition of slavery grew more vigorous. These issues created a sense of moral urgency for Christian women who saw themselves as responsible for protecting vulnerable groups.

This sociopolitical context created what Michel Foucault terms an "Event," "a singular moment in which the space of dissension opens" and the "arbitrariness" of rules that govern social life is revealed.[8] Within this context, women began to question the seemingly arbitrary discourse rules that "created friction" between what they believed they were called to do as Christians and the social customs that narrowly circumscribed their roles.[9] This situation, as Cathcart observes about the beginning of all social movements, raised questions about the "social reality" women had been "conditioned to accept."[10]

A Feminist Hermeneutic as a Rhetorical Resource

In grappling with the tension between their socially prescribed roles and their sense of moral agency and responsibility, women turned to scripture to discern their proper identity and obligations as Christians. With and through a feminist hermeneutic, they found warrants for themselves as preachers and public advocates with an important place in the public sphere. If Luther's intent was to reform the Church by providing a Bible in the common language, women's access to scripture and their ability to interpret through their own lens propelled them into advocacy for social reforms that profoundly transformed American life, including demands for their own empowerment.

Looking at scripture with fresh eyes, women found compelling examples of God's empowerment of women throughout Judeo-Christian history. With considerable expertise, Grimké deftly re-read the creation accounts of Genesis and other passages to argue for women's moral equality. She highlighted the first story of God's creating both women and men in the divine image and dispatched traditional male "mis-readings" of the second. Repeatedly Grimké, Mott, and Willard highlighted Deborah, called by God to serve as a judge in the years before the establishment of a kingdom, and Huldah, who was a prophet during King Josiah's short-lived reform efforts in Judah just prior to the Babylonian conquest. Clearly, they reasoned, God intended women to be full participants and leaders within their religious and social communities. Moreover, these authors, and Lee in particular, pointed to Mary Magdalene as the apostle to the apostles and Paul's commendation of the women who assisted him in his evangelistic ministry. If scripture was to be believed, women were clearly suited for and useful in the ministry of the church, including preaching. These examples, together with new understandings of the passages traditionally used to circumscribe their political life and their role in their religious communities, gave women a new sense of mission and empowerment. Joel's pronouncement, reiterated by Peter at Pentecost, became their watchword. God did pour out power on all people and daughters as well as sons were moved to prophesy. These uncovered and highlighted examples not only undercut traditional male interpretations with their attendant social proscriptions, but also produced a new view of Christian women's proper role.

Through and with their feminist biblical exegesis, these women developed a set of arguments that drew on what Martin Camper calls the stasis of jurisdiction. As Camper explains, legitimacy is at the heart of any jurisdictional dispute. Elaborating on a passage that echoes Foucault, Camper states that "the available lines of argument in the interpretive stasis of jurisdiction represent the range of rhetorical procedures by which individuals, communities, and institutions attempt to control, regulate, facilitate, and coordinate acts of textual interpretation."[11] He argues that "studying arguments in the stasis of jurisdiction reveals how the interpretation of texts is socially, culturally, and institutionally controlled through argument."[12] Providing their own commentaries and analyses, produced by using a new exegetical lens, the women in this volume revealed the clear biases and limitations in traditional male exegesis. In so doing, they explicitly and implicitly insisted on a reconsideration and loosening of socially constructed discursive rules that were grounded in male's selective interpretation of scripture.

In "Discourse on Language," Michel Foucault reflects on how commentary like that offered by these women "permits us to create new discourses ad infinitum: the top-heaviness of the original text, its permanence, its status as discourse ever capable of being brought up to date, the multiple or hidden meanings with which it is credited, the reticence and wealth it is believed to contain, all this creates an open possibility for discussion."[13] At the same time, "commentary's only role is to say *finally*, what has already been articulated *deep down*. . . . it gives us the opportunity to say something other than the text itself, but on condition that it is the text itself which is uttered and, in some ways, finalized."[14] In and through a feminist hermeneutic, these women did, indeed, express what had been "deep down" in scripture, largely buried under centuries of male interpretations. While these women affirmed the authority of the Bible, they disputed men's construal of it. Looking at scripture with fresh eyes, women came to understand their rightful place in God's divine plan.

Contributions to the Study of Social Movements

The case studies in this volume, which illustrate how women deployed biblical exegesis to craft persuasive texts in support of their rights, make important contributions to the study of social movements on several fronts. In particular, this study enhances our understanding of how the woman's movement achieved legitimacy and attracted members, growing from the sixty-eight women who signed the Declaration of Sentiments in 1848 to an estimated 7,000 when the National American Woman Suffrage Association was founded in 1890.[15] On a broader scale, insights into the rhetorical successes of this group can inform our understanding of other reform movements.

The Movement from Personal Awareness to Social Movement

As Stewart, Smith, and Denton note, a primary persuasive task of social movements is to "make people aware that the generally accepted view of social reality fostered by political, social, religious, education, legal, literary and media institutions is false and that something must be done about it."[16] Or as Linkugel, Allen, and Johannesen observe: "A problem is not really a problem to an audience until they perceive it as such. A situation may exist, and an audience may know that it does, but in their eyes it remains nothing more than a lifeless fact until they view it as something that threatens or violates their interest and values."[17] With and through scripture, these women performed important consciousness-raising work, particularly for the nascent movement, by enabling women to see their socially constructed identity, with its significant limitations, as a problem. Arguing that "consciousness-raising is an integral part of woman's subculture," Karlyn Campbell suggests that it "permeates" both the nineteenth century movement and modern feminist efforts.[18] Consciousness-raising in the earlier movement enabled women to become aware of their oppression and was "an essential element in the process of transforming women into agents of change."[19]

So, for example, Lee's autobiography demonstrated how women could experience and discern a divine call to preach despite ecclesial restrictions. She depicted herself a prophet called by God to preach the Gospel. Grimké's powerful arguments established women as moral agents with the same responsibilities as men. Significantly, she signs each letter "Thine in the bonds of womanhood" to highlight not only the ties that bind women into a sisterhood but also the conflict between God's intention for women and their greatly diminished status in contemporary culture. Following Grimké and influenced by her ideas, Mott boldly claims: "There is nothing of greater importance to the well-being of society at large—of man as well as woman—than the true and proper position of woman. . . . I have long wished to see woman occupying a more elevated position than that which custom for ages has allotted to her."[20] That "more elevated position" was, of course, as a full participant in American social and religious life. Willard also helped women perceive the tension between contemporary social stereotypes of women and a status closer to the original divine plan. With her call for "home protection," she urged women, accustomed to thinking their proper sphere was entirely domestic, to become political activists so that they could protect their beloved homes. And if women were working to elevate and purify American life, they should be able to proclaim the Gospel that guided their efforts in their churches. In every case, each woman warranted her appeals in scripture.

Previous scholarship on the woman's movement reveals how letter writing, journaling, participation in benevolent societies, and petitioning all helped women build a sisterhood network and recognize their political agency.[21] Campbell contends: "The communication in these small, supportive groups was the process by which women were transformed into feminists willing to speak and act for social change."[22] In their work on women's petitioning, Zaeske and Portnoy reveal how women's participation in the Indian removal and antislavery petition drives gave them an awareness of themselves as political agents. However, at this point, these women construed their political agency as actions *for others.* In contrast, this volume explores an argument that catalyzed them into advocating *for themselves.* The texts we have studied moved many women into being advocates *for their own rights.*

The consciousness-raising work of these women was also constitutive rhetoric; it called into being a new audience of women who saw advocating for their own rights as essential to fulfilling their responsibilities as Christians.[23] In this process, Mott was particularly important because through her approach and personal appearance she created an attractive persona that appealed to many women. Likewise, Willard was able to shift women's identity in subtle but significant ways, so that large numbers of largely conservative women who embraced the ideals of True Womanhood were transformed into advocates for woman's rights. In so doing, Mott and Willard helped foster what Edwin Black called a second persona, an implied audience that invited women to see themselves as agents of change, albeit operating with appropriate feminine decorum.[24] Charland, calling this process "interpellation," suggests it "occurs at the very moment one enters into a rhetorical situation, that is, as soon as an individual recognizes and acknowledges being addressed."[25]

What Charland observes about constitutive rhetoric is true, not only for these women, but also, we believe, for all reform movements: "this rhetoric of identification is ongoing, not restricted to one hailing, but usually part of a rhetoric of socialization."[26] In every case, the texts in this volume gently shifted the self-perceptions of many women and helped create and attract an audience, whose fundamental self-identity had been dramatically altered. With and through their rhetoric, women literally called themselves and others into being and came to see themselves as agents for their own improvement. The feminist hermeneutic was key to this process. The ability to call an audience into being is critical for social movements because social movements, as Stewart, Smith and Denton remind us, necessarily rely on changing self-perceptions of audiences and gaining adherents.[27] Future research could profitably explore the particular strategies other groups used to summon an audience into being.

Reform through Dissent

However successful these texts were in raising awareness and creating a potential audience, these women, particularly in the fragile stage of a nascent movement, needed to establish the legitimacy of their position to motivate adherents. As Stewart, Smith, and Denton note: "The moral nature of social movement rhetoric is critical to its claim of legitimacy as a social force."[28] Calling for women to mount the pulpit and claim the public platform flew in the face of powerful social norms. Thus, to prove their legitimacy, these women had to ground their appeals in widely accepted moral principles. In various ways, these women intuitively adopted a strategy of dissent to demonstrate their ethos.

Ivie explains that dissent allows a rhetor to express disagreement "without making a complete break with the prevailing viewpoint."[29] Indeed, rather than breaking with prevalent viewpoints entirely, these women artfully simultaneously reframed and affirmed them. Each woman remained true to her Christian roots, and each acknowledged her femininity through arguments, in appearance, and in the way she disseminated her message. Acknowledging their feminine moral natures, they argued only to be able to fulfill their Christian obligations outside the home and in service to others.

A rhetorical posture of dissent is the essence of any reform movement, which must "cut through political orthodoxies" in order to bring practices into better alignment with widely accepted values. Ivie suggests: "Dissent is a key word in the vocabulary of a democratic people. . . . It is a double-sided discourse with both a solid footing in public culture and sharp edge for cutting through political orthodoxies."[30] "The sharp edge" our women found was scripture, seen through the lens of a feminist hermeneutic and skillfully deployed to challenge the "political orthodoxies" of their day. In extending and deepening the meaning of key portions of scripture, the texts examined here allowed women to adopt a posture of dissent. In making their arguments for their proper place in the public sphere, these women drew attention to the tensions between their current social status and their roles as Christians, both in the home and in the public arena. They highlighted how the discursive rules consigned them to silence on important moral issues, in which they, as Christian women, should have a voice. They were not arguing for full equality and identical roles with men. Rather, they sought to expand their proper role as women, wives, and mothers, while still affirming their essential feminine identity.

Dissent was especially important not only to the individual women in this volume but also to the early woman's rights movement as a whole. At its inception, women did not see themselves as agents of change, they had no well-defined leaders, they had no platform, and they were arguably a minority voice. Dissent is, as Ivie opines, "argumentation that begins on the margins."[31] John Lucaites and Celeste Condit shed light on why dissent is an especially attractive strategy for such minority movements. They assert that the movement's goal is to "achieve legitimacy in the terms of the dominant ideology."[32] Rhetors in social movements who rely on dissent as their primary strategy are what Lucaites and Condit refer to as a "culturetypal rhetor." They explain: "Everyday, ordinary individuals, as well as social and political advocates" rely on "taken-for-granted" or "culturally sanctioned" narratives. "However, when conditions arise that invite or require social change, especially when a displaced group seeks to have its interests granted some kind of public legitimacy, the public vocabulary needs to be managed and reconstituted. Rhetors who successfully rearrange and revivify the culturally established public vocabulary to produce social change are masters of culturetypal rhetoric."[33] In other words, culturetypal rhetors employ dissent as a strategy and creatively draw upon the narratives, values, and characterizations of the dominant culture to point out inconsistencies between society's ideals and the lived realities of its citizens, particularly those of the group to which they belong.

This culturetypal rhetoric was critical to the success of the early movement for woman's rights. Lee, Grimké, Mott, and Willard all exemplify the culturetypal rhetor. They all draw upon and reinforce dominant perceptions of women as moral beings to point out the mistake in confining them to the domestic sphere when their responsibilities as Christians require them to act publicly on behalf of others. Before directly challenging social norms, they first had to establish their right to speak, to see themselves as agents of change and members of a social movement, and to enlist a critical mass of women (and men) who shared their views on expanding women's roles. The most expedient way of accomplishing these goals was to leverage socially accepted perceptions of male and female roles as warrants for public action.

In discussing how social movements struggle to remain viable, Stewart, Smith, and Denton contend that "Social movements have always sought out and attempted to utilize the *new* or *alternative media* of their day.[34] Although eventually these women did create periodicals of their own, the genius of these leaders was their adroitness in finding appropriate media to disseminate their messages that lay within the boundaries of traditional female decorum. Relying on forms of communication appropriate to their gender and the social expectations of their audience, they were able to maintain a "solid footing in public culture" while sharing messages that challenged the status quo.

When a change in leadership of the AME curtailed her preaching, Lee turned to the Methodist practice of writing spiritual autobiographies. This form was obviously well suited for her to make a convincing case for her divine call to preach. In and through a spiritual autobiography, Methodist readers could not only trace the author's dawning consciousness but could also see validation of her perspective in the success of her labors. Such autobiographies were commonplace within that denomination, and Methodists saw them as an appropriate expression of spiritual maturation. That medium was perfect for Lee's argument.

Long before the woman's rights movement, the United States had a rich history of public letters as a form of public persuasion. For example, John Dickinson's *Letters from a Farmer in Pennsylvania* helped foment support from the colonists' opposition to Great Britain and Tom Paine's *Common Sense* first appeared as a series of public letters.[35] The Grimké sisters proved adept in the art of the public letter; both wrote public letters that were widely circulated in abolitionist circles. By this time, an array of newspapers, including *The Liberator,* quickly published or republished such documents. Personal letters were decorous and commonplace for women. Adapting the spirit of the personal letter into a public document, Sarah Grimké ostensibly directed her *Letters on the Equality of the Sexes* to a well-established leader in women's abolitionist circles. Her letters were quickly published in sympathetic periodicals exactly as she intended.

Lucretia Mott, who had gained extensive experience in public speaking both in her role as a Quaker minister and in her work in female antislavery societies, was no stranger to the platform. By all accounts she was a polished and persuasive public speaker. However, in this case, she does not seek the platform to make her case. Rather, at the urging of friends, she responds to Dana's lecture. Thus, although women's presence on the public platform was generally accepted, Mott carefully situates her speaking in this case not as an assertive act on her part, but rather as a concerned response to the urgings of others.

By the time of Willard, women had access to a wide variety of media. Indeed, women's rights supporters had developed an extensive array of their own periodicals to disseminate their messages.[36] In addition, women were firmly ensconced in organizations dedicated to women's issues. Consequently, Willard had no difficulty finding media for her messages. Willard, a prolific writer, used her role as President of the WCTU to publish *Woman in the Pulpit* in addition to eight other books, an autobiography, and many pamphlets.[37] Significantly, however, and like Mott, she depicts the source of

Woman in the Pulpit as a request from others, and in this case, the editors of a periodical devoted to homiletics. By assembling and republishing her magazine articles as *Woman in the Pulpit* through the WCTU, she positions it, to some extent, under the aegis of that organization. The WCTU was widely recognized as an organization that was mobilizing women to protect their homes and reform American society. Her text appearing under that imprimatur undoubtedly made it seem less contentious than it was.

On another level, then, this study demonstrates how dissent, when grounded in scripture, may help reform movements gain adherents. In the case of the early woman's movement, the same gender stereotypes that had placed women firmly in the domestic sphere depicted them as the moral guardians and spiritual bastions within the home. The evangelical spirit of the era along with appeals to women to become involved in political issues with moral overtones encouraged women to shift their sense of identity. Political engagement through mechanisms such as petitioning and benevolent associations became a natural extension of their Christian responsibilities as wives and mothers. Almost without recognizing it, some women whose identity resided in the domestic realm were drawn to a progressive reform movement.

Although the early woman's movement may be one of the earliest, if not the first, to draw on the Bible as the "sharp edge" of dissent, more modern movements, also on societal margins, have adapted that strategy.[38] For example, the rhetoric of Martin Luther King Jr. is filled with appeals to biblical truths that challenged segregationist practices of his day. Arguably, two of his most famous pieces of discourse, his "I Have a Dream" speech and his "Letter from the Birmingham Jail," rely on dissent grounded in scripture just as these early women did. King's strategy of nonviolence also had deep biblical roots that both attracted and sustained the modern civil rights movement. As James A. Colaiaco observes in his book on the non-violent approach of King: "The black church played an essential role in the Montgomery bus boycott and in the struggle for civil rights in the South. As the centre of the black community, it provided both a refuge from a hostile white society and a place for political and social activities. . . . The black church also provided the spiritual basis for the nonviolent method of protest that transformed race relations in America."[39] The movement's grounding in the Bible empowered and attracted participants to do their part in perfecting the illusive American ideal of equality.

In a very different way, Phyllis Schlafly's efforts to stop passage of the Equal Rights Amendment relied implicitly on appealing to women who embraced traditional notions of femininity that were grounded in Christian scripture. Reviewing her political life at the time of her death in 2016, Donald T. Critchlow observed how her Stop Era campaign "tapped into evangelical Christians," a strategy quickly adopted by the Republican Party.[40] Moreover, like the leaders who urged women to petition Congress about Indian removal, Schlafly was conscious of adapting the strategies for advocacy to her followers' self-image. Thus, letter-writing and bringing baked goods to legislators allowed these women to engage in political advocacy while maintaining their womanly decorum.

Because reform groups must somehow find a "solid footing in public culture," attention to the sources and argumentative strategies they deploy may shed insight into how social change happens in American culture. Of course, scripture is not the only bulwark for reformers. But as these texts reveal, and as American history confirms, it is often effectively deployed. These women proved astute in understanding and successfully using its power.

Reformers as Prophets

This study underscores the role of prophetic ethos not only in the early woman's movement but all reform movements. In his article on early female public speakers, Casey suggests that such speakers were prophetic in claiming that they were directly empowered by God.[41] Indeed, that is precisely what Lee did. However, we argue that the arguments of these women were prophetic in contrasting current practices with the divine ideal. Moving beyond Casey's observations, we explore how women situated their calls for change within a salvific trajectory of restoring the divine plan much as the Hebrew prophets did.

Because reform movements always articulate a vision for the future by highlighting issues or concerns in the present, they are inherently prophetic. Different movements use different standards for exposing the inadequacies of current policies. A particular viewpoint may, in the eyes of the reformer, be in tension with fundamental principles of a democratic republic. In another instance, the reformer may insist that policies or institutions are immoral when judged by some sacred religious standard. Whatever standard the would-be reformers use to expose the weaknesses of the status quo, they must also craft a vision of the future. In his consideration of the place of the classical conception of invention (the finding of arguments), Phillips opines that "spaces of dissension" open freedom for "a reflective/inventional moment" where one can focus "on one's self and one's actions as a problem" as "some new way of living comes forth."[42] The women in this volume did precisely that.

By emphasizing their respect for scripture, these women built what Burke calls "identification" with their audiences. Burke writes: "You persuade a man only insofar as you can talk his language by speech, gesture, tonality, order image, attitude or idea, identifying your way with his."[43] Highlighting that their efforts were for the benefit of others, added to this process of identification. In essence, the Bible played a crucial role in connecting these women to their audiences. In every case, in making their arguments, our women's ability to read, interpret, and apply biblical truths as they perceived them to their situation was critical. Scripture was the cultural taken-for-granted discourse that connected them to other women and to the larger society. In the context of nineteenth-century culture, the Bible, seen through the lens of a feminist hermeneutic, was indeed a "revolutionary" document.

Part of the "revolutionary" potential of the Bible for these women lies in its empowerment of what contemporary theologian Walter Brueggemann calls "the prophetic imagination."[44] Within the Judeo-Christian tradition, the prophets' primary role as messengers of God is to juxtapose current practices and attitudes with divine truth. Brueggemann argues that "a prophetic understanding of reality is based in the notion that all social reality does spring fresh from the word."[45] In other words, prophets, drawing on scripture, find new insights to critique and urge correction of current social practices. Prophets always challenge the discursive communities of which they are a part. These empowered individuals both criticize society and offer a vision of "a new world."[46]

Brueggemann suggests that the role of such prophetic ministry is "to bring the claims of the tradition and the situation of enculturation into an effective interface. . . . The task of prophetic ministry is to nurture, nourish, and *evoke a consciousness and perception alternative to the consciousness and perception of the dominant culture around us.*"[47] Thus, Judeo-Christian prophecy draws on the past and, through commentary on sacred texts, hopes to illuminate and change the future. As Brueggeman explains in a later work: "the words of the text seize someone in the community who is a candidate for daring. In that moment of re-utterance, the present is freshly illuminated, reality is irreversibly transformed. The community comes to know or see or receive or decide afresh. What has been tradition, hovering in dormancy, becomes available *experience.*"[48] Within this tradition, both women and men could be prophets and, as Huldah from scripture did, guide their communities through difficult times.[49]

As we have seen, our women are prophetic: all speak for dramatic changes in their communities, and all envision or imply a better future. Each woman claims and exercises this prophetic role in a different way. In her only explicitly argumentative passage, Lee, like the Hebrew prophets, juxtaposes divine truth with human rules. She warns: the "by-laws of church government and discipline" can distort biblical truth and thwart God's plan for humankind.[50] Grimké at the very beginning of her first letter indicates that she plans to "advance arguments in opposition to a corrupt public opinion, and to the perverted interpretation of Holy Writ, which has so universally obtained."[51] Having established what she sees as the divine plan, most of her letters delineate how far contemporary society has deviated from God's original plan. In her last letter, she reports: "I have now, my dear sister, completed my series of letters. I am aware they contain some new views; but I believe they are based on the immutable truths of the Bible."[52] With grace and decorum, Mott gently chides Dana's interpretation of scripture and positions herself as leading an unenlightened man toward spiritual truth. At the same time, she looks eagerly toward a future when women may live out their divinely ordained role. Willard envisions a future where both men and women can live out their divine calling and interpret scripture. Their joint efforts will contribute to the "stereoscopic truth" and provide deeper understanding of God's plan for humankind.[53]

Our women realized they confronted the entrenched viewpoints and attitudes of their listeners and readers. Their antidote is to offer an alluring future that can energize change. As Brueggemann notes, while the alternative consciousness generated by the prophetic utterance "serves to *criticize* in dismantling the dominant consciousness," it also "serves to *energize* persons and communities by its promise of another time or situation toward which the community of faith may move."[54] In an entry in the *Woman's Bible*, Matilda Joslyn Gage summarizes and highlights the prophetic role of women like those in this study: "The wonderful progress and freedom of woman, as a woman, within the last half century, despite the false interpretation of the Bible by the Church and masculine power, is the result of a great battle; and all attempts to destroy her will be futile. Her day and hour have arrived; the dragon of physical power over her, the supremacy of the material things in the world, as depicted by male principle, are yielding to the spiritual, represented by woman."[55] In our view, these women did their work well. As prophetic voices, they helped uproot deeply entrenched social constraints and offered a compelling vision of a brighter future.

Interrelationship of Dissent, Prophetic Vision, and Constitutive Rhetoric in Reform Rhetoric

In his book on the prophetic tradition in American political life, James Darsey explores how radicals from Wendell Phillips to gay rights activists drew on their prophetic ethos either to construct a Jeremiad condemning American society or, in the alternative prophetic mode, to envision the perfecting of the culture through particular reforms.[56] Building on Darsey's work, this study reveals how prophetic discourse is inherently a rhetoric of dissent. And, conversely, dissent is inherently prophetic. The prophet must always embrace treasured cultural values and norms as a measuring stick for current practices and policies. The appeal of the prophet, whether condemnation via a Jeremiad or a promise of restoration and renewal as we see in the final sections of Isaiah, is inextricably linked to its cultural milieu. The prophet must try to constitute an audience capable of making the changes needed to restore or create a closer correspondence between actions and beliefs.

Moreover, in looking closely at the rhetoric of four women, this study has demonstrated the strong intrinsic linkages among constitutive rhetoric, the strategy of dissent, and the prophetic ethos within social movements. In so doing, it has added significantly to our understanding of how social movements come into being, attract members, achieve legitimacy, and sustain movement momentum over decades or even centuries.

For example, all social movements must constitute an audience for their message as well as gain and sustain legitimacy. Because "social movements champion *ordinary people* forming *great grassroots efforts* as the only forces that can bring about or resist change," acquiring a significant number of adherents is paramount to success.[57] Central to securing movement followers and legitimacy is building identification by connecting to and grounding appeals in widely shared values and ideals through the strategy of dissent.

In addition, all movements must alter perceptions of reality, maintain visibility, and sustain their efforts in the face of obstacles and public criticism. Building on the work of Michael Gurevitch and Mark R. Levy, Stewart, Smith, and Denton observe that "all social movements are essentially struggling 'over the definition and construction of social reality.'"[58] Dissent as a rhetorical strategy allows movement leaders to expose "paradoxes or inconsistencies in the rhetoric and practices of institutions . . . they oppose," and in so doing, changes perceptions of reality.[59] All social movements seek to keep their follower's attention on ultimate victory, either by purifying and correcting current social practices or by improving the community through their efforts. Either possibility relies on prophetic imagination.[60]

As we have seen, the thread of argument based on feminist exegesis that characterized early activists became less important as the movement gained momentum and attracted a critical mass of followers. By the dawn of the twentieth century, the suffrage movement was well-established and diverse enough in membership that the biblically based arguments became far less important and helpful. The women of the early woman's rights movement had succeeded in following Elizabeth Cady's advice of "Wiping the Dew" from their "spectacles."[61] What was needed at that point was strategic thinking and planning to push to the final goal. The ability of the suffrage movement to shift arguments and approaches over time encourages scholars to explore the dynamics of other movements to consider how they adapt to changing times and changing needs.

A Brief Epilogue

In *Writing a Woman's Life,* her study of the writings of George Sand, Virginia Wolff, and Dorothy Sayers, Carolyn Heilbrun considered how these women sought to break away from male scripts for their appropriate roles. She observes: "Power is the ability to take one's place in whatever discourse is essential to action and the right to have one's part matter."[62] Using the access to scripture that Erasmus could only imagine for them, the women in this volume, all roughly contemporary with George Sand, in very different ways sought to break away from the male scripts about their roles. In the end, through their individual and collective efforts, they achieved the power to take their place in the public arena and to have their voices matter. And their voices helped transform life in this country. Only at a distance can we begin to perceive how profound their contributions to social progress were. They were, indeed, prophetic voices, calling all Americans to a brighter future.

APPENDIX A

Brief Overview of Scholarship on Women and Rhetoric

Scholars have approached the woman's movement from a variety of perspectives. Excellent historical overviews of the nineteenth-century woman's movement abound.[1] A thorough overview of this work is beyond the scope of this project, but here we offer a brief sketch of scholarship that informed our thinking.

In their 2021 book, *Ethics and Representation in Feminist Rhetorical Inquiry,* Amy Dayton and Jennie Vaughn observe that scholarship on women's rhetoric, rhetorical methods, and rhetorical theory has grown significantly. Their volume builds on considerable rhetorical scholarship about women, which can be categorized into four main, often overlapping areas (1) recovering and revising women's voices and texts; (2) celebrating women's rhetorical practices; (3) challenging what counts as rhetoric; and (4) exploring women and their contributions as rhetorical theorists.[2]

Efforts to expand the rhetorical canon to recover and in some cases revise primary texts has been ongoing for decades.[3] Both volumes of Karlyn Kohrs Campbell's *Man Cannot Speak for Her,* Joy Ritchie and Kate Ronald's *Available Means: An Anthology of Women's Rhetoric,* Patricia Bizzell and Bruce Herzberg's *The Rhetorical Tradition: Readings from Classical Times to the Present,* and Cheryl Glenn's *Rhetoric Retold: Regendering the Tradition from Antiquity Through the Renaissance* illustrate work that recovers women's texts and voices.[4] Other anthologies like Shirley Wilson Logan's *"We are Coming": The Persuasive Discourse of Nineteenth-Century Black Women* expanded the rhetorical canon by including the texts of women of color. Special issues such as a 2002 *Rhetoric Society Quarterly* issue "Feminist Historiography in Rhetoric," an exchange by Xin Liu Gale, Cheryl Glenn, and Susan Jarratt in *College English,* and books like Lisa Tetrault's *The Myth of Seneca Falls,* raise questions about how to interpret, recover, and remember women's voices.[5] Together, this scholarship has overcome major obstacles to the study of women's rhetoric—recovering and gaining access to women rhetors and primary texts.

A second stream of scholarship focuses on women's rhetorical practices. Andrea Lunsford's 1995 *Reclaiming Rhetorica: Women in the Rhetorical Tradition* prompted an explosion of work that rewrote women into a rhetorical tradition that "has never recognized the forms, strategies, and goals used by many women as 'rhetorical.'"[6] Jacqueline Jones Royster's *Traces of a Stream: Literacy and Social Change Among African American Women,* Lindal Buchanan's *Regendering Delivery: The Fifth Canon and Antebellum Women Rhetors,* Molly Meijer Wertheimer's edited volume, *Listening to Their Voices: The Rhetorical Activities of Historical Women,* and Jaqueline Royster and Geza Kirsch's *Feminist Rhetorical Practices: New Horizons for Rhetoric, Composition and Literacy Studies* all enlarged the scope of rhetoric by highlighting women's sometimes distinctive practices. Special issues such as the 2011 *College Composition and Communication* issue on "Indigenous and Ethnic Rhetorics" edited by Kathleen Blake Yancey underscored the growing interest in the diversity and intersectionality of women's practice within the rhetorical tradition.

A third stream of scholarship questions what counts as rhetoric.[7] A 1992 *Rhetoric Society Quarterly* special issue on "Performing Feminism, Histories, Rhetorics," asked "How does gender give meaning to the organization and perception of historical knowledge?"[8] A 2003 special issue in *Philosophy and Rhetoric* interrogated "What counts as 'the tradition'?"[9] These special issues reflect significant interest in women's rhetoric as well as debates that percolate within this scholarship.

One debate focused on what constitutes a rhetorical text.[10] Barbara Berg locates the roots of feminism and a feminist consciousness in discourses not traditionally seen as rhetorical such as memoirs, diaries, women's fiction, and voluntary associations.[11] In *Women Speak: The Eloquence of Women's Lives,* Karen and Sonja Foss suggest that poetry, quilting and needlework, photography, baking, and architecture, among others reveal important aspects of women's communication.[12] In *Anglo-American Feminist Challenges to the Rhetorical Traditions,* Krista Ratcliffe urges scholars to examine texts such as etiquette manuals, cookbooks, and fiction to discover women's rhetorical practices and theories of rhetoric. Increased attention to these and other private discourses has led to an appreciation of women as both rhetorical practitioners and rhetorical theorists. As Carol Mattingly concludes: "traditional ways of assessing rhetoric cannot provide effective understandings or appreciations of women's rhetoric. Women's forms of rhetoric have been devalued, not only the shape their words have taken—in letters, diaries, protests, and other forms—but their physical forms as well, and their needs differ widely from the needs and expectations espoused in the traditional canon. . . . We need time to see rhetoric in new ways."[13]

A fourth strand of work explores women as theorists and women's contributions to rhetorical theory. Ritchie and Ronald caution: "Women's rhetorical acts cannot be neatly separated from women's rhetorical theory despite the existence of these categories in the masculinist rhetorical tradition, where rhetorical theory arises from practices within specific contexts and communities . . . women have purposefully sought to keep the context, the immediacy of experience, attached to the theorizing rather than creating an abstract set of prescriptions disconnected from the contexts or stripped of the exigencies of everyday life."[14] Not surprisingly then, much scholarship on women and rhetorical theory draws on women's personal experiences.[15] Edited volumes such as Cindy Griffin, Karen Foss, and Sonja Foss's *Readings in Feminist Rhetorical Theory* and Hilda Miller and Lillian Bridwell-Bowles' *Rhetorical Women: Roles and Representations*; anthologies such as Jane Donawerth's *Rhetorical Theory by Women Before 1900*; books like Cheryl Glenn's *Rhetorical Feminism and This Thing Called Hope;* and essays like Karlyn Kohrs Campbell's "Theory Emergent from Practice: The Rhetorical Theory of Frances Wright" and Christine Sutherland's "Mary Astell: Reclaiming Rhetorica in the Seventeenth Century" are all examples of scholarship that focus on women as rhetorical theorists.

Together, this research reveals a burgeoning interest in rhetorical feminism, which embraces nontraditional forms of rhetoric and experiences even as it challenges traditional understandings of rhetorical theory and practice. As Glenn summarizes: "rhetorical practices should *do* something . . . rhetorical inquiry should make a difference in the world." She suggests that this happens when scholars use their agency to "redefine rhetorical history, theory, and praxis to the end of representing and including more users and uses of rhetoric; to represent more ethically and accurately the dominant and the marginalized alike (even as we rethink this metaphor); and to prepare the next generation of rhetorically empowered scholars, feminists, teachers, and citizens."[16]

APPENDIX B

Contested Passages in Scripture

Throughout the struggles for woman's rights, certain Bible passages became the focal point of debate and contention. Below are those passages in the King James Version, which was the standard among Protestants until modern times.

Passages Urging Women's Submission and Silence

Genesis 3:16: Unto the woman he said, I will greatly multiply thy sorrow and thy conception; in sorrow thou shalt bring forth children; and thy desire shall be to thy husband, and he shall rule over thee.

1 Corinthians 11:3: But I would have you know, that the head of every man is Christ; and the head of the woman is the man; and the head of Christ is God.

1 Corinthians 14:34–35: Let your women keep silence in the churches: for it is not permitted unto them to speak; but they are commanded to be under obedience as also saith the law. And if they will learn anything, let them ask their husbands at home: for it is a shame for women to speak in the church.

Ephesians 5:23: For the husband is the head of the wife, even as Christ is the head of the church: and he is the savior of the body.

1 Timothy 2:11–14: Let the woman learn in silence with all subjection. But I suffer not a woman to teach, nor to usurp authority over the man, but to be in silence. For Adam was first formed, then Eve. And Adam was not deceived, but the woman being deceived was in the transgression.

Passages Suggesting Women's Equality

Genesis 1:27: So God created man in his own image, in the image of God created he him; male and female created he them.

Joel 2:28: And it shall come to pass afterward, that I will pour out my spirit upon all flesh; and your sons and your daughters shall prophesy, your old men shall dream dreams, your young men shall see visions. (Peter quotes this passage in his Pentecost sermon in Acts 2:17.)

Galatians 3:28: There is neither Jew nor Greek, there is neither bond nor free, there is neither male nor female: for ye are all one in Christ Jesus.

Examples Used by Women

Deborah: judge and prophet; Judges 4 and 5

Hulda: prophet; 2 Kings 22:14–20; 2 Chronicles 34:22–28

Mary Magdalene: preacher and apostle; particularly John 20:17–18

Co-workers with Paul:

>   Junia: Romans 16:7
>
>   Phoebe: Romans 16:1–2
>
>   Priscilla: Romans 16:3–4
>
>   Tryphaena and Tryphosa: Romans 16:12

NOTES

PREFACE

1. Schuessler, "Complex History."

2. Tetrault, *Myth of Seneca Falls*, 1–10. Stanton, Anthony, and Gage, eds. *History of Woman Suffrage*. Following the preface title, the first epigraph is from Coogan, ed., *New Oxford Annotated Bible*. Peter quotes this passage in his sermon to a crowd in Acts 2: 17-18. It became a staple quotation for women in arguing for a voice. The second epigraph shows a slight misquotation of Genesis 2:18 as provided in the two translations available to Shaw. The King James rendered the verse: "It is not good for man to be alone." The Revised version (1881–1885) offered: "It is not good for the man to be alone."

3. These citations are all from the King James translation, which was the standard at the time.

4. Brekus, *Strangers and Pilgrims,* 3. Casey, "First Female Public Speakers," 1–28. For a detailed study of one such woman, see Brekus, *Sarah Osborn's World.*

5. Casey, "First Female Public Speakers," 3.

6. Brekus, *Strangers and Pilgrims,* 4.

7. Perkins, "Impact of the 'Cult of True Womanhood,'" 18. As Perkins points out, this concept of True Womanhood applied to upper- and middle-class White women. For free Black women, womanhood was linked to "racial uplift."

8. Stanton, *Woman's Bible*, viii.

9. Welter, "Cult of True Womanhood," 151–74. In offering another analysis of nineteenth-century models for feminine behavior, Frances B. Cogan praises Welter's "excellent scholarship" and limns what she terms women in the ideal of the Real Woman. This ideal, Cogan argues, encouraged women to engage in physical fitness, attain education, become employed when necessary for financial reasons, and learn how to choose a good marriage partner. Like Welter, Cogan largely refers to middle- and upper-class White women. Cogan acknowledges that the notion of the Real Woman was relatively short lived (1840–80) and faded even as the cult of True Womanhood persisted into the twentieth century. See Cogan, *All American Girl.*

10. Welter, "Cult of True Womanhood," 152.

11. Roberts, "True Womanhood Revisited," 150.

12. E. Gold, "Grimké Sisters," 344.

13. Roberts, "True Womanhood Revisited," 151. Carolyn Eastman observes that the restrictions the Cult of True Womanhood placed on women represented a dramatic shift in social expectations for women. Eastman explains that gender roles became more sharply delineated in the early nineteenth century. "Common-school and female education likewise underwent related shifts in the early nineteenth century that reconceived the way ordinary people participated in public. At the same time that schoolbooks began teaching students to venerate their

164 : Notes to Pages xiii–2

national leaders' oratory and wise guidance—imagining a more passively patriotic public—popular literature began to advance a model of girlhood and womanhood that was less public and less political than before." Eastman, *A Nation of Speechifiers*, 82.

14. Stanley, *Holy Boldness*, 19.

15. Perkins, "Impact of the 'Cult of True Womanhood,'" 18.

16. We are aware of the sensitivities around the use of the word "Indian" to refer to Indigenous people. However, since that was the term used at the time, we are adopting it here, with apologies.

17. Florence, *Preaching as Testimony*, 40.

18. Nathan O. Hatch labels these changes "the democratization of American Christianity." We will explain this more fully in Chapter 1. Hatch, *Democratization of American Christianity*, 220.

19. Donawerth, *Conversational Rhetoric*, 73–74; Trible, "Five Loaves and Two Fishes," 279–95. Apparently unaware of the texts we will study, Trible seems to consider the emergence of feminist hermeneutics and theology as a twentieth-century phenomenon.

20. Dissent as a rhetorical strategy is explained in further detail in Chapter 1. Within a rhetorical context, Robert L. Ivie defines dissent as follows: "Dissent means advancing a significant difference of opinion or expressing a substantial disagreement without making a complete break with the prevailing viewpoint." Ivie, "Enabling Democratic Dissent," 50. Eric Doxtader elaborates on that definition, noting that dissent "is a moment of conflict in which the taken-for-granted rules, topics and norms of public deliberation are contested, opposed, or transgressed." Doxtader, "Characters in the Middle of Public Life," 337.

21. Spitzack and Carter, "Women in Communication Studies," 405.

22. Although scholars are inconsistent in how they refer to the nineteenth-century movement, the women themselves seem to prefer "woman's rights" to "women's rights." So, for example, both suffrage movements after the Civil War were "woman suffrage" associations and the collection of documents that Elizabeth Cady Stanton coedited was called *History of Woman Suffrage*.

23. Although Sarah was not married and had no children, she was an integral part of Angelina and Theodore Weld's household with an active role in rearing their offspring. Thus, her primary role for much of her life was within a domestic setting.

CHAPTER 1: WELLSPRING OF ARGUMENT

1. Donawerth also observes that the Reformation was a "model for women's claiming the right to preach" but does not develop that idea nor does she explore fully the strand of argument we identify. Donawerth, *Conversational Rhetoric*, 75.

2. John 10:11–18. This story was highly significant for Jarena Lee, one of the women discussed in this volume, and will be explored much more fully in that chapter.

3. Romans 16:1. The King James translates this title as "servant." When the word is used in relation to Timothy in 1 Timothy 4:6, the translation is "minister." Sarah Grimké and other women will note the apparent discrepancy and attribute it to the prejudice of male interpreters.

4. Cardman, "Women, Ministry, and Church Order," 300.

5. Throughout the struggles for woman's rights, certain Bible passages became the focal point of debate and contention. Following are passages from the King James

Notes to Pages 2–6 : 165

Version, which was the standard among Protestants until modern times. Passages urging women's submission and silence: Genesis 3:16: Unto the woman he said, I will greatly multiply thy sorrow and thy conception; in sorrow thou shalt bring forth children; and thy desire shall be to thy husband, and he shall rule over thee; 1 Corinthians 11:3: But I would have you know, that the head of every man is Christ; and the head of the woman is the man; and the head of Christ is God; 1st Corinthians 14:34–35: Let your women keep silence in the churches: for it is not permitted unto them to speak; but they are commanded to be under obedience as also saith the law. And if they will learn anything, let them ask their husbands at home: for it is a shame for women to speak in the church; Ephesians 5:23: For the husband is the head of the wife, even as Christ is the head of the church: and he is the savior of the body; 1 Timothy 2:11–14: Let the woman learn in silence with all subjection. But I suffer not a woman to teach, nor to usurp authority over the man, but to be in silence. For Adam was first formed, then Eve. And Adam was not deceived, but the woman being deceived was in the transgression.

6. This authority came from Matthew 16:19 where Jesus gives Peter the keys of the kingdom and the power to pronounce forgiveness.

7. Marshall, *Reformation,* 13.

8. McGrath, *Christianity's Dangerous Idea,* 45.

9. Daniell, "William Tyndale," 39. The Vulgate is the Latin translation of the Bible that was and is the standard within the Roman Catholic Church.

10. Foucault, "The Discourse on Language," 216 (emphasis in original).

11. Phillips, "Event of Dissension," 62.

12. Phillips, "Event of Dissension," 62.

13. D. Wilson, *Out of the Storm,* 345 (emphasis in original).

14. Luther, *To the Christian Nobility,* 26.

15. Because individuals studied in this book used different translations, the precise wording of biblical quotations will vary considerably. When we quote their usage directly, we will use the wording they provide without identifying the particular translation. However, when we are referring to passages they address, we will use what is a widely adopted modern version: the New Revised Standard Version. In particular, our citations will be from the *The New Oxford Annotated Bible,* 3rd edition.

16. Luther, *To the Christian Nobility,* 21.

17. Luther, *To the Christian Nobility,* 21.

18. Luther, *To the Christian Nobility,* 23.

19. Luther, *To the Christian Nobility,* 27.

20. Camper, *Arguing Over Texts,* 91–113. Martin Camper labels this strategy the "stases of conflicting passages." "Stasis" (plural "stases") is a rhetorical term that identifies the possible issues of dispute in a situation. When disputants are looking at differing passages in a work to make an argument, that interpretive struggle is around the stasis of conflicting passages. This will be a key element in women's struggle for full participation in the church and in the public arena.

21. D. Wilson, *Out of the Storm,* 345.

22. McGrath, *Christianity's Dangerous Idea,* 2–3.

23. Phillips, "Event of Dissension," 65.

24. Duerden, "Equivalence of Power," 15. Here Duerden is quoting two different sources for Foucault. The first internal quote is to Foucault, "What Is an Author?," 108. The second quote is to "Nietzsche, Genealogy, History," 86.

25. See Mathieson, *Woman's Voice,* for both a copy of von Grumbach's most notable publication and a careful analysis of it.

26. Fell, "Womens Speaking Justified," 157. In the 1666 edition, the title is *Womens Speaking,* although subsequent editions, including the online version at Quaker Heritage, insert the apostrophe *Women's Speaking.* We will follow the original edition.

27. In discussing early women public speakers, Michael W. Casey suggests "they defended their right to speak using biblical precedents of women leaders and speakers." His focus is simply on how they used these examples to defend their own speaking. However, he does not connect this to exegetical practice nor does he consider how these women developed arguments based on their exegesis. See Casey, "First Female Public Speakers," 9–13.

28. M. Solomon, "Role of the Suffrage Press," 1, 4.

29. Quoted in Hatch, *Democratization of American Christianity,* 220.

30. Rossel and Dupuis, *Memoirs of Charles G. Finney,* xix.

31. McCook, "Second Great Awakening," 252.

32. Mathews, "Second Great Awakening," 30. [see query, p. 30]

33. Hatch, *Democratization of American Christianity,* 6.

34. Hatch, *Democratization of American Christianity,* 22.

35. Hatch, *Democratization of American Christianity,* 3.

36. Hatch, *Democratization of American Christianity,* 4. See also Carwardine, "Second Great Awakening in the Urban Centers," 337.

37. Gonzalez, *Story of Christianity,* 228.

38. See Brekus, *Strangers and Pilgrims,* for a discussion of the impact of evangelicalism in the First and Second Great Awakenings in empowering women.

39. Berg, *Remembered Gate,* 8.

40. Tinkler, "Renaissance Humanism," 283–84.

41. Sutherland and Sutcliffe, *Changing Tradition.*

42. Zboray and Zboray, *Voices without Votes,* 3.

43. Zboray and Zboray, *Voices without Votes,* 12.

44. Smith-Rosenberg, "Female World of Love and Ritual."

45. Zboray and Zboray, *Voices without Votes,* 12. The frequent correspondence between Antoinette Brown Blackwell and Lucy Stone from 1846 to 1850 is a case in point. In "Writing Themselves into Consciousness," Lisa Gring-Pemble argues their letters served as a form of consciousness raising: "In and through the letters, the women transform[ed] themselves from private individuals to social activists," 42. Such testing grounds were vital to the growth and maintenance of the nascent woman's movement. As Gerda Lerner observes "Thinking women, like men, not only needed other thinkers against whom to argue in order to test out their ideas, but they needed audiences, whether private or public." *The Creation of a Feminist Consciousness from the Middle-Ages to Eighteen-Seventy* (New York: Oxford University Press, 1993), 221.

46. Flexner, *Century of Struggle,* 41–42.

47. Flexner, *Century of Struggle,* 42.

48. Melder, *Beginnings of Sisterhood,* 39.

49. Bogin and Yellin, "Introduction," 9.

50. K. Campbell, *Man Cannot Speak for Her,* Vol. 1, 49.

51. Ray, "What Hath She Wrought?" 187. For more information on the lyceum movement, see also Ray, *Lyceum and Public Culture* and Wright, *Cosmopolitan Lyceum.*

Notes to Pages 10–12 : 167

52. Ray, "What Hath She Wrought?" 204.

53. N. Johnson, *Gender and Rhetorical Space.* Although Johnson's work focuses on how spaces were gendered in the aftermath of the Civil War, her concept applies to attitudes from earlier in the century. Karlyn Kohrs Campbell's notion that public speaking required qualities of expertise and authority at odds with the qualities associated with True Womanhood reflects the same gendering of rhetorical spaces. See K. Campbell, *Man Cannot Speak for Her,* Vol. 1, 10.

54. Flexner, *Century of Struggle,* 44. See Kerber, "Separate Spheres," 9–39, for a thoughtful analysis of the resonances of this concept in the writing of women's history. See also Kerber et al., "Beyond Roles, Beyond Spheres," 565–85. In her comments, Kerber urges scholars to consider the "hegemonic" power of such metaphors.

55. Several scholars have noted that the lines between public and private spheres were sometimes blurred, pointing to the elocutionary education of young women, female educators as lecturers, and women exhorters as examples. See, for example, Kelley, *Learning to Stand and Speak* and Ganter, "Women's Entrepreneurial Lecturing," 42–55. Carolyn Eastman also traces the rise of a more active female public space in the late eighteenth century to a more circumscribed, less political, and less public role in the early nineteenth centuries in *A Nation of Speechifiers.*

56. Welter, "Cult of True Womanhood," 174.

57. K. Campbell, *Man Cannot Speak for Her,* Vol. 1, 10.

58. Beecher, "Circular," 4, 17. The circular is also reprinted in *Christian Advocate,* September 9, 1826, n.p.

59. Beecher, "Circular."

60. Zaeske, *Signatures of Citizenship,* 2.

61. Zaeske, *Signatures of Citizenship,* 109.

62. Zaeske, *Signatures of Citizenship,* 142.

63. Portnoy, "'Female Petitioners,'" 608.

64. In time, women realized that they needed their own newspapers to reach beyond the confines of public meetings or conventions. Beginning in 1849, Amelia Bloomer, who was married to a newspaper publisher, started *The Lily,* which gradually moved from a focus on temperance to a broader agenda of woman's rights (Chambers, Steiner, and Fleming, *Women and Journalism,* 147–48). Eventually, other periodicals, published by women themselves, provided conduits for the ideas of and developments about the woman's movement to reach wider audiences. These periodicals included *The Una, The Revolution, The Woman's Tribune, The Agitator, The Woman's Journal,* and *Farmer's Wife,* to name a few. See M. Solomon's *Voice of Their Own* for an exploration of the various journals and newspapers involved with suffrage.

65. Zaeske, "'Promiscuous Audience,'" 203; Flexner, *Century of Struggle,* 82.

66. Stewart, Smith, and Denton, *Persuasion and Social Movements,* 23.

67. Cathcart, "Confrontation Perspective," 72. See also Cathcart, "Defining Social Movements," 267–73; Cathcart, "New Approaches to the Study of Movements," 82–88; Cathcart, "Movements," 233–47.

68. Interest in the woman's rights movement and individual women in it helped catalyze interest in women as rhetors and as theorists. Such scholarship not only expanded our notion of the forms rhetorical practice can take and of the history of women's rhetorical theory, but also enriched our understanding of the many ways women found to engage each other and the issues of their day. Although

much of this work is beyond the scope of this project, Appendix A suggests some of the richness of that scholarship.

69. In addition to Flexner and Lerner, see, for example, Cott, *Bonds of Womanhood* and Ryan, *Women in Public*. Logan's *With Pen and Voice* is an example of the recovery of work by women of color. Donawerth's scholarship explores women's contributions to rhetorical theory. See, for example, *Conversational Rhetoric* and *Rhetorical Theory*.

70. See Browne, *Angela Grimké*; E. Gold, "Grimké Sisters"; Daughton, "Fine Texture of Enactment"; Japp, "Esther or Isaiah?"

71. Dow, "Spectacle, Spectatorship, and Gender Anxiety," 143–57.

72. K. Campbell's work (*Man Cannot Speak for Her*, Vol. 1 and Vol. 2) is groundbreaking in its exploration of the rhetorical dimensions of the woman's rights movement. See also DuBois, *Feminism and Suffrage*; Melder, *Beginnings of Sisterhood*; Matthews, *Rise of the Public Woman*; Mattingly, *Well-Tempered Women*.

73. Kraditor, *Ideas of the Woman Suffrage Movement*, 43–75.

74. Zaeske, "'Promiscuous Audience,'" 192.

75. Zaeske, "'Promiscuous Audience,'" 203.

76. Ivie, "Enabling Democratic Dissent," 50.

77. Doxtader, "Characters in the Middle of Public Life," 336.

78. Ivie, "Enabling Democratic Dissent," 51. The internal quote is from Bleiker, *Popular Dissent*, 269.

79. Ivie, "Toward a Humanizing Style," 454.

80. Ivie, "Toward a Humanizing Style," 455.

81. Doxtader, "Characters in the Middle of Public Life," 336.

82. Ivie, "Enabling Democratic Dissent," 50.

83. Lucaites and Condit, "Reconstructing *Equality*," 18 (emphasis in original).

84. In his discussion of early female public speakers, Casey explains how they claimed to be prophets in that their call to preach came directly from God. Rather than focusing on their perception of the source of their calls, our discussion will explore how their discourse reflected the pattern of the Hebrew prophets in comparing current practices to the divine plan. See Casey, "First Female Public Speakers," especially 4–9.

85. D. Peterson, "Prophecy," 621, 648.

86. Darsey, *Prophetic Tradition*, 17.

87. Chittester, *Time Is Now*, 103.

88. Bercovitch, *American Jeremiad*, 7. There is a vast literature on the Jeremiad in American political discourse. The form has been particularly useful in considering the discourse of African Americans in their struggle for full citizenship rights. See, for example, Howard-Pitney, "Enduring Black Jeremiad," 482.

89. Hays, *Message of the Prophets*, 22.

90. Ruether, *Introducing Redemption in Christian Feminism*, 13.

91. Stewart, Smith, and Denton, *Persuasion and Social Movements*, 62.

92. Stewart, Smith, and Denton, *Persuasion and Social Movements*, 65.

93. Stewart, Smith, and Denton, *Persuasion and Social Movements*, 67.

94. Stewart, Smith, and Denton, *Persuasion and Social Movements*, 65.

95. Kenneth Burke, *Rhetoric of Motives*, 46.

96. Black, "Second Persona," 113.

97. Charland, "Constitutive Rhetoric," 138–40. Charland is drawing on the work of Louis Althusser.

Notes to Pages 17–21 : 169

98. Charland, "Constitutive Rhetoric," 143.

99. Charland, "Constitutive Rhetoric," 142.

CHAPTER 2: JARENA LEE'S *RELIGIOUS EXPERIENCE AND JOURNAL*

1. Bassard, *Spiritual Interrogations,* 87. Apparently, the African Methodist Episcopal Church hierarchy had forbidden itinerant preachers like Lee to publish books or pamphlets without formal approval. Despite this prohibition, Lee published the expanded version at her own expense in 1849. Andrews, *Sisters of the Spirit,* 6.

2. Florence, *Preaching as Testimony,* 47.

3. Florence, *Preaching as Testimony,* 47.

4. Andrews, *Sisters of the Spirit,* 2.

5. Jones, *All Bound Up Together,* 40, 66.

6. Joel 2:28. This is from the King James Translation, which is almost certainly the one Lee would have known. Peter quotes this passage in his Pentecost sermon in Acts 2.

7. Andrews notes that Lee's minimal attention to her early life is typical of American spiritual autobiographies. He writes of the three women, whose autobiographies he collects, that "For each of these women her life before conversion was of no real significance except insofar as it could be used as a kind of negative moral object lesson for her reader." Andrews, *Sisters of the Spirit,* 11.

8. Lee, *Religious Experience and Journal,* 3.

9. Hubert, "Testimony and Prophecy," 46. See also Florence, *Preaching as Testimony,* 41.

10. Lee, *Religious Experience and Journal,* 97. Perhaps because of her lack of education, she "enlisted the aid of an unnamed editor to reshape a portion of her religious journal into a narrative form suitable for publication." Andrews, *Sisters of the Spirit,* 6. In light of her accomplishments, it is difficult to take at face value Lee's assertion that she had only "three months of schooling." Although she may have lacked formal education, she clearly had educated herself.

11. Lee, *Religious Experience and Journal,* 97–98.

12. Allen had established the Bethel African Methodist Episcopal Church in 1793. Later in 1815, that group and others joined to form the African Methodist Episcopal Church. See "Our History."

13. Andrews, *Sisters of the Spirit,* gives this date as 1811. However, Dodson gives the date as 1809 in *Engendering Church,* 90. Neither source footnotes these dates and Lee's narrative is not specific. Dodson indicates that Lee was the first to petition for a *license* to preach "even before the denomination formally existed"(90). Andrews, *Sisters of the Spirit,* notes that Allen had denied an English woman's *request* to preach to his congregation, 5.

14. Lee, *Religious Experience and Journal,* 11.

15. Westerkamp, *Women and Religion,* 115. Westerkamp argues: "The Methodist Connection that Asbury established in the United States was far less open to women's leadership" in part because they placed "a premium on respectability," 114–15.

16. Lee, *Religious Experience and Journal,* 15.

17. In *Taking Heaven by Storm,* Wigger explains how this role emerged: "Seizing on the democratic and leveling impulses of the age, American Methodists offered new roles for zealous lay men and women as local preachers, lay exhorters, class leaders, and a host of semi-official positions," 29.

18. Lee, *Religious Experience and Journal,* 29.

170 : Notes to Pages 21–25

19. Giver-Johnston, *Claiming the Call to Preach*, 125.
20. Collins, "Walking in Light," 344.
21. Bassard, *Spiritual Interrogations*, 99, 90 (emphasis in original).
22. Lee, *Religious Experience and Journal*, 97.
23. Stanley, *Holy Boldness*, 209–10.
24. Newman, *Freedom's Prophet*, 232.
25. C. Peterson, "Secular and Sacred Space," 45.
26. Wills, "Women and Domesticity," 137.
27. C. Peterson, "Secular and Sacred Space," 44; See also Washington, *Sojourner Truth's America*, 261.
28. Tabraham, *Making of Methodism*, 8.
29. Wesley, *Works of John Wesley*, 134–35.
30. Tabraham, *Making of Methodism*, 15–21; Chilcote, *Early Methodist Spirituality*, 10–13. In its break with the Roman Catholic Church in the sixteenth century, Anglicanism retained a respect for tradition as a source of spiritual discernment. Inspired by Protestant reformers, the Anglican Church embraced an emphasis on scripture as a vital grounding for theological thinking and added reason to mediate tensions between the other two. Together, these enabled clear spiritual understanding and sound doctrine. Wesley added experience to this three-pronged approach.
31. Chilcote, *Early Methodist Spirituality*, 7–8; Tabraham, *Making of Methodism*, 10.
32. Tabraham, *Making of Methodism*, 31–40.
33. Stanley, *Holy Boldness*, 91.
34. Andrews, *Sisters of the Spirit*, 15.
35. Taves, *Fits, Trances, & Visions*, 75.
36. Andrews, *Sisters of the Spirit*, 14–15.
37. Chilcote, *Early Methodist Spirituality*, 32.
38. Collins, "Walking in Light," 337.
39. Chilcote, *Early Methodist Spirituality*, 12–13.
40. Batty, "Origins," 12–14.
41. Kaplan and Kaplan, *Black Presence*, 98; Graham, "Women Local Preachers," 165–67; Gonzalez, *Story of Christianity*, 210; Payne, *History of the African Methodist Episcopal Church*, 71–93. Payne contains an account, largely in the form of a letter from Allen, about his ministry. Significantly, Payne does not mention Lee in his history although he certainly knew of her and her work.
42. Wesley, "Sermon 98."
43. Quoted in Heitezenrater, *Wesley and the People*, 248.
44. Wesley, "June 13 1771," 143.
45. Chilcote, *Early Methodist Spirituality*, 170. As Collins concludes in "Walking in Light," 342: "The central truth behind the empowerment of women in early Methodism is that John Wesley enjoyed and respected women."
46. Quoted in Richey, *Methodism in the American Forest*, 13.
47. Richey, *Methodism in the American Forest*, 13–14.
48. Richey, *Methodism in the American Forest*, 17.
49. Richey, *Methodism in the American Forest*, 22.
50. Quoted in Richey, *Methodism in the American Forest*, 22 (emphasis in original).
51. Newman, *Freedom's Prophet*, 39.
52. Dickerson, *African Methodist*, 19.
53. Taves, *Fits, Trances, & Visions*, 75.

Notes to Pages 25–31 : 171

54. M. Noll, *America's God,* 167, 169.

55. Hatch, *Democratization of American Christianity, 3.*

56. Newman, *Freedom's Prophet,* 40–43.

57. Asbury, who is credited with being a founder of the American Methodist Church, began as an itinerant lay preacher in England. In 1771 Wesley sent him to North America, where he continued his work. At the 1784 meeting, Thomas Coke, an Anglican clergyman sent over by Wesley, ordained him a deacon, priest and deacon on subsequent days. See Wigger, *American Saint,* 33–46 (an account of his work in England and commission to North America) and 142–43.

58. Newman, *Freedom's Prophet,* 53.

59. Newman, *Freedom's Prophet,* 54.

60. Newman, *Freedom's Prophet,* 58–59.

61. Newman, *Freedom's Prophet,* 62–63.

62. Newman, *Freedom's Prophet,* 63–65.

63. Reported in Newman, *Freedom's Prophet,* 63–64.

64. Newman, *Freedom's Prophet,* 70–72.

65. Quoted in Hatch, *Democratization of American Christianity,* 109.

66. Newman, *Freedom's Prophet,* 162–65.

67. Newman, *Freedom's Prophet,* 172–78.

68. J. Campbell, *Songs of Zion,* 48. Allen also encouraged his wife, Sarah, to engage in charitable work outside of the home and assisted her in establishing a free Black female benevolent society. Newman, *Freedom's Prophet,* 232–34.

69. Giver-Johnston, *Claiming the Call to Preach,* 128.

70. Matthew 7:15–120: "Beware of false prophets, which come to you in sheep's clothing, but inwardly they are ravening wolves. Ye shall know them by their fruits. Do men gather grapes of thorns, or figs of thistles? Even so every good tree bringeth forth good fruit; but a corrupt tree bringeth forth evil fruit. A good tree cannot bring forth evil fruit, neither can a corrupt tree bring good fruit. Every tree that bringeth not forth good fruit is hewn down, and cast into the fire. Wherefore by their fruits ye shall know them."

71. Lee, *Religious Experience and Journal,* 3. Italics and misspelling ("prophecy" for "prophesy") in the original.

72. Ben Zvi, *Jewish Study Bible,* 1172. Notably, in this version, this passage begins a new chapter in Joel. In most Christian versions, the passage is the ending of the previous description of destruction. See also, Mobley, notes to Joel, *New Oxford Annotated Bible,* 1299.

73. Aquinas, *Lectures,* caput 20, lectio 3.

74. Ehrman, *Peter, Paul, and Mary Magdalene,* 251–53; 256.

75. Lee, *Religious Experience and Journal,* 11–12. Interestingly, Casey reports that Harriet Livermore made a very similar argument in her defense of her own preaching. Casey, "First Female Public Speakers," 13.

76. Lee, *Religious Experience and Journal,* 11.

77. Lee, *Religious Experience and Journal,* 3. Italics and misspelling ("prophecy" for "prophesy") in the original.

78. Lee, *Religious Experience and Journal,* 97.

79. Lee, *Religious Experience and Journal,* 3.

80. Lee, *Religious Experience and Journal,* 3.

81. Lee, *Religious Experience and Journal,* 3.

82. Lee, *Religious Experience and Journal,* 4.

83. Lee, *Religious Experience and Journal*, 4.
84. Lee, *Religious Experience and Journal*, 4.
85. Lee, *Religious Experience and Journal*, 29.
86. Acts 8:21.
87. Lee, *Religious Experience and Journal*, 5.
88. Lee, *Religious Experience and Journal*, 34. This reference of withdrawing to a secret place to pray clearly alludes to Jesus's admonition to his disciples in Matthew 6:6: "But whenever you pray, go into your room and shut the door and pray to your Father who is in secret; and your Father who sees in secret will reward you."
89. Lee, *Religious Experience and Journal*, 10.
90. Andrews, *Sisters of the Spirit*, 15–16.
91. Exodus 3:1–4.
92. Exodus 3:11.
93. Exodus 4:10.
94. Exodus 4:12.
95. Lee, *Religious Experience and Journal*, 11.
96. Lee, *Religious Experience and Journal*, 17.
97. Lee, *Religious Experience and Journal*, 10.
98. Jeremiah 1:9.
99. Lee, *Religious Experience and Journal*, 11.
100. C. Peterson, "Secular and Sacred Space," 53.
101. Brekus, *Strangers and Pilgrims*, 172.
102. Stanley, *Holy Boldness,* 198–200.
103. Lee, *Religious Experience and Journal*, 12.
104. Allen and Tapisco, *Doctrines and Discipline,* 76.
105. Lee, *Religious Experience and Journal*, 18.
106. Lee, *Religious Experience and Journal*, 17. Florence, *Preaching as Testimony*, 43, sees Allen's reaction as implicitly granting Lee the right to preach.
107. Lee, *Religious Experience and Journal*, 17.
108. Lee, *Religious Experience and Journal*, 23.
109. Lee, *Religious Experience and Journal*, 20.
110. Lee, *Religious Experience and Journal*, 36.
111. Lee, *Religious Experience and Journal*, 88.
112. Allen and Tapisco, *Doctrines and Disciplines,* 92–93.
113. Bassard, *Spiritual Interrogations*, 90 (emphasis in original).
114. Bassard, *Spiritual Interrogations*, 92.
115. Bassard, *Spiritual Interrogations*, 92.
116. Lee, *Religious Experience and Journal*, 6.
117. Lee, *Religious Experience and Journal*, 8.
118. Allen and Tapisco, *Doctrines and Disciplines,* 93–94.
119. Minifee, "'I Took Up the Hymn-Book,'" 18.
120. Lee, *Religious Experience and Journal*, 6. The hymn is "Come Thou Fount of Every Blessing" by Robert Robinson.
121. Lee, *Religious Experience and Journal*, 7.
122. Bassard, *Spiritual Interrogations*, 93-94, 95.
123. Minifee, "'I Took Up the Hymn-Book,'" 1.
124. Minifee, "'I Took Up the Hymn-Book,'" 12.
125. Lee, *Religious Experience and Journal*, 97.
126. Gaines, "No Half Savior," 64.

Notes to Pages 39–45 : 173

127. Brekus, *Strangers and Pilgrims*, 6.
128. Lee, *Religious Experience and Journal*, 97.
129. Giver-Johnston, *Claiming the Call to Preach*, 131.
130. Bassard, *Spiritual Interrogations*, 87. As explained in note 1 (chap. 2) the AME forbade itinerant preachers from publishing materials without approval. Defying this rule, Lee published her expanded version in 1849 with no apparent consequences.
131. Howard, "Legacy Profile," 89. See also Dodson, "Nineteenth Century A.M.E. Preaching Women," 280–82.
132. Howard, "Legacy Profile," 89. Foote, who was a member of the African Methodist Episcopal Zion Church, faced her own struggles within that denomination in defending her call to preach. Foote was forty years younger than Lee. In 1894, she became the first woman ordained a deacon in the AME Zion Church and six years later was ordained an elder, the second woman to hold that office in her denomination. See Andrews, *Sisters of the Spirit*, 9–10.
133. Schmidt, *Grace Sufficient*, 79.
134. Newman, "Freedom's Prophet," 234.
135. Wills, "Women and Domesticity," 138.
136. Wills, "Women and Domesticity," 138.
137. Women in Ministry, "The Herstory of AMEWIM."
138. Payne, *History of the African Methodist Episcopal Church*, 301.
139. Payne, *History of the African Methodist Episcopal Church*, 237.
140. Andrews, *Sisters of the Spirit*, 6–7.
141. Andrews, *Sisters of the Spirit*, 6–7.
142. Payne, *History of the African Methodist Episcopal Church*, 301.
143. Payne, *History of the African Methodist Episcopal Church*, 273.
144. Women in Ministry, "The Herstory of AMEWIM."
145. Richey et al., *Methodist Experience in America*, 242. For more information, see Chilcote, *Methodist Defense of Women in Ministry*, 99–101.
146. Brekus, *Strangers and Pilgrims*, 180.
147. Dodson, "Nineteenth Century A.M.E. Preaching Women," 277–78.
148. Brekus, *Strangers and Pilgrims*, 134.
149. Dodson, "Nineteenth Century A.M.E. Preaching Women," 277.
150. Giver-Johnston, *Claiming the Call to Preach*, 122.
151. Matthew 7:17; 20.
152. Collins, "Walking in Light," 340.
153. Painter, *Sojourner Truth*, 198.
154. Painter, "Representing Truth," 482–88.
155. Brekus, *Strangers and Pilgrims*, 260.
156. Mattingly, *Appropriate[ing] Dress*, 7. In *Sojourner Truth*, Painter makes a similar point about Sojourner Truth's photographs. Painter observes that the photos "allowed Truth to circumvent . . . the racial stereotype embedded in her nation's language." 198.
157. Collier-Thomas, *Daughters of Thunder*, 12.
158. Darsey, *Prophetic Tradition*, 16.
159. Lee, *Religious Experience and Journal*, 11.
160. J. Campbell, *Songs of Zion*, calls the technique Lee uses a strategy of reversal, or "appropriating Christian ideals and turning them back against their professors," 23. For more examples of how Lee uses the strategy of reversal consult Cullen, "Holy Fire," 143–14.

161. Providing additional reasons to believe that Jarena Lee knew Quaker reformers such as Lucretia Mott and the Grimké sisters, Emma Jones Lapsansky observes in her study of women activists in Philadelphia that Black and White reformers developed strong relationships and frequently interacted with one another. Her study of Charlotte Forten, a free Black woman in nineteenth-century Philadelphia whose aunts were involved in the "establishment and maintenance of a female antislavery society in the city," reveals that Forten's family entertained "anyone who was associated with progressive political, social, and educational reform," including Lucretia Mott, William Lloyd Garrison, Angelina Grimké, and Lydia Maria Child. Drawing on Forten's diary, Lapsansky adds that religious leaders like Lee, Julia Foote, and Frances Ellen Watkins Harper would have been part of "Forten's round of meetings and activities." Lapsansky, "Feminism, Freedom, and Community," 4–6, 10. Nancy Hewitt points out that "Mott was introduced to a range of black religious beliefs and institutions," suggesting that she encountered Jarena Lee and Maria Stewart among others. Hewitt, "Race, Class, Region, and Activism," 130.

162. Knight, "Many Names for Jarena Lee," 61.

163. Angell, "Controversy Over Women's Ministry," 96. See also Lindley, *"You Have Stept Out of Your Place,"* 181.

164. Angell, "Controversy Over Women's Ministry," 101.

165. Jones, *All Bound Up Together,"* 185.

166. Prescott, "Imagining 'Sweet Fellowship,'" 80. See also Florence, *Preaching as Testimony,* 40.

167. Women in Ministry, *Celebrating the Reverend Jarena Lee,* 45.

CHAPTER 3: SARAH MOORE GRIMKÉ'S *LETTERS ON THE EQUALITY OF THE SEXES*

1. Lerner, *Grimké Sisters from South Carolina,* 41. Catharine H. Birney suggests that Israel Morris had encouraged Sarah to follow the spirit in her discernments, perhaps including this move, *The Grimké Sisters,* 31. Birney, a former student and friend and their first biographer, had access to their diaries and letters for her work.

2. Birney, *The Grimké Sisters,* 32.

3. Durso, *Power of Woman,* 54; Perry, *Lift Up Thy Voice,* 68.

4. Durso, *Power of Woman,* 55.

5. Sarah Grimké's diary, dated 1827 in Lerner, *Grimké Sisters from South Carolina,* 42.

6. Lerner, *Grimké Sisters from South Carolina,* 42.

7. Faulkner, *Lucretia Mott's Heresy,* 42. Here Faulkner is quoting an article from *The Lily,* the first newspaper in the United States edited for and by women. It was initially established by Amelia Jenks Bloomer and published from 1849 to 1853.

8. Faulkner, *Lucretia Mott's Heresy,* 42.

9. Lerner, *Grimké Sisters from South Carolina,* 42–43. Unfortunately, the leadership in her meeting were Orthodox Quakers, who did not support the abolitionism of the Hicksite Quakers and particularly eschewed political activity.

10. Lerner, *Grimké Sisters from South Carolina,* 139.

11. To avoid confusion between the sisters, in the initial phases of this essay we will refer to her as Sarah. The article is W. H. J. (William H. Johnson) "Lucretia Mott," *The Lily* (February 1, 1854), 19.

12. Durso, *Power of Woman,* 20.

13. Lerner, *Grimké Sisters from South Carolina,* 15.

14. Birney, *The Grimké Sisters,* 10.

Notes to Pages 51–54 : 175

15. Perry, *Lift Up Thy Voice,* 2.
16. Perry, *Lift Up Thy Voice,* 3.
17. Perry, *Lift Up Thy Voice,* 23.
18. She would certainly have been familiar with Ephesians 6:5–8, which was used to defend slavery: "Servants, be obedient to them that are your masters according to the flesh, with fear and trembling, in singleness of your heart, as unto Christ; Not with eyeservice, as menpleasers; but as the servants of Christ, doing the will of God from the heart; With good will doing service, as to the Lord, and not to men: Knowing that whatsoever good thing any man doeth, the same shall he receive of the Lord, whether he be bond or free." Further, she would be cognizant that the Israelites practiced slavery without divine reproach. The Ten Commandments even implies that slavery is acceptable since they order that slaves be accorded a sabbath along with all others.
19. Birney, *The Grimké Sisters,* 45–46. Birney suggests that Angelina was quicker to condemn the entire institution and see the need for its eradication than Sarah.
20. Durso, *Power of Woman,* 15.
21. Lerner, *Grimké Sisters from South Carolina,* 245.
22. Durso, *Power of Woman,* 14.
23. Birney, *The Grimké Sisters,* 23; 17–18.
24. S. Grimké, *Letters on the Equality of the Sexes,* 114.
25. Lumpkin, *Emancipation of Angelina Grimké,* 9.
26. Birney, *The Grimké Sisters,* 13.
27. Birney, *The Grimké Sisters,* 12–14.
28. Lerner, *Grimké Sisters from South Carolina,* 228. Lerner goes on to assert that close relationship was "the blight of their middle years."
29. Birney, *The Grimké Sisters,* 16.
30. Birney, *The Grimké Sisters,* 11.
31. Lumpkin, *Emancipation of Angelina Grimké,* 11.
32. Birney, *The Grimké Sisters,* 27.
33. Birney, *The Grimké Sisters,* 19.
34. Birney, *The Grimké Sisters,* 25–27. Kollock was especially well-known for his fervent and effective preaching. See Waugh, "Henry Kollock, 1778–1819."
35. David Hempton suggests Sarah's encounter with evangelicalism and her struggle with it were not unique. In particular, he argues that Elizabeth Cady Stanton and Frances Willard underwent similar engagements and contestations. See Hempton, *Evangelical Disenchantment,* 92–113.
36. Birney, *The Grimké Sisters,* 27.
37. Birney, *The Grimké Sisters,* 27.
38. Birney, *The Grimké Sisters,* 34; Durso, *Power of Woman,* 32. Later, Israel, who was a widower with eight children, proposed to Sarah, but she refused. Durso, *Power of Woman,* 88–90, offers an analysis for the various possible reasons for Sarah's refusal.
39. Birney, *The Grimké Sisters,* 28–29.
40. Perry, *Lift Up Thy Voice,* 54.
41. Soderlund, *Quakers and Slavery,* 17. In *Slavery and the Meetinghouse,* Jordan provides an excellent discussion of the nuances and tensions among the Quakers in regard to slavery and abolitionism.
42. Sarah Grimké, "Letter on the Subject of Prejudice," cited in Durso, *Power of Woman,* 74.

176 : Notes to Pages 54–57

43. Durso, *Power of Woman,* 68.
44. Although Quakers universally opposed slavery, they were not united in their support for abolitionism, which was a form of political activism that some thought contaminated their meetings.
45. Durso, *Power of Woman,* 70–71.
46. A. Grimké, "Letter to William Lloyd Garrison."
47. Lerner, *Feminist Thought of Sarah Grimké,* 12.
48. During the 1820s, a breach developed in Quakerism between orthodox Quakers, who dominated the meeting the Grimkés attended, and Hicksites. The orthodox Quakers were, in general, less sympathetic to non-birthright Quakers and women's leadership. See Durso, *Power of Woman,* 57–60.
49. A. Grimké, "Appeal to the Christian Women of the South," 36, 16-18, (emphasis in original).
50. S. Grimké, "An Epistle to the Clergy of the Southern States." Lerner, *Grimké Sisters from South Carolina,* provides an intriguing comparison of Sarah's epistle with a document developed by Theodore Weld, 104–106.
51. Grimké, "Letter to Theodore Weld," quoted in Durso, *Power of Woman,* 72.
52. S. Grimké, *Letters on the Equality of the Sexes,* 20.
53. Birney, *The Grimké Sisters,* 168. Although Birney attributes the letter to Angelina, it uses "we" throughout and both sisters sign it.
54. Quoted in Melder, *Beginnings of Sisterhood,* 78.
55. Bogin and Yellin, "Introduction," 9–10.
56. Durso, *Power of Woman,* 112–15.
57. Durso, *Power of Woman,* 116.
58. Lerner, *Grimké Sisters from South Carolina,* 127–28.
59. Beecher, "Essay on Slavery and Abolitionism."
60. A. Grimké, *Letters to Catherine E. Beecher;* Perry, *Lift Up Thy Voice,* 152–56. For a comprehensive and insightful analysis of this exchange between Angelina Grimké and Catherine Beecher, see Portnoy, *Their Right to Speak,* 203–43.
61. The rapidity with which the letters made it into print suggests she certainly intended publication.
62. S. Grimké, *Letters on the Equality of the Sexes,* 37. The pastoral letter referred to is "Pastoral Letter of the Generational Association of [Congregational Ministers of] Massachusetts."
63. Lerner, *Feminist Thought of Sarah Grimké,* 21. Angelina responded in two of her letters.
64. Sarah and Angelina Grimké to Henry Clarke Wright reprinted in Ceplair, *Public Years of Sarah and Angelina Grimké,* 129. Wright was a Congregationalist minister who was close friends with William Lloyd Garrison. John Greenleaf Whittier was a Quaker poet involved in the founding of the American Anti-Slavery Society. Theodore Weld, who later became Angelina's husband, was an active and successful antislavery activist. He conducted the training sessions Angelina and Sarah attended. Until his marriage to Angelina, Weld supported their abolitionist activism but was uncomfortable with their discussions of women's rights. See Durso, *Power of Woman,* 105–6.
65. Henry Clarke Wright was an ardent abolitionist and woman's rights advocate who was a close friend of William Lloyd Garrison and became a strong supporter of the Grimké sisters. The poet John Greenleaf Whitter was also a strong abolitionist. For an excellent account of Sarah's gradual emergence into an advocate

Notes to Pages 57–63 : 177

for abolition, consult Durso, *Power of Woman;* Lerner, *Grimké Sisters from South Carolina;* and Perry, *Lift Up Thy Voice.*

66. On pages 6–15, Bartlett provides an analysis of the "Intellectual and Social Origins" of Grimké's thinking, giving surprisingly short shrift to the religious currents. She also asserts, erroneously we think, that Quakerism introduced her to the "Puritan idea" of individual interpretation of the Bible. That notion did not originate with the Puritans nor was it restricted to Quakerism. See Bartlett, *Sarah Grimké,* 17.

67. See Ramsey, *Anglican Spirit,* especially 30–34 for a discussion of the role of reason in Anglican thought.

68. *Articles of Religion.*

69. Heyrman, "First Great Awakening."

70. Waugh, "Henry Kollock, 1778–1819."

71. Birney, *The Grimké Sisters,* 20–22.

72. Dandelion, *Quakers,* 2.

73. Soderlund, *Quakers and Slavery,* 34–35; 120.

74. Ingle, *First Among Friends,* 252.

75. Braithwaite, *Second Period of Quakerism,* 273.

76. Kunze, *Margaret Fell and the Rise of Quakerism,* 13.

77. Kunze, *Margaret Fell and the Rise of Quakerism,* xii.

78. Ruether, *Introducing Redemption in Christian Feminism,* 13.

79. Kruczek-Aaron, *Everyday Religion,* 2.

80. As indicated in note 16 (preface), we understand the problems with using the word "Indian" to refer to Indigenous people. At the time, the controversy bore that label and, thus, we use it here.

81. Hershberger, "Mobilizing Women, Anticipating Abolition," 18.

82. Ivie, "Enabling Democratic Dissent," 50.

83. The title of this section comes from "Pastoral Letter," 366.

84. "Pastoral Letter," 363.

85. "Pastoral Letter," 366.

86. "Pastoral Letter," 366–67.

87. "Pastoral Letter," 367.

88. "Pastoral Letter," 367.

89. "Pastoral Letter," 366.

90. "Pastoral Letter," 366.

91. Although a full consideration of the debates that swirled around women's involvement in drives to petition Congress about slavery and Indian removal are beyond the scope of this project, they were a significant part of the context that produced concerns about women's rights. For comprehensive consideration of those discussions, see Zaeske, *Signatures of Citizenship,* and Portnoy, *Their Right to Speak.* Zaeske demonstrates convincingly how women's efforts in the petitioning drive began to craft a new public role for them. Significantly, both Grimkés were engaged in petition efforts.

92. S. Grimké, *Letters on the Equality of the Sexes,* 31.

93. S. Grimké, *Letters on the Equality of the Sexes,* 102.

94. S. Grimké, *Letters on the Equality of the Sexes,* 31–32.

95. S. Grimké, *Letters on the Equality of the Sexes,* 31–32. However, her reading of the second creation story, particularly Genesis 3, suggests that she not only had access to a copy of the Hebrew text, but also knew enough Hebrew to do her own translation.

178 : Notes to Pages 63–67

96. Grimké advocated that women's learning these languages had decided advantages. "I am inclined to think, when we are admitted to the honor of studying Greek and Hebrew, we shall produce some various readings of the Bible a little different from those we now have." S. Grimké, *Letters on the Equality of the Sexes*, 38.

97. S. Grimké, *Letters on the Equality of the Sexes*, 31.

98. Grimké signs every letter but the first with "Thine in the bonds of womanhood."

99. S. Grimké, *Letters on the Equality of the Sexes*, 38 (emphasis in original). In the discussion that follows, distinctive font such as small caps are, unless otherwise noted, in the original. The section title above quotes S. Grimké, *Letters on the Equality of the Sexes*, 32.

100. Bartlett, *Sarah Grimké*, 22.

101. We are aware that using the term "feminist" to Grimké's approach is somewhat anachronistic. However, Carol A. Newsom and Sharon H. Ringe identify Elizabeth Cady Stanton's *Woman's Bible* as a precursor for modern feminist criticism, even adapting the name of her work for their own. Grimké's work, which antedates Stanton by almost fifty years, definitely reflects what modern scholars would term a "feminist" perspective. See Newsom and Ringe, *Women's Bible Commentary*, xx–xxi.

102. Genesis 1:28.

103. Fell, "Womens Speaking Justified," 157. As mentioned in note 26 (chap. 1), we have chosen to identify the text as "Womens Speaking" to honor Fell's original wording in the 1666 edition. Later editions will refer to the title as "Women's Speaking." Lerner, *Feminist Thought of Sarah Grimké*, 21–22.

104. S. Grimké, *Letters on the Equality of the Sexes,* 35. She is referring to Genesis 9 where Noah and his sons are instructed to be fruitful and multiply and are told all animals are subject to them.

105. S. Grimké, *Letters on the Equality of the Sexes,* 35. The Matthew passage is, in fact, a paraphrase of Deuteronomy 6: 13.

106. S. Grimké, *Letters on the Equality of the Sexes,* 38.

107. S. Grimké, *Letters on the Equality of the Sexes,* 80.

108. S. Grimké, *Letters on the Equality of the Sexes,* 32.

109. S. Grimké, *Letters on the Equality of the Sexes*, 32 (emphasis in original).

110. S. Grimké, *Letters on the Equality of the Sexes*, 33 (emphasis in original).

111. S. Grimké, *Letters on the Equality of the Sexes*, 98. Isaiah 43:27: "Your first ancestor sinned and your interpreters transgressed against me." Romans 5:12: "Therefore, just as sin came into the world through one man, and death came through sin, and so death spread to all because all have sinned."

112. S. Grimké, *Letters on the Equality of the Sexes*, 33 (emphasis in original).

113. We are grateful to Amanda Beckenstein Mbuvi, Vice President for Academic Affairs at Reconstructionist Rabbinical College for her help with this translation issue.

114. The relevant verse in regard to Cain is Genesis 4:12. Interestingly, the New Revised Standard Version, the most widely used modern translation, preserves the distinction to which Grimké objects.

115. The section title above quotes S. Grimké, *Letters on the Equality of the Sexes*, 35.

116. Ruether, "Subordination and Liberation of Women," 177.

117. S. Grimké, *Letters on the Equality of the Sexes*, 35.

118. Hirsch, Seligsohn, and Bacher, "Nimrod."

Notes to Pages 67–69 : 179

119. S. Grimké, *Letters on the Equality of the Sexes*, 35. The upas tree (Antiaris toxicaria) has seeds that yield strychnine. Antislavery tracts in the nineteenth century used it as a symbol of slavery; see "The friends of humanity laying the axe."

120. S. Grimké, *Letters on the Equality of the Sexes*, 35–36. Grimké is referring to the story of the visitation of three mysterious strangers during their time in Mamre, some twenty-four years after the initial promise of an heir. The story is recorded in Genesis 18. In that account, Abraham consigns Sarah to the tent to prepare food, but she manages to eavesdrop and hear the promise of the strangers.

121. Rebekah's name is spelled various ways. Grimké uses Rebecca. We are using the spelling preferred in the New Revised Standard Version.

122. S. Grimké, *Letters on the Equality of the Sexes*, 36. The incident is in Genesis 24:47. Interestingly, Grimké reports he offered an earring, but the Hebrew is quite clear it was a ring for her nose.

123. S. Grimké, *Letters on the Equality of the Sexes*, 81. Acts 16:3 details this incident.

124. S. Grimké, *Letters on the Equality of the Sexes*, 81.

125. Corinthians 11:3; Ephesians 5:23.

126. Camper, *Arguing Over Texts*, 91–132.

127. Camper, *Arguing Over Texts*, 132.

128. John 10:30.

129. S. Grimké, *Letters on the Equality of the Sexes*, 82.

130. S. Grimké, *Letters on the Equality of the Sexes*, 83. The passages she pairs are Ephesians 5:22 and Ephesians 5:25; Colossians 3:18 and Colossians 3:19; and 1 Peter 3:2 and 1 Peter 3:7. The last of these is not attributed to Paul but to Peter, although modern scholars doubt that attribution. See Coogan, ed., *New Oxford Annotated Bible*, 394–95 (1 Peter). Similarly, scholars are somewhat skeptical of Paul's actual authorship of Ephesians or Colossians. See Coogan, ed., *New Oxford Annotated Bible*, 320–21 (headnote to Ephesians) and 334–35 (headnote to Colossians).

131. Child, *Brief History of the Condition of Women*.

132. S. Grimké, *Letters on the Equality of the Sexes*, 44.

133. According to Ceplair, Sarah's discussion of women around the world was "largely derived" from Child. Letters V, VI and VII, contain large blocks of quoted but unattributed material (*Public Years of Sarah and Angelina Grimké,* 204). However, at the end of Letter VI she does acknowledge her general indebtedness to Child's work. Durso (*Power of Woman,* 128) reports that Lydia Child was one of the persons who welcomed the Grimké's to Boston in 1837. Durso (*Power of Woman,* 105–107) also quotes a letter from Theodore Weld to the sisters on August 15, 1837 that compares their work to Child's. In his opinion, they can do more for abolition than she had done (apparently with her 1833 *An Appeal of that Class of Americans Called Africans*) but they risk that contribution if they continue to raise the issue of women's rights in their work.

134. S. Grimké, *Letters on the Equality of the Sexes*, 41–42.

135. S. Grimké, *Letters on the Equality of the Sexes*, 72 (emphasis in original).

136. Blackstone, "Of Husband and Wife."

137. S. Grimké, *Letters on the Equality of the Sexes*, 72.

138. S. Grimké, *Letters on the Equality of the Sexes*, 74–75.

139. S. Grimké, *Letters on the Equality of the Sexes*, 77.

140. S. Grimké, *Letters on the Equality of the Sexes*, 72.

180 : Notes to Pages 70–78

141. S. Grimké, *Letters on the Equality of the Sexes,* 38 (emphasis in original). Here Sarah may be echoing the words of the Declaration of Independence, which speaks of "a long train of abuses and usurpations, pursuing invariably the same Object . . ."

142. The section title above quotes S. Grimké, *Letters on the Equality of the Sexes,* 38.

143. S. Grimké, *Letters on the Equality of the Sexes,* 48–49 (emphasis in original).

144. S. Grimké, *Letters on the Equality of the Sexes,* 47–48.

145. S. Grimké, *Letters on the Equality of the Sexes,* 62. As colorful as the story about Cochrane's daughter may be, we can find no historical source that validates it.

146. S. Grimké, *Letters on the Equality of the Sexes,* 63.

147. S. Grimké, *Letters on the Equality of the Sexes,* 64.

148. S. Grimké, *Letters on the Equality of the Sexes,* 85 (emphasis in original). Her statement is a bit inaccurate and unclear. Although in some Methodist churches, women could serve as exhorters, this was not the principle preaching activity. We are uncertain what group she means by "Christians."

149. S. Grimké, *Letters on the Equality of the Sexes,* 86.

150. S. Grimké, *Letters on the Equality of the Sexes,* 86. In regard to Noah, Sarah is apparently referring to 2 Peter 2:5.

151. S. Grimké, *Letters on the Equality of the Sexes,* 86–87.

152. Here, she is quoting the King James Version.

153. S. Grimké, *Letters on the Equality of the Sexes,* 87.

154. Luke 2:38.

155. Acts 2:17.

156. S. Grimké, *Letters on the Equality of the Sexes,* 89.

157. S. Grimké, *Letters on the Equality of the Sexes,* 90–91.

158. S. Grimké, *Letters on the Equality of the Sexes,* 91. Philip's daughters are mentioned in Acts 21:8–9. Paul refers to Priscilla in Romans 16:3 and Phoebe in Romans 16:1.

159. S. Grimké, *Letters on the Equality of the Sexes,* 96.

160. S. Grimké, *Letters on the Equality of the Sexes,* 99.

161. S. Grimké, *Letters on the Equality of the Sexes,* 99.

162. S. Grimké, *Letters on the Equality of the Sexes,* 34.

163. Ivie, "Enabling Democratic Dissent," 46.

164. Welter, "Cult of True Womanhood," 152.

165. Welter, "Cult of True Womanhood," 153.

166. S. Grimké, *Letters on the Equality of the Sexes,* 97.

167. S. Grimké, *Letters on the Equality of the Sexes,* 100–101.

168. S. Grimké, *Letters on the Equality of the Sexes,* 44.

169. S. Grimké, *Letters on the Equality of the Sexes,* 68 (emphasis in original).

170. Mattingly, *Appropriate[ing] Dress,* 29.

171. Mattingly, *Appropriate[ing] Dress,* 30.

172. Vonnegut, "Poison or Panacea?" 76, 77.

173. Kohrs and Jerry, "Woman and Speaker," 123–33.

174. Wasco, "Angel in the Envelope," 4.

175. Vonnegut, "Poison or Panacea?" 82.

176. *The New England Spectator 1834–1838.*

177. Ceplair, *Public Years of Sarah and Angelina Grimké,* 204 fn.

178. Quoted in S. Grimké, *Letters on the Equality of the Sexes,* 25–26.

179. Sarah is referring to the King James translation, which does indeed make that distinction. Many modern translations do not.

180. S. Grimké, *Letters on the Equality of the Sexes,* 31.

Notes to Pages 78–84 : 181

181. S. Grimké, *Letters on the Equality of the Sexes*, 92. The men, as mentioned earlier, are John Locke, the well-known British scholar, and Adam Clarke, a noted biblical scholar.

182. S. Grimké, *Letters on the Equality of the Sexes*, 36–37.

183. S. Grimké, *Letters on the Equality of the Sexes*, 35–36.

184. S. Grimké, *Letters on the Equality of the Sexes*, 38.

185. S. Grimké, *Letters on the Equality of the Sexes*, 40–41.

186. S. Grimké, *Letters on the Equality of the Sexes*, 100.

187. Aristotle, *Poetics and Rhetoric*, 105–106. In this annotated volume Garver incorporates the classic translation by W. Rhys Roberts.

188. Aristotle, *Poetics and Rhetoric*, 245.

189. Gring-Pemble, "Writing Themselves into Consciousness," 42.

190. Gring-Pemble, "Writing Themselves into Consciousness," 41–42.

191. Lerner, *Grimké Sisters from South Carolina*, xix; xviii.

192. Lerner, *Grimké Sisters from South Carolina*, xix.

193. M. Bacon, *Mothers of Feminism*, 105.

194. Durso, *Power of Woman*, 155–56.

195. Lerner, *Grimké Sisters from South Carolina*, 141–42.

196. Melder, *Beginnings of Sisterhood*, 90.

197. Angelina Grimké to Jane Smith, August 26, 1837, in Ceplair, *Public Years of Sarah and Angelina Grimké*, (italics in original) 286.

198. For a full and insightful analysis of the debates at that meeting around the topic of women, see Hogan, "A Time for Silence," 63–79.

199. William Lloyd Garrison to an unidentified friend, September 12, 1835, quoted in Ceplair, *Public Years of Sarah and Angelina Grimké*, 21.

200. Lerner, *Grimké Sisters from South Carolina*, xv. Lerner's original edition in 1967 stimulated scholarship on the sisters in the twentieth century. Other scholars had given them passing attention; see for example, Barnes and Dumond (*Letters of Theodore Dwight Weld*). Similarly, in addition to miscellaneous references, Benjamin Thomas (*Theodore Weld*) devotes an entire chapter to them (133–49) in his biography of Weld. Dwight Lowell Dumond (*Antislavery*) devoted an entire chapter to Angelina's work (190–97) and included both of them in a later chapter on women in the movement.

CHAPTER 4: LUCRETIA COFFIN MOTT'S *DISCOURSE ON WOMAN*

1. K. Campbell, *Man Cannot Speak for Her*, Vol. 1, 38. While Mott was supportive of a wide variety of issues involving women, she was not initially in favor of suffrage. Even with the "Discourse on Woman" she refrains from encouraging women to vote because of the current state of political affairs. See Mott, "Discourse on Woman," 90.

2. K. Campbell, *Man Cannot Speak for Her, Vol. 1*, 38.

3. Mott, "Discourse on Woman," 76.

4. W. Johnson, "Lucretia Mott," 19. In 1849, Amelia Jenks Bloomer established *The Lily*, the first woman's newspaper.

5. See Hogan and Solomon, "Extending the Conversation," 32–46, for a discussion of the influence of these two works on her speech.

6. Palmer, ed., *Selected Letters of Lucretia Coffin Mott*, 392.

7. Quoted in Cromwell, *Lucretia Mott*, 145.

8. M. Bacon, *Valiant Friend*, 9.

9. M. Bacon, *Valiant Friend*, 8.

10. M. Bacon, *Valiant Friend*, 13. Wakefield, *Beauties and Wonders*, 162–63. Wakefield was a British Quaker, philanthropist, and prolific author. Interestingly, most of the entries in the two volumes are far less tendentious and much more focused on natural subjects.

11. Faulkner and Hewitt, "Introduction," 12.

12. Faulkner, *Lucretia Mott's Heresy*, 26.

13. M. Bacon, *Valiant Friend*, 21–22.

14. Faulkner, *Lucretia Mott's Heresy*, 26–27.

15. Faulkner, *Lucretia Mott's Heresy*, 25.

16. Faulkner and Hewitt, "Introduction," 12.

17. M. Bacon, *Valiant Friend*, 23–24.

18. M. Bacon, *Valiant Friend*, 23–24.

19. Faulker, *Lucretia Mott's Heresy*, 30.

20. Faulkner, *Lucretia Mott's Heresy*, 30. Apparently, this quotation was part of a series of questions that were taught to students in a sort of catechism.

21. J. Mott, *Hints to Young People*, 23–24. Although it is somewhat unclear, the date of this publication suggests this is James Mott Sr. and not Lucretia Mott's husband. Faulkner incorrectly attributes this directly to Abigail Mott, his daughter. She and her husband Lindley Murray Moore were also graduates of Nine Partners. See Faulkner, *Lucretia Mott's Heresy*, 31 footnote 17.

22. Faulkner, *Lucretia Mott's Heresy*, 59.

23. M. Bacon, *Valient Friend*, 26.

24. M. Bacon, *Valiant Friend*, 20–21.

25. Faulkner, *Lucretia Mott's Heresy*, 33; M. Bacon, *Valiant Friend*, 22.

26. M. Bacon, *Valiant Friend*, 22. Both Bacon and Faulkner contend that Mott memorized all of William Cowper's *The Task*. Having looked at the text of that poem, which runs 5,000 lines, we find that claim difficult to accept.

27. Faulkner, *Lucretia Mott's Heresy*, 37 (emphasis in original).

28. Faulkner, *Lucretia Mott's Heresy*, 41.

29. M. Bacon, *Valiant Friend*, 36–37.

30. M. Bacon, *Valiant Friend*, 37.

31. M. Bacon, *Valiant Friend*, 37.

32. Faulkner, *Lucretia Mott's Heresy*, 42.

33. M. Bacon, *Valiant Friend*, 44–45. James Mott's mother took the other side and a considerable rupture occurred in their relationship.

34. Faulkner, *Lucretia Mott's Heresy*, 62.

35. Quoted in Faulkner, *Lucretia Mott's Heresy*, 62. She was writing to a school friend, Phebe Post Willis, and he to his wife, Helen E. Garrison.

36. Hamm, "George F. White," 44.

37. "Declaration of Sentiments and Resolutions," in *Man Cannot Speak for Her: Key Texts of the Early Feminists,* compiled by Karlyn Kohrs Campbell (Westport: Praeger, 1989), 33–40.

38. Faulkner, *Lucretia Mott's Heresy*, 64–65.

39. I. Brown, "Cradle of Feminism," 144.

40. I. Brown, "Cradle of Feminism," 145.

41. Faulkner, *Lucretia Mott's Heresy*, 63.

42. Faulkner, *Lucretia Mott's Heresy*, 66–67.

Notes to Pages 89–94 : 183

43. Quoted in I. Brown, "Cradle of Feminism," 145.
44. Minutes of the Philadelphia Female Anti-Slavery Society, December 14, 1833. Quoted in I. Brown, "Cradle of Feminism," 146.
45. I. Brown, "Cradle of Feminism," 150.
46. I. Brown, "Cradle of Feminism," 144.
47. Quoted in I. Brown, "Cradle of Feminism," 151.
48. According to Faulkner, Mott was a delegate from at least three groups: the American Anti-Slavery Society, the Philadelphia Female Anti-Slavery Society, and the American Free Produce Association. She also carried documentation from her Monthly Meeting, which authorized her to speak in Quaker meetings. Seven other women almost went as delegates but they, too, were refused seats. Faulkner, *Lucretia Mott's Heresy*, 92.
49. See Hogan, "A Time for Silence," 63–79, for a full and insightful analysis of the debates at that meeting around the topic of women.
50. Sarah Pugh, June 11, 1840, reported in L. Mott, *Lucretia Mott's Diary*, 28.
51. Faulkner, *Lucretia Mott's Heresy*, 140.
52. Unger, "Mott, Lucretia Coffin."
53. Faulkner, *Lucretia Mott's Heresy*, 2.
54. Duyckinck and Duyckinck, "Richard Henry Dana," 91.
55. Quoted in K. Campbell, *Man Cannot Speak for Her*, Vol. 2, 72.
56. Quoted in K. Campbell, *Man Cannot Speak for Her*, Vol. 2, 73.
57. Sillars, "Romantic Idealism to Romantic Rationalism," 47–55.
58. Cartwright, "On the Marriage of the Lady Mary." We have included in brackets the two lines previous to Dana's citation for more context.
59. Dana, "Woman," 1.
60. Dana, "Woman," 1.
61. Dana, "Woman," 7.
62. Dana, "Woman," 10.
63. Dana, "Woman," 13.
64. Dana, "Woman," 14.
65. Dana, "Woman," 19.
66. Dana, "Woman," 2.
67. Dana, "Woman," 3.
68. Dana, "Woman," 20.
69. Dana, "Woman," 29.
70. Dana, "Woman," 33.
71. Kraditor, *Ideas of the Woman Suffrage Movement*, 15.
72. Dana, "Woman," 10.
73. Kraditor, *Ideas of the Woman Suffrage Movement*, 18.
74. Kraditor, *Ideas of the Woman Suffrage Movement*, 22.
75. Kraditor, *Ideas of the Woman Suffrage Movement*, 24.
76. K. Campbell suggests that Mott's persona was "that of a minister, as understood by the Quakers"; see *Man Cannot Speak for Her*, Vol. 1, 45. While we generally agree with this, we think that in this speech Mott evinces both pastoral and prophetic dimensions of that role that are significant. Hence, we think that it is more accurate to describe her persona in this speech as prophetic pastor.
77. L. Mott, "Discourse on Woman," 75.
78. L. Mott, "Discourse on Woman," 74.

184 : Notes to Pages 94–97

79. L. Mott, "Discourse on Woman," 75.
80. Zulick and Leff, "Time and the 'True Light,'" delineate clearly how Mott develops the metaphor of "up and forward" in this speech.
81. L. Mott, "Discourse on Woman," 74.
82. L. Mott, "Discourse on Woman," 74.
83. L. Mott, "Discourse on Woman," 74–75.
84. Dandelion, *Introduction to Quakerism*, 22.
85. L. Mott, "Discourse on Woman," 75.
86. K. Campbell, *Man Cannot Speak for Her*, Vol. 1, 45.
87. Dandelion, *Introduction to Quakerism*, 22.
88. K. Campbell suggests the speech was "extemporaneous," drawing on previously used materials. See *Man Cannot Speak for Her*, Vol. 1, 39. This is undoubtedly true since that was the style preferred by Quakers in their meetings. However, Faulkner and Hewitt note that this is one of only a few cases with evidence that Mott revised it before publication. They opine she may have taken the opportunity to insert the long verbatim quotations at that point. See Densmore et al., *Lucretia Mott Speaks*, 19.
89. Dandelion, *Introduction to Quakerism*, 5.
90. Dandelion, *Introduction to Quakerism*, 22–23.
91. Dandelion, *Introduction to Quakerism*, 32.
92. Sillars in "Romantic Idealism to Romantic Rationalism" labels her view "Enlightenment Rationalism." For our part, we think that characterization locates her orientation in the intellectual climate of the day. Instead, we believe that her viewpoint is firmly grounded in and animated by Quaker theology.
93. Zulick and Leff discuss the metaphor of upward and forward in relation to this speech. Although we agree with Zulick and Leff's identification of the metaphor of upward and forward in this speech and generally with their idea that her view of history is progressive, we disagree that this makes her treatment of scripture "problematic" ("Time and the 'True Light,'" 22). We will argue that her view of history is progressive but that it traces a salvific arc that begins in what is depicted in scripture and moves toward the future when the original divine plan is restored.
94. Dana, "Woman," 1.
95. Genesis 1:27.
96. L. Mott, "Discourse on Woman," 75. For reasons that are unclear, she has altered the passage slightly by adding the phrase "and called their name Adam."
97. In contrast, Grimké explicated this sometimes-troublesome passage quite effectively, focusing on God's intention to create a helpmeet for man. See S. Grimké, *Letters on the Equality of the Sexes*, 31–34.
98. Genesis 3:16.
99. L. Mott, "Discourse on Woman," 76 (emphasis added).
100. L. Mott, "Discourse on Woman," 76; S. Grimké, *Letters on the Equality of the Sexes*, 38.
101. The story of Miriam can be found in several places in scripture, most notably in Exodus 2 and 15; Deborah's is in Judges 4 and 5; and Huldah's in 2 Kings 22:14–20 and 2 Chronicles 34:22–28. New Standard Version Exodus. 2, Judges 4–5, Kings. 22:14, Chronicles. 34:22–28
102. L. Mott, "Discourse on Woman," 76. Miriam hides Moses in a reed basket on the river to save his life and then, when pharaoh's daughter rescues him, Miriam identifies his own mother as a wet nurse (Exodus 2:1–10). Micah 6:4 identifies

Miriam, along with Moses and Aaron, as being sent before the Israelites to lead them out of Egypt. King James Version Exodus 2:1–10, Micah 6:4.

103. Mott provides a scriptural reference to Deborah's story: Judges 4 and 5.

104. L. Mott, "Discourse on Woman," 77.

105. Kings 22 and 2 Chronicles 34 relate Huldah's story.

106. L. Mott, "Discourse on Woman," 77. Grimké had used these same examples.

107. See the *Greek Interlinear Bible* for a way to examine the Greek with the interlinear English.

108. Mott was probably using the King James Version of the Bible, which does make that difference. Some modern translations, like the New Revised Standard Version, label Phoebe as a "deacon" and Tychicus as a "minister."

109. The Timothy passage is the only place in scripture where this word occurs in any reference to women.

110. I Timothy 2:11–12.

111. Strong, *Strong's New Exhaustive Concordance of the Bible*, 38, 5.

112. Margaret Fell does not deal with the word "profess." However, she disputes the universal application of this passage to all women, since it particularly mentions the marital relationship and not the church environment.

113. L. Mott, "Discourse on Woman," 78.

114. L. Mott, "Discourse on Woman," 78 (emphasis in original).

115. L. Mott, "Discourse on Woman," 78.

116. L. Mott, "Discourse on Woman," 78.

117. L. Mott, "Discourse on Woman," 79.

118. Her omission of these women may reflect their associations with prostitution in Rahab's case or sexual manipulation in Tamar's. Mary Magdalene has, without biblical warrant, almost been characterized as a prostitute on the basis of that attribution by Pope Gregory the Great in 591 in his Homily 33. Interestingly, she does allude to the Samaritan woman at the well who seems to be linked in scripture to sexual promiscuity; L. Mott, "Discourse on Woman," 77.

119. L. Mott, "Discourse on Woman," 80. The title of the section title above is from Mott, "Discourse on Woman," 71.

120. Beecher, *Suggestions Respecting Improvements in Education,* 53; 54–55. Quoted in L. Mott, "Discourse on Woman," 81.

121. L. Mott, "Discourse on Woman," 83.

122. L. Mott, "Discourse on Woman," 83.

123. L. Mott, "Discourse on Woman," 83–84.

124. Dana, "Woman," 14; L. Mott, "Discourse on Woman," 84–85.

125. L. Mott, "Discourse on Woman," 84.

126. L. Mott, "Discourse on Woman," 87.

127. L. Mott, "Discourse on Woman," 88.

128. L. Mott, "Discourse on Woman," 89.

129. L. Mott, "Discourse on Woman," 96.

130. L. Mott, "Discourse on Woman," 97.

131. L. Mott, "Discourse on Woman," 97.

132. L. Mott, "Discourse on Woman," 97. This is a quotation from Nathaniel Parker Willis, *Dashes at Life*, Volume I: *Inklings of an Adventure,* 109.

133. Quoted in M. Bacon, *Valiant Friend,* 104–5.

134. K. Campbell, *Man Cannot Speak for Her,* Vol. 1, 48.

135. K. Campbell, *Man Cannot Speak for Her,* Vol. 1, 47.

136. Trible, "Five Loaves and Two Fishes," 289–95.
137. Sillars, "Romantic Idealism to Romantic Rationalism," 54.
138. K. Campbell, *Man Cannot Speak for Her,* Vol. 1, 38, 45.
139. K. Campbell, *Man Cannot Speak for Her,* Vol. 1, 47.
140. L. Mott, "Discourse on Woman," 79.
141. For a full discussion of dissent, see Chapter 1 of this volume.
142. L. Mott, "Discourse on Woman," 81.
143. L. Mott, "Discourse on Woman," 96.
144. Mattingly, *Appropriate[ing]Dress,* xiii.
145. Quoted in Mattingly, *Appropriate[ing] Dress,* 28.
146. Doxtader, "Characters in the Middle of Public Life," 337.
147. Greene, "Quaker Feminism," 148.
148. L. Mott, "Discourse on Woman," 74.
149. Pushon, *Portrait in Grey,* 180.

CHAPTER 5: FRANCES WILLARD'S *WOMAN IN THE PULPIT*

1. Willard, *Glimpses of Fifty Years,* 360. The subtitle of this chapter paraphrases the words of Edward Wheeler's eulogy for Willard, as quoted in Bordin, *Frances Willard,* 4.
2. Willard, *Woman in the Pulpit,* 62.
3. Bordin, *Francis Willard,* 117.
4. Zimmerelli, "'Stereoscopic View of Truth,'" 354.
5. Willard, *Woman in the Pulpit,* 5.
6. Evans, *Do Everything,* 198.
7. Willard, *Glimpses of Fifty Years,* v.
8. Bordin, *Frances Willard,* 112.
9. Bordin, *Frances Willard,* 5.
10. Bordin, *Frances Willard,* 4.
11. Quoted Earhart, *Frances Willard,* 372; Dow, "'Womanhood' Rationale," 299; Hempton, *Evangelical Disenchantment,* 105.
12. Bordin, *Frances Willard,* 6. Toward the end of her life, and under Willard's leadership, WCTU women "authored and successfully supported an impressive body of legislation" related to some of these issues (Bordin, *Frances Willard,* 175). Beyond temperance, and consistent with her "Do Everything" policy, Willard was a champion of and influencer for many social causes including dress reform, "putting a monetary value on housework," women's control of reproduction, women police officers, "strengthening rape laws," an eight-hour workday, and full access to education. See for example, K. Campbell, *Man Cannot Speak for Her, Vol. 1,* 122, 123; Fletcher, *Gender and the American Temperance Movement,* 108. Slagell explains that Willard's "Do Everything" policy initially encouraged women to do whatever they could to support temperance but "soon evolved into a much broader reform agenda." Slagell, "'Making the World More Homelike,'" 160.
13. Bordin, *Frances Willard,* 4.
14. During Willard's lifetime, several separate realizations of Methodism existed, each with a different history in regard to the integration of women into the ministry. Her branch of Methodism was the Methodist Episcopal Church. For a fuller discussion of these groups, see "Timeline of Women in Methodism."
15. Willard, *How to Win,* 51.
16. Bordin, *Frances Willard,* 21.

Notes to Pages 111–114 : 187

17. Evans, *Do Everything*, 23.
18. Evans, *Do Everything*, 23.
19. Willard, *Glimpses of Fifty Years,* 69.
20. Evans, *Do Everything*, 29.
21. Willard, *Glimpses of Fifty Years,* 69.
22. Willard, *Glimpses of Fifty Years,* 76.
23. Schmidt, "Reexamining the Public/Private Split," 237.
24. Bordin, *Frances Willard*, 29.
25. Willard, *Glimpses of Fifty Years,* 69–70. See also Hardesty, *Women Called to Witness,* 6.
26. Willard, *Glimpses of Fifty Years,* 76.
27. Bordin, *Frances Willard*, 21–23. See also Evans, *Do Everything*, 21, 22.
28. Willard, *Glimpses of Fifty Years*, 100. The name of this school is rendered in various ways. We have chosen to follow Willard's usage.
29. Willard, *Glimpses of Fifty Years,* 100. Some of Willard's autobiographers have speculated about her sexual identity. See Donawerth, *Conversational Rhetoric*, 97; Hempton, *Evangelical Disenchantment*, 107–8. Others maintain that "Willard's affectional ties with women moved through a pattern quite normal for her time." Bordin, *Frances Willard*, 44–47. Evans writes in his biography: "A frequently debated question about Willard relates to her sexual orientation. The fact that Willard loved women is beyond doubt. The exact meaning of that love, will likely never be understood" (*Do Everything*, 11).
30. Evans, *Do Everything*, 35.
31. Bordin, *Frances Willard,* 31. Unfortunately, a bout of typhoid prevented her reading her valedictory address.
32. Bordin, *Frances Willard,* 31.
33. Willard, "23 July 1859," 45.
34. Bordin, *Frances Willard,* 27.
35. Willard, *Glimpses of Fifty Years*, 121.
36. Willard, *Glimpses of Fifty Years,* 622–23.
37. Willard, *Glimpses of Fifty Years,* 622.
38. Only when her former fiancé Charles Fowler, who had become bishop, denied her and four other elected women seats at the Methodist General Conference did Willard threaten in her WCTU presidential address in 1888 "to withdraw from the Methodist Church and found her own." Hardesty, *Women Called to Witness,* 10.
39. Willard and Lathbury, *Work and Workers.*
40. Willard, *Woman in the Pulpit,* 62.
41. Willard, *Woman in the Pulpit,* 62.
42. Evans, *Do Everything,* 35.
43. Quoted in Bordin, *Frances Willard*, 30 (emphasis in original). The Ephesians 5 passage in question: "Wives, submit yourselves unto your own husbands, as unto the Lord. For the husband is the head of the wife, even as Christ is the head of the church: and he is the saviour of the body. Therefore as the church is subject unto Christ, so let the wives be to their own husbands in everything."
44. Bordin, *Frances Willard*, 34.
45. Willard, "Journal 18," 17.
46. Willard, *Glimpses of Fifty Years*, 645. Scholars speculate about the sexuality of other suffrage leaders. Susan Ware identifies both Anna Howard Shaw and Carrie

188 : Notes to Pages 114–119

Chapman Catt as having an "unconventional lifestyle" that found safety within the suffrage movement. See https://www.pbs.org/wgbh/americanexperience/features/vote-carrie-mollie-anna-lucy/.

47. Willard, *Glimpses of Fifty Years,* 169. See also Evans, *Do Everything,* 52–53.
48. Evans, *Do Everything,* 57.
49. Evans, *Do Everything,* 53. See also Bordin, *Frances Willard,* 39–44.
50. Bordin, *Frances Willard,* 42.
51. Bordin, *Frances Willard,* 54.
52. B. Solomon, *In the Company of Educated Women,* 47.
53. Bordin, *Frances Willard,* 57.
54. Bordin, *Frances Willard,* 55.
55. *On the Same Terms.*
56. *On the Same Terms.* See also Bordin, *Women at Michigan,* 6.
57. Hardesty, *Women Called to Witness,* 5.
58. Evans, *Do Everything,* 74.
59. Willard, *Glimpses of Fifty Years,* 201.
60. Willard, *Glimpses of Fifty Years,* 209–10.
61. Willard, *Glimpses of Fifty Years,* 229–30. See also Evans, *Do Everything,* 80–81.
62. Willard, *Glimpses of Fifty Years,* 226–31.
63. Willard, *Glimpses of Fifty Years,* 231. Bordin, *Frances Willard,* 32, 63. See also Hardesty, *Women Called to Witness,* 5; A. Parker, "'Hearts Uplifted and Minds Refreshed,'" 137.
64. For a full description of this movement, see Maxwell, "Washingtonian Society," 410–51.
65. Willard, *Glimpses of Fifty Years,* 331.
66. Willard, *Glimpses of Fifty Years,* 332.
67. Bordin, *Woman and Temperance,* 16–18 (quotation is on page 18).
68. Willard, *Glimpses of Fifty Years,* 334 (emphasis in original).
69. Willard, *Glimpses of Fifty Years,* 337–38.
70. Willard, *Glimpses of Fifty Years,* 339.
71. Bordin, *Frances Willard,* 87.
72. Bordin, *Frances Willard,* 87.
73. Bordin, *Frances Willard,* 87.
74. Bordin, *Frances Willard,* 88.
75. Bordin, *Frances Willard,* 89.
76. Gifford, "Home Protection," 109.
77. Brekus, "Female Evangelism," 136.
78. Brekus, "Female Evangelism," 145.
79. Long, "Consecrated Respectability," 284; 385. Bizzell, "Frances Willard," 385.
80. Long, "Consecrated Respectability," 282.
81. Bizzell, "Frances Willard," 386; 384–85; 378. Bizzell makes a compelling argument that Palmer was in fact a role model "and spiritual mentor" for Willard, although biographer Ruth Bordin tends to minimize their connection.
82. Chaves, *Ordaining Women,* 10.
83. At this point, there were several branches of Methodism, most of which would eventually unite into the United Methodist Church in the twentieth century. Mary Oliver and Anna Howard Shaw were preceded by Maggie Newton Van Cott with whom Willard was acquainted. Van Cott was a "sought after evangelist" who received a local preacher's license in 1869 and was one of about seventy

Notes to Pages 119–121 : 189

women who secured local preacher's licenses in the 1870s. Schmidt, *Grace Sufficient*, 181–82. Her preaching caused quite a controversy according to a *New York Times* article on April 25, 1869. The article begins: "Our readers will remember the excitement caused in the late New York Methodist Episcopal Conference held at Sing Sing, by the announcement . . . that the Quarterly Conference . . . had licensed a female preacher, one 'Widow Van Cott.' The Conference immediately became greatly agitated over the subject, about one-half being in favor of continuing the "widow" in the good cause of converting souls, while the other half were strenuously opposed to such a proceeding, avowing openly and above-board that it was a female suffrage movement, with which they would have nothing to do." Apparently, there was a motion to disprove the licensing of female preachers, but it did not succeed, and the matter of licensing was referred to a special committee. With the support of Methodist Episcopal Church pastor Joseph Crane Hartzell and the San Francisco District Conference, a recommendation was made to support Van Cott's ordination in 1874. Bishop Stephen Merrill who presided over the California Conference, "rejected the recommendation, ruling that lower judicatories had no right to grant women licenses to preach" (Richey et al., *Methodist Experience in America*, 242). An appeal of Merrill's decision to the 1876 General Conference failed.

84. Rowe, ed., "Ordination of Women," 301–02.
85. Chilcote, *Methodist Defense of Women in Ministry*, 99.
86. Schmidt, *Grace Sufficient*, 185.
87. "Timeline of Women in Methodism." According to this timeline, the United Brethren Church, which consolidated with the Methodist Episcopal Church in 1968 to form the current United Methodist Church, was more progressive in including women as preachers and ministers.
88. W. Noll, "Women as Clergy," 11; See also Schmidt, *Grace Sufficient*, 189–92 and Chilcote, *Methodist Defense of Women in Ministry*, 99.
89. Gifford, *Debate in the Methodist Episcopal Church*, np. See also Rowe, ed., "Ordination of Women," 298–304.
90. Bordin, *Frances Willard*, 160.
91. Bordin, *Frances Willard*, 160.
92. Bordin, *Frances Willard*, 161. See also Richey et al., *Methodist Experience in America*, 278.
93. Richey et al., *Methodist Experience in America*, 278. Bordin, *Frances Willard*, 161 surmises why Willard "declined the privilege so reluctantly offered." According to Bordin, she received a similar rebuff from the Presbyterians a bit later. Bordin, *Francis Willard*, 161–62.
94. Gifford, *Debate in the Methodist Episcopal Church*, np.
95. Richey et al., *Methodist Experience in America*, 278.
96. Gifford, *Debate in the Methodist Episcopal Church*, np.
97. Bordin, *Frances Willard*, 164. Evans, *Do Everything*, 201. Willard was not able to follow through with her plans because before the General Conference began, she was called home as a result of her mother's serious illness. Bordin, *Frances Willard*, 165.
98. Evans, *Do Everything*, 202.
99. Richey et al., *Methodist Experience in America*, 279–80.
100. Willard, "Annual Address," 45-46. See also Willard, *Glimpses of Fifty Years*, 465.
101. Evans, *Do Everything*, 195.

190 : Notes to Pages 121–131

102. Evans, *Do Everything,* 8.

103. Bordin, *Frances Willard,* 162.

104. Bordin, *Frances Willard,* 162. Bordin reports that it was not until 1896 when the "full Conference voted to accept women as delegates to the 1904 assembly where they took their seats long after Willard's death," *Frances Willard,* 167.

105. Hempton, *Evangelical Disenchantment,* 110.

106. Evans, *Do Everything,* 196.

107. *Union Signal,* July 2, 1885, 3.

108. Augustine Jones, "Early Beginnings," *Union Signal,* May 20, 1886, 5.

109. Donawerth, *Conversational Rhetoric,* 101.

110. Willard, *Woman in the Pulpit,* 6 (emphasis in original).

111. Willard, *Woman in the Pulpit,* 9.

112. Willard, *Woman in the Pulpit,* 10.

113. Willard, *Woman in the Pulpit,* 11–12.

114. Willard, *Woman in the Pulpit,* 10–13.

115. Willard, *Woman in the Pulpit,* 15.

116. Willard, *Woman in the Pulpit,* 73–75.

117. William Ingraham Haven, quoted in Willard, *Woman in the Pulpit,* 93.

118. Willard, *Woman in the Pulpit,* 73.

119. Willard, *Woman in the Pulpit,* 94.

120. Willard, *Woman in the Pulpit,* 103, 106.

121. Willard, *Woman in the Pulpit,* 100.

122. Willard, *Woman in the Pulpit,* 116.

123. Camper, *Arguing Over Texts,* 106–11.

124. Camper, *Arguing Over Texts,* 110.

125. Camper, *Arguing Over Texts,* 108–11.

126. Hawthorne, who died in 1864, did not write these words for *Woman in the Pulpit.* Willard apparently chose to include this quote in support of her case for women preaching. The reference is to Hawthorne, *The Blithedale Romance,* 1852.

127. Heading attribution from Willard, *Woman in the Pulpit,* 26; Hempton, *Evangelical Disenchantment,* 111.

128. Hempton, *Evangelical Disenchantment,* 111.

129. Outler, "Wesleyan Quadrilateral," 8, 9.

130. Camper, *Arguing Over Texts,* 139–62.

131. Willard, *Woman in the Pulpit,* 17.

132. Willard, *Woman in the Pulpit,* 17–18.

133. Willard, *Woman in the Pulpit,* 18.

134. Willard, *Woman in the Pulpit,* 20.

135. Willard, *Woman in the Pulpit,* 20 (emphasis in original).

136. Willard, *Woman in the Pulpit,* 21.

137. Willard, *Woman in the Pulpit,* 23.

138. Willard, *Woman in the Pulpit,* 26.

139. Zimmerelli, "'Stereoscopic View of Truth,'" 363.

140. Willard, *Woman in the Pulpit,* 27.

141. Willard, *Woman in the Pulpit,* 40.

142. Gifford and Slagell, eds., *Let Something Good Be Said,* 103.

143. Gifford and Slagell, eds., *Let Something Good Be Said,* 113.

144. Willard, "White Life for Two," 325.

145. Willard, *Woman in the Pulpit,* 33–34.

Notes to Pages 131–137 : 191

146. Willard, *Woman in the Pulpit*, 34.
147. Camper, *Arguing Over Texts*, 69.
148. Willard, *Woman in the Pulpit*, 41.
149. She is referring to John 11:27. Prior to the raising of Lazarus, Martha affirms that she believes Jesus is the Messiah. This parallels Peter's pronouncement in Matthew 16:17.
150. Willard, *Woman in the Pulpit*, 43–44 (emphasis in original).
151. Willard, *Woman in the Pulpit*, 43–44 (emphasis in original).
152. These quotes are respectively from Revelation 21:5 and 2 Corinthians 3:6. Although Willard seems to suggest that Jesus spoke these words ("these are his words"), he did not speak them. Willard, *Woman in the Pulpit*, 52.
153. The section title above quotes Willard, *Woman in the Pulpit*, 54.
154. K. Campbell, *Man Cannot Speak for Her*, Vol. 1, 123.
155. Willard, *Woman in the Pulpit*, 47, 48.
156. Willard, *Woman in the Pulpit*, 39.
157. Willard, *Woman in the Pulpit*, 28.
158. Willard, *Woman in the Pulpit*, 46.
159. Willard, *Woman in the Pulpit*, 46–47.
160. Willard, *Woman in the Pulpit*, 62.
161. Zimmerelli, "'Stereoscopic View of Truth,'" 368.
162. Willard, *Woman in the Pulpit*, 51.
163. Willard, *Woman in the Pulpit*, 65.
164. Willard, *Woman in the Pulpit*, 66. In support of her claims, she also cites a "leading woman preacher" as well as Senator Henry W. Blair who is arguing for woman's right to vote, but Willard insists that there is an analogy between the right to vote and the right to preach.
165. Willard, *Woman in the Pulpit*, 54.
166. Willard, *Woman in the Pulpit*, 54–55.
167. Willard, *Woman in the Pulpit*, 21.
168. Willard, *Woman in the Pulpit*, 49.
169. Willard, *Woman in the Pulpit*, 49.
170. "Timeline of Women in Methodism."
171. For a fuller discussion of dissent, see Chapter 1 of this volume.
172. Hempton, *Evangelical Disenchantment*, 111.
173. Hempton, *Evangelical Disenchantment*, 111–13.
174. Gifford, "Home Protection," 100.
175. "Frances Willard," *The Outlook*.
176. K. Campbell, *Man Cannot Speak for Her, Vol. 1*, 126; Dow, "Frances E. Willard." "Frances E. Willard," *Methodist Magazine and Review;* Bordin, *Frances Willard*, makes a similar point noting that Willard's "emphasis on womanliness" may have been "a way to clothe new answers in old garments," demonstrating her ability to use "conservative values to promote radical ends," 10.
177. Schmidt, "Reexamining the Public/Private Split," 238.
178. Bordin, *Frances Willard*, 9, See also DuBois "Radicalism of the Woman Suffrage Movement."
179. Slagell, "Making the World More Homelike,'" 175. Slagell provides a thorough analysis of how Willard used "home protection" as a rhetorical strategy, 164–88.
180. Mattingly, *Well-Tempered Women*, 67.
181. *Christian Advocate.*

192 : Notes to Pages 137–140

182. Evans, *Do Everything,* 322.
183. Hardesty, *Women Called to Witness,* 129.
184. Bordin, *Frances Willard,* 39.
185. Evans, *Do Everything,* 323.
186. Slagell, "'Making the World More Homelike,'" 159.
187. Giver-Johnston, *Claiming the Call to Preach,* 155. Slagell makes a similar point noting that "[S]he maintained an aura of womanliness that brought her accolades from conservative audiences before whom speakers such as Elizabeth Cady Stanton and Susan B. Anthony could never dream to gain a hearing." "'Making the World More Homelike,'" 162.
188. Gifford, "Home Protection," 97.
189. Stewart, Smith, and Denton, *Persuasion and Social Movements,* 49–62.
190. As Slagell notes, Willard played a "major role in creating an environment in which the early twentieth-century movement could succeed," "Rhetorical Structure," 20.
191. Slagell, "Rhetorical Structure," 19.
192. Evans, *Do Everything,* 326.
193. "Frances E. Willard," *Methodist Magazine,* April 1898, 374.
194. Willard, "President's Annual Address," *Minutes of the National Woman's Christian Temperance Union,* Fourteenth Convention, November 16-21, 1887. Chicago: Woman's Temperance Publication Association, 1888 (emphasis in original).
195. Zimmerelli, "'Stereoscopic View of Truth,'" 364 (emphasis in original).
196. Hardesty, *Women Called to Witness,* 131.
197. Willard, *How to Win,* 54–55, 57. Willard says something similar in "Annual Address of Frances E. Willard, President of the National W.C.T.U., At Eleventh Annual Convention at St. Louis, MO October 20, 23, 24, 25, 1884," the *Union Signal,* October 30, 1884, 2: "Woman will bless and brighten every place she enters, and she will enter every place."
198. Ackerman, "Noble Women."
199. "Frances Willard," *The Outlook,* 58, no. 9, February 26, 1898, 514.
200. Kraditor, *Ideas of the Woman Suffrage Movement,* 43–75.
201. Although most members of the WCTU were White women, it was one of a few national organizations that Black women could join. The National WCTU seated Black and White women together and some scholars note that under Willard, the WCTU did become more inclusive of women of color and immigrants (Gifford and Slagell, *Let Something Good Be Said,* 193, 203–5.) Although Willard maintained she was not racist, evidence suggests otherwise. For example, the WCTU tacitly condoned segregation, making accommodations for Southern WCTU women to organize segregated state and local chapters. Moreover, Willard clearly held prejudices against immigrants, poor and working-class people, and Black Americans as demonstrated by an interview entitled "The Race Problem: Miss Willard on the Political Puzzle of the South," given to *The New York Voice,* a pro-prohibition newspaper at an 1890 WCTU Convention in Atlanta. During the interview, Willard indicated support for the "Back to Africa" movement, which advocated for the relocation of Black Americans to West Africa. She further stated that the WCTU "had irreparably wronged ourselves by putting no safeguard on the ballot-box at the North that would sift out alien illiterates. . . . It is not fair that they should vote, nor is it fair that a plantation Negro, who can neither read nor write, whose ideas are bounded by the fence of his own field and the price

Notes to Pages 140–145 : 193

of his own mule, should be entrusted with the ballot" ("The Race Problem: Miss Willard on the Political Puzzle of the South," *The New York Voice*, October 28, 1890, 8). She also indicated, without any supporting evidence, that Black voters were the reason why the South defeated some prohibition bills. Most damning were statements she made and attributed to what her White-middle class Southern friends told her: "The problem on their hands is immeasurable. The colored race multiplies like the locusts of Egypt. The grog shop is its centre of power. The safety of woman, of childhood, of home, is menaced in a thousand localities at this moment, so that men dare not go beyond the sight of their own roof-tree" ("The Race Problem," 8). Willard's inflammatory remarks incurred the wrath of Ida B. Wells, a civil rights activist and journalist who advocated tirelessly for anti-lynching legislation. She was infuriated by the refusal of well-known White reformers like Willard to support her anti-lynching cause. Following Willard's infamous interview, Wells engaged in a four-year long debate with her, accusing her of promoting harmful stereotypes about Black people such as the commonly held belief that Black men raped White women, a fiction perpetrated by White people to maintain power and to justify violence and lynching. In her fifteenth presidential address in 1894, Willard defended her statements about Black voting and prohibition, tempering her statement by acknowledging that she wished she had also mentioned the sexual assault of White men against Black women and girls. The WCTU passed anti-lynching resolutions beginning in 1894, resolutions which Willard endorsed. She never recanted the statements she made in her interview. Frances Willard House Museum, "Truth-Telling." For more information, see also August, "Strained Sisterhood in the WCTU," 1–15; Fletcher, *Gender and the American Temperance Movement,* 120.

202. Hardesty, *Women Called to Witness,* 11–12.

203. Elizabeth Cady Stanton," Letter to the Editors," *Woman's Journal,* February 28, 1898, reprinted in Gordon, ed., *Selected Papers,* 206–8.

CONCLUSION

1. We are grateful to Professor Mitzi Budde, head librarian at the Bishop Payne Library at the Virginia Theological Seminary, for helping us locate the source of the first epigraph. It is frequently used but without proper citation.

2. D. Wilson, "Luther Legacy," 34.

3. D. Wilson, *Out of the Storm,* 358.

4. McCook, "Second Great Awakening," 252.

5. Zaeske, *Signatures of Citizenship,* 21, 22.

6. Article 1, section 2, clause 3 provided that for purposes of congressional representation would be "determined by adding the whole Number of free Persons, including those bound to Service for a Term of Years and excluding Indians not taxed, three fifths of all persons." This became knowns as the 3/5ths compromise.

7. See Portnoy, *Their Right to Speak,* especially Chapter 1 for a full discussion of the emergence of Indian removal as a political issue.

8. Phillips, "Event of Dissension," 65.

9. Phillips, "Event of Dissension," 66.

10. Cathcart, "Confrontation Perspective," 72.

11. Camper, *Arguing over Texts,* 142.

12. Camper, *Arguing Over Texts,* 161.

13. Foucault, *Archaeology of Knowledge,* 221.

194 : Notes to Pages 145–155

14. Foucault, *Archaeology of Knowledge,* 221 (emphasis in original).
15. "On Her Own Wings."
16. Stewart, Smith, and Denton, *Persuasion and Social Movements,* 49–50.
17. Linkugel, Allen, and Johannesen, *Contemporary American Speeches,* 208.
18. K. Campbell, "Femininity and Feminism," 104. Throughout this article, Campbell refers to some women as "feminists." For us, that terminology seems anachronistic.
19. K. Campbell, "Femininity and Feminism," 104, 107.
20. K. Campbell, *Man Cannot Speak for Her,* Vol. 2, 72.
21. K. Campbell, "Femininity and Feminism," 104.
22. K. Campbell, "Femininity and Feminism," 105.
23. Charland, "Constitutive Rhetoric," 133–50.
24. Black, "Second Persona."
25. Charland, "Constitutive Rhetoric," 138.
26. Charland, "Constitutive Rhetoric," 138.
27. Stewart, Smith, and Denton, *Persuasion and Social Movements,* 58–62.
28. Stewart, Smith, and Denton, *Persuasion and Social Movements,* 15.
29. Ivie, "Enabling Democratic Dissent," 50.
30. Ivie, "Enabling Democratic Dissent," 46.
31. Ivie, "Argument from Similitude," 311–23.
32. Lucaites and Condit, "Reconstructing *Equality,*" 5.
33. Lucaites and Condit, "Reconstructing *Equality,*" 8.
34. Stewart, Smith, and Denton, *Persuasion and Social Movements,* 81 (emphasis in original).
35. Kathryn Burke, "Letter Writing in America."
36. See M. Solomon, *Voice of Their Own.*
37. Slagell, "'Making the World More Homelike,'" 160.
38. Ivie, "Argument from Similitude," 311–23.
39. Colaiaco, *Martin Luther King Jr.,* 7.
40. Chritchlow, "Phyllis Schlafly."
41. Casey, "First Female Public Speakers," 4–10.
42. Phillips, "Spaces of Invention," 339.
43. Kenneth Burke, *Rhetoric of Motives,* 46.
44. Brueggemann, *Prophetic Imagination.*
45. Brueggemann, *Prophetic Imagination,* xiii.
46. Eaton, *Mysterious Messengers,* 5.
47. Brueggemann, *Prophetic Imagination,* 2, 3 (emphasis in original).
48. Brueggemann, *Texts that Linger,* 1 (emphasis in original).
49. Newsom, "Introduction to the Prophetic Books," 970.
50. Lee, *Religious Experience and Journal,* 11.
51. S. Grimké, *Letters on the Equality of the Sexes,* 31.
52. S. Grimké, *Letters on the Equality of the Sexes,* 102.
53. Zimmerelli, "'Stereoscopic View of Truth.'"
54. Brueggemann, *Prophetic Imagination,* 3 (emphasis in original).
55. Stanton, *Woman's Bible,* 2: 151.
56. Darsey, *Prophetic Tradition,* 1997.
57. Stewart, Smith, and Denton, *Persuasion and Social Movements,* 73 (emphasis in original).

58. Stewart, Smith, and Denton, *Persuasion and Social Movements,* 49. See also Gurevitch and Levy, *Mass Communication Review Yearbook,* 19.
59. Stewart, Smith, and Denton, *Persuasion and Social Movements,* 73.
60. Stewart, Smith, and Denton, *Persuasion and Social Movements,* 82.
61. Stanton, *Woman's Bible,* ix.
62. Heilbrun, *Writing a Woman's Life,* 18.

APPENDIX A

1. In addition to Lerner's *Creation of a Feminist Consciousness,* see also Flexner, *Century of Struggle;* Cott, *Bonds of Womanhood;* DuBois, *Feminism and Suffrage;* Hewitt and Valk, *Companion to American Women's History;* Melder, *Beginnings of Sisterhood;* Matthews, *Rise of the Public Woman;* and Ryan, *Women in Public.*
2. For a representative example of a text that addresses all four of these areas, see Buchanan and Ryan, *Walking and Talking Feminist Rhetorics.*
3. See, for example, Wood, "Women and Communication," 99.
4. Bizzell and Herzberg's first edition of *Rhetorical Tradition* was published in 1990. The second edition was published in 2001 and the third edition (with a third coeditor) was published in 2020.
5. Bizzell, "Feminist Methods of Research," 7; Gale, "Historical Studies"; Glenn, "Truth, Lies, and Method, 387-89; Jarratt, "Rhetoric and Feminism," 390–93.
6. Lunsford, *Reclaiming Rhetorica,* 6.
7. For example, see Self, "What Distinguishes."
8. Jarratt, "Performing Feminisms," 1.
9. Portnoy, "Defining, Using, and Challenging the Rhetorical Tradition," 103.
10. See, for example, Tinkler's discussion of *contentio* and *sermo* in "Renaissance Humanism," 283. See also Sutherland and Sutcliffe, *Changing Tradition,* 11.
11. Berg, *Remembered Gate.*
12. Foss and Foss, *Women Speak;* Zboray and Zboray, *Voices without Votes.*
13. Mattingly, "Telling Evidence," 107.
14. Ritchie and Ronald, *Available Means,* xxvii.
15. See, for example, Donawerth, *Conversational Rhetoric,* 74.
16. Glenn, *Rhetorical Feminism,* 4.

BIBLIOGRAPHY

Abzug, Robert H. *Cosmos Crumbling: American Reform and the Religious Imagination.* New York: Oxford University Press, 1994.

Ackerman, Amy. "Noble Women." *The Presbyterian Messenger,* April 6, 1894.

Allen, Richard, and John Tapisco. *The Doctrines and Discipline of the African Methodist Episcopal Church.* Philadelphia: John H. Cunningham, 1817. https://docsouth.unc .edu/church/ame/ame.html.

Andrews, William L. *Sisters of the Spirit: Three Black Women's Autobiographies of the Nineteenth Century.* Bloomington: Indiana University Press, 1986.

Angell, Stephen. "The Controversy Over Women's Ministry in the African Methodist Episcopal Church During the 1880s: The Case of Sarah Ann Hughes." In *This Far by Faith: Readings in African-American Women's Religious Biography,* edited by Judith Weisenfeld and Richard Newman, 95–104. New York: Routledge, 1996.

Anthony, Susan B., Matilda Joslyn Gage, and Elizabeth Cady Stanton, eds. *History of Woman Suffrage,* Vol. 1, *1848–1861.* Project Gutenberg. https://www.gutenberg.org/ ebooks/28020

Anthony, Susan B., and Ida Husted Harper, eds. *The History of Woman Suffrage*, Vol. IV, *1883–1900.* Indianapolis: Hollenbeck Press, 1902. http://www.gutenberg.org/ files/29870-h/29870-h.htm

Aristotle. *Poetics and Rhetoric.* Edited by Eugene Garver. New York: Barnes and Noble Classics, 2005.

Articles of Religion. *Book of Common Prayer.* http://justus.anglican.org/resources/ bcp/1928/Articles.htm.

Aquinas, Thomas., Cai, P. Raphaelis. *Super Evangelium S. Ioannis Lectura.* Caputo 20, Lecture 3. Italy: Marietti, 1952.

August, Anita. "Strained Sisterhood in the WCTU: The Lynching and Suffrage Rivalry between Ida B. Wells and Frances E. Willard." *Rhetoric Review* 40, no. 1 (February 2021): 1–15.

Bacon, Jacqueline. "'God and a Woman': Women Abolitionists, Biblical Authority and Social Activism." *Journal of Communication and Religion* 2, no. 1 (March 1999): 10–20.

Bacon, Jacqueline. *The Humblest May Stand Forth.* Columbia: University of South Carolina Press, 2002.

Bacon, Margaret Hope. *Mothers of Feminism: The Story of Quaker Women in America.* San Francisco: Harper and Row, 1986.

Bacon, Margaret Hope. *Valiant Friend: The Life of Lucretia Mott.* New York: Walker, 1980.

Baker, Frank. *Charles Wesley as Revealed by His Letters.* London: Epworth Press, 1948.

Baker, Jean H. *The Lives of America's Suffragists.* New York: Hill and Wang, 2005.

Baker, Jean H. ed. *Votes for Women: The Struggle for Suffrage Revisited.* New York: Oxford, 2002.

198 : Bibliography

Baliff, Michelle. "Re/Dressing Histories: Or, on Re/Covering Figures Who Have Been Laid Bare by Our Gaze." *Rhetoric Society Quarterly* 22, no. 1 (Winter 1992): 91–98.

Baliff, Michelle, Diane Davis, and Roxanne Mountford. *Women's Ways of Making It in Rhetoric and Composition.* New York: Routledge, 2008.

Barnes, Gilbert Hobbes, and Dwight Lowell Dumond, eds. *The Letters of Theodore Dwight Weld, Angelina Grimké and Sarah Grimké, 1822–1844.* Gloucester: P. Smith, 1965.

Bartlett, Elizabeth Ann, ed. *Sarah Grimké Letters on the Equality of the Sexes and Other Essays.* New Haven: Yale University Press, 1988.

Bassard, Katherine Clay. *Spiritual Interrogations: Culture, Gender, and Community in Early African American Women's Writing.* Princeton: Princeton University Press, 1999.

Batty, Margaret. "Origins: The Age of Wesley." In *Workaday Preachers: The Story of Methodist Local Preachers,* edited by Geoffrey Milburn and Margaret Batty, 11–34. Peterborough: Methodist Publishing House, 1995.

Beecher, Catharine. "Circular: Addressed to Benevolent Ladies of the United States." *Christian Advocate,* September 9, 1826. https://teachingamericanhistory.org/docu ment/circular-addressed-to-benevolent-ladies-of-the-united-states/.

Beecher, Catharine. "Essay on Slavery and Abolitionism Addressed to Miss A.D. Grimké," section 104–105, http://utc.iath.virginia.edu/abolitn/abesceba2t.html.

Beecher, Catharine. *Suggestions Respecting Improvements in Education.* Hartford: Packer and Butler, 1829.

Bercovitch, Sacvan. *The American Jeremiad, Anniversary Edition.* Madison: University of Wisconsin Press, 2012.

Berg, Barbara J. *The Remembered Gate: Origins of American Feminism—Woman and the City, 1800–1860.* Oxford: Oxford University Press, 1980.

Birney, Catharine H. *The Grimké Sisters: Sarah and Angelina Grimké, the First American Women Advocates of Abolition and Woman's Rights.* Boston: Lee and Shepard, 1885.

Bitzer, Lloyd F. "The Rhetorical Situation." *Philosophy & Rhetoric* 1, no. 1 (January 1968): 1-14.

Bizzell, Patricia. "Editing the Rhetorical Tradition." *Philosophy and Rhetoric* 36, no. 2 (2003): 109–18.

Bizzell, Patricia. "Feminist Methods of Research in the History of Rhetoric: What Difference Do They Make." *Rhetoric Society Quarterly* 30, no. 4 (Autumn 2004): 5–17.

Bizzell, Patricia. "Frances Willard, Phoebe Palmer, and the Ethos of Methodist Preachers." *Rhetoric Society Quarterly* 36, no. 4 (Fall 2006): 377–98.

Bizzell, Patricia. "Opportunities for Feminist Research in the History of Rhetoric." *Rhetoric Review* 11, no. 1 (1992): 50–58.

Bizzell, Patricia, Bruce Herzberg, Robin Reames, eds. *The Rhetorical Tradition: Readings from Classical Times to the Present.* Boston: Bedford/St. Martin's, 2020.

Black, Edwin. "The Second Persona." *Quarterly Journal of Speech* 56, no. 2 (April 1970): 109–19.

Blackstone, William. "Of Husband and Wife." In *Commentaries on the Laws of England (1765–1769)*—Book 1, Chapter 15. https://lonang.com/library/reference/blackstone -commentaries-law-England/bla-115/.

Bleiker, Roland. *Popular Dissent, Human Agency and Global Politics.* Cambridge: Cambridge University Press, 2000.

Bogin, Ruth, and Jean Fagan Yellin. "Introduction." In *The Abolitionist Sisterhood: Women's Political Culture in Antebellum America,* edited by Jean Fagan Yellin and John C. Van Horne, 1–19. Ithaca: Cornell University Press, 1994.

Bordin, Ruth. *Frances Willard: A Biography.* Chapel Hill: University of North Carolina Press, 1986.

Bordin, Ruth. *Woman and Temperance: The Quest for Power and Liberty, 1873–1900.* New Brunswick: Rutgers University Press, 1990.

Bordin, Ruth. *Women at Michigan: The "Dangerous Experiment," 1870s to the Present.* Ann Arbor: University of Michigan Press, 1999.

Braithwaite, William C. *The Second Period of Quakerism.* London: MacMillan, 1919. https://archive.org/details/secondperiodofquoobrai.

Brekus, Catherine. "Female Evangelism in the Early Methodist Movement." In *Methodism and the Shaping of American Culture,* edited by Nathan O. Hatch and John H. Wigger, 135–74. Nashville: Kingswood Books, 2001.

Brekus, Catherine. *Sarah Osborn's World: The Rise of Evangelical Christianity in Early America.* New Haven: Yale University Press, 2013.

Brekus, Catherine. *Strangers and Pilgrims: Female Preaching in America, 1740–1845.* Chapel Hill: University of North Carolina Press, 1998.

Brown, Ira V. "Cradle of Feminism: The Philadelphia Female Anti-Slavery Society 1833–1840." *The Pennsylvania Magazine of History and Biography* 102, no. 2 (April 1978): 143–66.

Brown, Joanne Carlson. "Protestant Women and Social Reform." In *In Our Own Voices: Four Centuries of American Women's Writing,* edited by Rosemary Skinner Keller and Rosemary Radford Ruether, 247–90. San Francisco: Harper Collins, 1995.

Browne, Stephen Howard. *Angelina Grimké: Rhetoric, Identity, and the Radical Imagination.* East Lansing: Michigan State University Press, 1999.

Brueggemann, Walter. *The Prophetic Imagination.* 2nd ed. Minneapolis: Augsburg Fortress, 2001.

Brueggemann, Walter. *Texts that Linger, Words that Explode: Listening to Prophetic Voices,* edited by Patrick D. Miller. Minneapolis: Fortress Press, 2000.

Buchanan, Lindal. *Regendering Delivery: The Fifth Canon and Antebellum Women Rhetors.* Carbondale: Southern Illinois University Press, 2005.

Buchanan, Lindal, and Kathleen J. Ryan, eds. *Walking and Talking Feminist Rhetorics: Landmark Essays and Controversies.* Anderson: Parlor Press, 2010.

Burke, Kathryn. "Letter Writing in America." *Smithsonian National Postal Museum.* https://postalmuseum.si.edu/research-articles/letter-writing-in-america

Burke, Kenneth. *A Rhetoric of Motives.* Berkeley: University of California Press, 1969.

Burton, Vicki Tolar. *Spiritual Literacy in John Wesley's Early Methodism.* Waco: Baylor University Press, 2008.

Campbell, James T. *Songs of Zion: The African Methodist Episcopal Church in the United States and South Africa.* New York: Oxford University Press, 1995.

Campbell, Karlyn Kohrs. "Femininity and Feminism: To Be or Not to Be a Woman." *Communication Quarterly* 31, no. 2 (Spring 1983): 101–108.

Campbell, Karlyn Kohrs. "Gender and Genre: Loci of Invention and Contradiction in the Earliest Speeches by U.S. Women." *Quarterly Journal of Speech* 81, no. 4 (November 1995): 479–95.

Campbell, Karlyn Kohrs. "Inventing Women: From Amaterasu to Virginia Woolf." *Women's Studies in Communication* 21, no. 2 (Fall 1998): 111–26.

Campbell, Karlyn Kohrs. "The Rhetoric of Women's Liberation: An Oxymoron." *Quarterly Journal of Speech* 59, no. 1 (February 1973): 74–86.

Campbell, Karlyn Kohrs. "Rhetorical Feminism." *Rhetoric Review* 20, no. 1 (Spring 2001): 9–12.

Campbell, Karlyn Kohrs. "Theory Emergent from Practice: The Rhetorical Theory of Frances Wright." In *Rhetorical Women: Roles and Representations,* edited by Lillian Bridwell-Bowles and Hildy Miller, 125–41. Tuscaloosa: University of Alabama Press, 2005.

Campbell, Karlyn Kohrs, ed. *Man Cannot Speak for Her.* Vol. 1, *A Critical Study of Early Feminist Rhetoric.* Westport: Praeger, 1989.

Campbell, Karlyn Kohrs, ed. *Man Cannot Speak for Her.* Vol. 2, *Key Texts of the Early Feminists.* Westport: Praeger, 1989.

Campbell, Karlyn Kohrs, ed. *Women Public Speakers in the United States: 1800–1925.* Westport: Greenwood Press, 1993.

Campbell, Karlyn Kohrs, and E. Claire Jerry. "Woman and Speaker: A Conflict in Roles." In *Seeing Female: Social Reality and Personal Lives,* edited by Sharon S. Brehm, 123–34. New York: Greenwood Press, 1988.

Camper, Martin. *Arguing Over Texts: The Rhetoric of Interpretation.* New York: Oxford University Press, 2018.

Cardman, Francine. "Women, Ministry, and Church Order in Early Christianity." In *Women and Christian Origins,* edited by Ross Shepherd Kraemer and Mary Rose D'Angelo, 299–329. New York: Oxford University Press, 1999.

Carey, Brycchan, and Geoffrey Plank. *Quakers and Abolition.* Urbana: University of Illinois Press, 2014.

Cartwright, William. "On the Marriage of the Lady Mary to the Prince of Aurange His Son. 1641." In *Spenser and the Tradition: English Poetry 1579–1830,* compiled by David Hill Radcliffe. Center for Applied Technologies in the Humanities, Virginia Tech. http://spenserians.cath.vt.edu/TextRecord.php?action=GET&textsid=33413.

Carwardine, Richard. "The Second Great Awakening in the Urban Centers: An Examination of Methodism and the 'New Measures.'" *Journal of American History* 59, no. 2 (September 1972): 327–40.

Casey, Michael W. "The First Female Public Speakers in America (1630–1840): Searching for Egalitarian Christian Primitivism." *Journal of Communication and Religion* 23, no. 1 (March 2000): 1–27.

Cathcart, Robert S. "A Confrontation Perspective on the Study of Social Movements." *Communication Studies* 34, no. 1 (Spring 1983): 69–74.

Cathcart, Robert S. "Defining Social Movements by their Rhetorical Form." *Central States Speech Journal* 31, no. 4 (Winter 1980): 267–73.

Cathcart, Robert S. "Movements: Confrontation as Rhetorical Form." *Southern States Communication Journal* 43, no. 3 (Spring 1978): 233–47.

Cathcart, Robert S. "New Approaches to the Study of Movements: Defining Movements Rhetorically." *Western Speech* 36, no. 2 (Spring 1972): 82–88.

Ceplair, Larry, ed. *The Public Years of Sarah and Angelina Grimké: Selected Writings, 1835–1839.* New York: Columbia University Press, 1989.

Chambers, Deborah, Linda Steiner, and Carole Fleming. *Women and Journalism.* London and New York: Routledge, 2004.

Charland, Maurice. "Constitutive Rhetoric: The Case of the Peuple Quebecois." *Quarterly Journal of Speech* 73, no. 2 (May 1987): 133–50.

Chaves, Mark. *Ordaining Women: Culture and Conflict in Religious Organizations.* Cambridge: Harvard University Press, 1997.

Chavéz, Karma R., Cindy L. Griffin, and Marsha Houston. *Standing in the Intersection: Feminist Voices, Feminist Practices in Communication Studies.* Albany: State University of New York Press, 2012.

Bibliography : 201

Chilcote, Paul Wesley. *Early Methodist Spirituality: Selected Women's Writings.* Nashville: Kingswood Books, 2007.

Chilcote, Paul Wesley. *John Wesley and the Women Preachers of Early Methodism.* Metuchen: American Theological Library Association, 1991.

Chilcote, Paul Wesley. *The Methodist Defense of Women in Ministry: A Documentary History.* Eugene: Cascade Books, 2017.

Child, Lydia Maria. *Appeal in Favor of that Class Called Africans.* Boston: Allen and Ticknor, 1833.

Child, Lydia Maria. *Brief History of the Condition of Women, in Various Ages and Nations.* New York: C. S. Francis, 1835.

Chittester, Joan. *The Time Is Now: A Call to Uncommon Courage.* New York: Convergent Books, 2019.

Christian Advocate (New Orleans) 31, no. 19 (March 5, 1896).

Church, A.M.E. (2017). *The Doctrines and Discipline of the African Methodist Episcopal Church.* Chapel Hill: University of North Carolina Press. https://muse.jhu.edu/book/52336.

Clarkson, Thomas. *An Essay on Slavery and Commerce of the Human Species, Particularly Africans: In Three Parts.* Philadelphia: Nathaniel Wiley, 1804.

Cogan, Frances B. *All American Girl: The Ideal of Real Woman-Hood in Mid-Nineteenth-Century America.* Athens: University of Georgia Press, 1989.

Colaiaco, James A. *Martin Luther King, Jr.: Apostle of Militant Nonviolence.* London: MacMillan Press, 1988.

Collier-Thomas, Bettye. *Daughters of Thunder: Black Women Preachers and Their Sermons, 1850–1979.* San Francisco: Jossey-Bass, 1998.

Collins, Vicki Tolar. "Walking in Light, Walking in Darkness: The Story of Women's Changing Rhetorical Space in Early Methodism." *Rhetoric Review* 14, no. 2 (1996): 336–54.

Cone, James. *For My People: Black Theology and the Black Church.* New York: Orbis, 1984.

Coogan, Michael D., ed. *The New Oxford Annotated Bible.* 3rd ed. Oxford: Oxford University Press, 2001.

Cott, Nancy. *The Bonds of Womanhood: "Woman's Sphere" in New England, 1780–1835.* New Haven: Yale University Press, 1977.

Crawford, Elizabeth. *The Women's Suffrage Movement: A Reference Guide 1866–1928.* London: University of London Press, 1999.

Critchlow, Donald T. "Phylis Schlafly: The Mother of Right Wing Populism: Donald Trump is the Anti-Globalist Candidate She's Been Waiting For." *Washington Post,* September 8, 2016.

Cromwell, Otelia. *Lucretia Mott.* Cambridge: Harvard University Press, 1958.

Cullen, Margaret. "Holy Fire: Biblical Radicalism in the Narratives of Jarena Lee and Zilpha Elaw." In *The Force of Tradition: Response and Resistance in Literature, Religion, and Cultural Studies,* edited by Donald G. Marshall, 143–64. Lanham: Rowman and Littlefield, 2005.

Dana, Richard Henry, Sr. "Woman." *Lectures on Shakespeare, 1838–1847.* Massachusetts Historical Society, Dana papers, Box 37, 1.

Dandelion, Ben Pink. *An Introduction to Quakerism.* Cambridge: Cambridge University Press, 2007.

Dandelion, Ben Pink. *Quakers: A Very Short Introduction.* Oxford: Oxford University Press, 2008.

Daniell, David. "William Tyndale, the English Bible, and the English Language." In *The Bible as Book: Reformation,* edited by Orlaith O'Sullivan and Ellen N. Herron, 39–50. London: British Library, 2000.

Darsey, James. *The Prophetic Tradition and Radical Rhetoric in America.* New York: New York University Press, 1997.

Daughton, Suzanne M. "The Fine Texture of Enactment: Iconicity as Empowerment in Angelina Grimké's Pennsylvania Hall Address." *Women's Studies in Communication* 18, no. 1 (Spring 1995): 19–43.

Dayton, Amy E., and Jenny L. Vaughan, eds. *Ethics and Representation in Feminist Rhetorical Inquiry.* Pittsburgh: University of Pittsburgh Press, 2021.

Densmore, Christopher, Carol Faulkner, Nancy Hewitt, and Beverly Wilson Palmer, eds. *Lucretia Mott Speaks: The Essential Speeches and Letters.* Urbana: University of Illinois Press, 2017.

Dickerson, Dennis C. *The African Methodist Episcopal Church: A History.* Cambridge: Cambridge University Press, 2020.

"Declaration of Sentiments and Resolutions." In *Man Cannot Speak for Her: Key Texts of the Early Feminists,* compiled by Karlyn Kohrs Campbell, 33–39. New York: Greenwood Press, 1989.

Dodson, Jualynne E. *Engendering Church: Women, Power, and the AME Church.* New York: Rowman & Littlefield, 2002.

Dodson, Jualynne, E. "Nineteenth Century A.M.E. Preaching Women." In *Women in New Worlds: Historical Perspectives on the Wesleyan Tradition,* edited by Hilah E. Thomas and Rosemary Skinner Keller, 276–89. Nashville: Abingdon, 1981.

Donawerth, Jane. *Conversational Rhetoric: The Rise and Fall of a Women's Tradition, 1600–1900.* Carbondale: Southern Illinois University Press, 1992.

Donawerth, Jane, ed. *Rhetorical Theory by Women before 1900: An Anthology.* New York: Rowman and Littlefield, 2002.

Dorrien, Gary. *The Making of American Liberal Theology: Imagining a Progressive Religion 1805–1900.* Louisville: Westminster John Knox Press, 2001.

Dow, Bonnie J. "Frances E. Willard (1839–1898): Reinventor of 'True Womanhood.'" In *Women Public Speakers in the United States, 1800–1925: A Biocritical Sourcebook,* edited by Karlyn Kohrs Campbell, 476–89. Westport: Greenwood Press, 1993.

Dow, Bonnie J. "Spectacle, Spectatorship, and Gender Anxiety in the Television News Coverage of the 1970 Women's Strike for Equality." *Communication Studies* 50, no. 2 (Summer 1999): 143–57.

Dow, Bonnie J. "The 'Womanhood' Rationale in the Woman Suffrage Rhetoric of Frances E. Willard." *Southern Communication Journal* 56, no. 4 (Summer 1991): 298–307.

Doxtader, Erik W. "Characters in the Middle of Public Life: Consensus, Dissent, and Ethos." *Philosophy and Rhetoric* 33, no. 4 (2000): 336–39.

DuBois, Ellen Carol. *Feminism and Suffrage: The Emergence of an Independent Women's Movement in America.* Ithaca: Cornell University Press, 1978.

DuBois, Ellen Carol. "The Radicalism of the Woman Suffrage Movement: Notes Toward the Reconstruction of Nineteenth-Century Feminism." *Feminist Studies* 3, no. 1–2 (Autumn 1975): 63–71.

Dubois, Ellen Carol. *Woman Suffrage and Woman's Rights.* New York: New York University Press, 1998.

Bibliography : 203

Duerden, Richard. "Equivalence of Power: Authority and Reformation Bible Translation." In *The Bible as Book: The Reformation,* edited by Orlaith O'Sullivan and Ellen N. Norton, 9–23. London: British Library, 2000.

Dumond, Dwight Lowell. *Antislavery: The Fight for Freedom in America.* Ann Arbor: University of Michigan Press, 1961.

Durso, Pamela. *The Power of Woman: The Life and Writings of Sarah Moore Grimké.* Macon: Mercer University Press, 2003.

Duyckinck, Evart A., and George L. Duyckinck. "Richard Henry Dana." *The Cyclopedia of American Literature: Embracing Personal and Critical Notices of Authors, and Selections from Their Writings. From the Earliest Period to the Present Day; with Portraits, Autographs, and Other Illustrations,* 91. New York: Charles Scribner, 1856.

Earhart, Mary. *Frances Willard: From Prayers to Politics.* Chicago: University of Chicago Press, 1944. https://archive.org/details/franceswillardfr00earh/page/n9/mode/2up.

Eastman, Carolyn. *A Nation of Speechifiers: Making an American Republic After the Revolution.* Chicago: University of Chicago Press, 2010.

Eaton, John. *Mysterious Messengers: A Course on Hebrew Prophecy from Amos Onwards.* London: SCM Press, 1997.

Edwards Jr., Mark U. *Printing, Propaganda, and Martin Luther.* Minneapolis: Fortress Press, 2005.

Ehrman, Bart D. *Peter, Paul, and Mary Magdalene: The Followers of Jesus in History and Legend.* Oxford: Oxford University Press, 2006.

Enoch, Jessica. *Refiguring Rhetorical Education: Women Teaching African American, Native American, and Chicanola Students, 1865–1911.* Carbondale: Southern Illinois University Press, 2008.

Epstein, Barbara Leslie. *The Politics of Domesticity: Women, Evangelism and Temperance in Nineteenth-Century America.* Middletown: Wesleyan University Press, 1981.

Evans, Christopher Hodge. *Do Everything: The Biography of Frances Willard.* New York: Oxford University Press, 2022.

Faulkner, Carol. *Lucretia Mott's Heresy: Abolition and Women's Rights in 19th Century America.* Philadelphia: University of Philadelphia Press, 2011.

Faulkner, Carol, and Nancy Hewitt. "Introduction." In *Lucretia Mott Speaks: The Essential Speeches and Sermons,* edited by Christopher Densmore, Carol Faulkner, Nancy Hewitt, and Beverly Wilson Palmer, 10–24. Urbana: University of Illinois Press, 2017.

Fell, Margaret. "Womens Speaking Justified, Proved and Allowed of by the Scriptures, and how Women Were the First that Preached the Tidings of the Resurrection of Jesus, and Were Sent by Christ's own Command, before He Ascended to the Father John 20.17." 1666. In *Women's Speaking Justified and Other Pamphlets,* edited by Jane Donawerth and Rebecca M. Lush, 157–76. Toronto: Iter Press, 2018.

Fiorenza, Elisabeth Schüssler. *In Memory of Her: A Feminist Theological Reconstruction of Christian Origins.* 10th Anniversary Edition. New York: Crossroad, 1994.

Fletcher, Holly Berkley. *Gender and the American Temperance Movement of the Nineteenth Century.* New York: Routledge, 2008.

Flexner, Eleanor. *Century of Struggle: The Woman's Rights Movement in the United States.* Cambridge: Belknap Press of Harvard University Press, 1975.

Florence, Anna Carter. *Preaching as Testimony.* Louisville: Westminster John Knox, 2007.

Foss, Karen A. *Women Speak: The Eloquence of Women's Lives Prospect Heights*. Long Grove: Waveland Press, 1991.

Foucault, Michel. *The Archaeology of Knowledge and the Discourse on Language*. Translated by A.M. Sheridan Smith. New York: Pantheon Books, 1972.

Foucault, Michel. "Nietzsche, Genealogy, History." In *The Foucault Reader*, edited by Paul Rabinow, 76–100. New York: Pantheon, 1984.

Foucault, Michel. "The Discourse on Language." In *The Archaeology of Knowledge and the Discourse on Language*, Translated by A.M. Sheridan Smith. New York: Pantheon Books, 1972.

Foucault, Michel. "What Is an Author." In *The Foucault Reader*, edited by Paul Rabinow, 101–20. New York: Pantheon, 1984.

Foust, Christina R., Amy Pason, and Kate Zittlow Rogness, eds. *What Democracy Looks Like: The Rhetoric of Social Movements and Counterpublics*. Tuscaloosa: University of Alabama Press, 2017.

"Frances E. Willard." *The Methodist Magazine and Review*, April 1898, 374.

"Frances Willard." *The Outlook* 58, no. 9 (February 26, 1898).

Frances Willard House Museum. "Truth-Telling: Frances Willard and Ida B. Wells: Frances Willard and the 'Race Problem.'" https://scalar.usc.edu/works/willard-and-wells/introduction?path=index

Gaines, Steven Tramel. "No Half Savior: Jarena Lee's Autobiography as Prophetic Rhetoric." *Carolinas Communication Annual* XXXIII, 2017.

Gale, Xin Liu. "Historical Studies and Postmodernism: Rereading Aspasia of Miletus." *College English* 62, no. 3 (January 2000): 361–86.

Ganter, Granville, "Women's Entrepreneurial Lecturing in the Early National Period." In *Thinking Together: Lecturing, Learning, and Difference in the Long Nineteenth Century*, edited by Angela Ray and Paul Stob, 42–55. University Park: University of Pennsylvania Press, 2018.

General Association of Congregational Churches. "Pastoral Letter." In *American Rhetorical Discourse*, 2nd ed., edited by Ronald Reid and James Klumpp, 363–67. Long Grove: Waveland Press, 1995.

Gifford, Carolyn De Swarte, ed. *The Debate in the Methodist Episcopal Church Over Laity Rights for Women*. New York: Garland, 1987.

Gifford, Carolyn De Swarte. "Home Protection: The WCTU's Conversion to Woman Suffrage." In *Gender, Ideology, and Action: Historical Perspectives on Women's Public Lives*, edited by Janet Sharistanian, 95–120. New York: Greenwood, 1986.

Gifford, Carolyn De Swarte. "Women in Social Reform Movements." In *Women and Religions in America: The Nineteenth Century*, Vol. 1, edited by Rosemary Radford Ruether and Rosemary Skinner Keller, 294–303. San Francisco: Harper & Row, 1981.

Gifford, Carolyn De Swarte, and Amy R. Slagell, eds. *Let Something Good Be Said: Speeches and Writing of Frances E. Willard*. Chicago: University of Illinois Press, 2007.

Giver-Johnston, Donna. *Claiming the Call to Preach: Four Female Pioneers of Preaching in Nineteenth-Century America*. New York: Oxford University Press, 2021.

Glenn, Cheryl. *Rhetorical Feminism and This Thing Called Hope*. Carbondale: Southern Illinois University Press, 2018.

Glenn, Cheryl. *Rhetoric Retold: Regendering the Tradition from Antiquity Through the Renaissance*. Carbondale: Southern Illinois University Press, 1997.

Glenn, Cheryl. "Truth, Lies, and Method: Revisiting Feminist Historiography." *College English* 62, no. 3 (January 2000): 387–89.

Bibliography : 205

Glenn, Cheryl. *Unspoken: The Rhetoric of Silence.* Carbondale: Southern Illinois University Press, 2004.

Gold, David, and Catherine L. Hobbs, eds. *Rhetoric and Women's Oratorical Education: American Women Learn to Speak.* New York: Routledge, 2013.

Gold, Ellen Reid. "The Grimké Sisters and the Emergence of the Woman's Rights Movement." *Southern Speech Communication Journal* 46, no. 4 (Summer 1981): 341–60.

Gonzalez, Justo L. *The Story of Christianity,* Vol. 1 and 2, *The Early Church to the Reformation.* New York: HarperCollins Publishers, 2010.

Gordon, Ann D., ed. *The Selected Papers of Elizabeth Cady Stanton and Susan B. Anthony: An Awful Hush, 1895 to 1906.* New Brunswick: Rutgers University Press, 2013.

Graham, E. Dorothy. "Women Local Preachers." In *Workaday Preachers: The Story of Methodist Local Preaching,* edited by Geoffrey Milburn and Margaret Batty, 165–90. Peterborough: Methodist Publishing House, 1995.

Greek Interlinear Bible. http://www.scripture4all.org/OnlineInterlinear/Greek_Index.htm.

Greene, Dana. "Quaker Feminism: The Case of Lucretia Mott." *Pennsylvania History: A Journal of Mid-Atlantic Studies* 48, no. 2 (April 1981):143–54.

Griffin, Cindy, Karen A. Foss, and Sonja K. Foss, eds. *Readings in Feminist Rhetorical Theory.* Thousand Oaks: Sage, 2004.

Grimké, Angelina Emily. *Appeal to the Christian Women of the South.* Edinburgh: William Oliphant, Jun. &, Co., 1837.

Grimké, Angelina Emily. *Letters to Catherine E. Beecher, in Response to an Essay on Slavery and Abolitionism, Addressed to A. E. Grimké.* Boston: Knapp, 1838.

Grimké, Angelina Emily. "Letter to William Lloyd Garrison, 1835." https://www.loc.gov/resource/rbpe.05601500/.

Grimké, Sarah M. "An Epistle to the Clergy of the Southern States." https://en.wikisource.org/wiki/An_Epistle_to_the_Clergy_of_the_Southern_States

Grimké, Sarah M. "Letters on the Equality of the Sexes," edited by Elizabeth Ann Bartlett, 31–103. New Haven: Yale University Press, 1988.

Grimké, Sarah, and Angelina Grimké, "Letter to Henry C. Wright, August 27, 1837." In *The Public Years of Sarah and Angelina Grimké : Selected Writings 1835-1849,* edited and annotated by Larry Ceplair, 287-288. New York: Columbia University Press, 1989.

Gring-Pemble, Lisa. "Writing Themselves into Consciousness: Creating a Rhetorical Bridge between the Public and Private Spheres." *Quarterly Journal of Speech* 84, no. 1 (February 1998): 41–61.

Gurevitch, Michael, and Mark R. Levy, eds. *Mass Communication Review Yearbook.* Vol. 5. Beverly Hills: Sage, 1985.

Hamm, Thomas D. "George F. White and the Hicksite Opposition to Abolitionism." In *Quakers and Abolition,* edited by Brycchan Carey and Geoffrey Plank, 43–55. Chicago: University of Illinois Press, 2017.

Hardesty, Nancy A. "Evangelical Women." In *In Our Own Voices: Four Centuries of American Women's Writing,* edited by Rosemary Skinner Keller and Rosemary Radford Ruether, 207–246. San Francisco: Harper Collins, 1995.

Hardesty, Nancy A. *Women Called to Witness: Evangelical Feminism in the Nineteenth Century.* Knoxville: University of Tennessee Press, 1999.

Hardesty, Nancy A. *Your Daughters Shall Prophesy: Revivalism and Feminism in the Age of Finney.* New York: Carlson Publishing, 1991.

Hatch, Nathan O. *The Democratization of American Christianity.* New Haven: Yale University Press, 1989.

Hawthorne, Nathaniel. *The Blithedale Romance.* Boston: Ticknor, Reed, and Fields, 1852. Project Gutenberg. https://www.gutenberg.org/files/2081/2081-h/2081-h.htm

Hays, J. Daniel. *The Message of the Prophets: A Survey of Prophetic and Apocalyptic Books of the Old Testament.* Grand Rapids: Zondervan, 2010.

Heilbrun, Carolyn G. *Writing a Woman's Life.* New York: Norton, 1988.

Heitzenrater, Richard P. *Wesley and the People Called Methodists.* Nashville: Abingdon Press, 1995.

Hempton, David. *Evangelical Disenchantment: Nine Portraits of Faith and Doubt.* New Haven: Yale University Press, 2008.

Hempton, David. *Methodism: Empire of the Spirit.* New Haven: Yale University Press, 2005.

Hempton, David. "The People Called Methodists: Transitions in Britain and North America." In *The Oxford Handbook of Methodist Studies,* edited by William J. Abraham and James E. Kirby, 67–84. Oxford: Oxford University Press, 2009.

Hershberger, Mary. "Mobilizing Women, Anticipating Abolition: The Struggle Against Indian Removal in the 1830s." *Journal of American History* 86, no. 1 (June 1999): 15–40.

Hewitt, Nancy. "Abolition and Suffrage." Supplementary Material in PBS "Not for Ourselves Alone: The Story of Elizabeth Cady Stanton and Susan B. Anthony." A film by Ken Burns and Paul Barnes. http://www.pbs.org/stantonanthony/.

Hewitt, Nancy. "Race, Class, Region, and Activism, 1820s–1870s." In *A Companion to American Women's History,* 2nd ed., edited by Nancy A. Hewitt and Anne M. Valk, 123–40. Hoboken: John Wiley & Sons, 2021.

Hewitt, Nancy. "Taking the True Woman Hostage." *Journal of Women's History* 14, no. 1 (Spring 2002): 156–62.

Hewitt, Nancy, and Anne M. Valk, eds. *A Companion to American Women's History.* 2nd ed. Hoboken: John Wiley & Sons, 2021.

Heyrman, Christine Leigh. "The First Great Awakening." *National Humanities Center.* https://nationalhumanitiescenter.org/tserve/eighteen/ekeyinfo/.

Hirsch, Emil G., Maz Seligsohn, and Wilhelm Bacher. "Nimrod." *Jewish Encyclopedia.* https://www.jewishencyclopedia.com/articles/11548-nimrod.

Hogan, Lisa Shawn. "A Time for Silence: William Lloyd Garrison and the 'Woman Question' at the 1840 World Anti-Slavery Convention." *Gender Issues* 25, no. 2 (August 2008): 63–79.

Hogan, Lucy, and Martha Solomon. "Extending the Conversation Sharing the Inner Light." *Rhetoric Society Quarterly* 25 (1995): 32–46

Holborn, Louise W. "Printing and the Growth of a Protestant Movement in Germany from 1517 to 1524." *Church History* 11, no 2 (June 1942): 123–47.

Hoover, Theresa. "Black Women and the Churches: Triple Jeopardy." In *Black Theology: A Documentary History, 1966–1979,* edited by Gayraud S. Wilmore and James H. Cone, 377–88. Maryknoll: Orbis Books, 1979.

Howard, Joy A. J. "Legacy Profile: Julia A. J. Foote (1823–1901)." *Legacy* 23, no. 1 (2006): 86–93.

Howard-Pitney, David. "The Enduring Black Jeremiad: The American Jeremiad and Black Protest Rhetoric, from Frederick Douglass to W. E. B. Du Bois, 1841–1919." *American Quarterly* 38, no. 3 (1986): 481–92.

Hubert, Susan J. "Testimony and Prophecy in the Life and Religious Experience of Jarena Lee." *Journal of Religious Thought* 54/55, no. 2/1 (Spring–Fall 1998): 45–52.

Hunter, Sheryl. "Discursive Identity Formation for Suffrage Women: Reframing the 'Cult of True Womanhood' Through Song." *Western Journal of Communication* 70, no. 3 (July 2006): 234–60.

Ingle, H. Larry. *First Among Friends: George Fox & the Creation of Quakerism.* New York: Oxford University Press, 1994.

Ivie, Robert L. "Argument from Similitude in Martin Luther King, Jr.'s Deliberative Dissent from War." *Argumentation* 34, no. 3 (2020): 311–23.

Ivie, Robert L. "Enabling Democratic Dissent." *Quarterly Journal of Speech* 10, no.1 (February 2015): 46–59.

Ivie, Robert L. "Toward a Humanizing Style of Democratic Dissent." *Rhetoric and Public Affairs* 11, no. 3 (2008): 454–58.

Japp, Phyllis. "Esther or Isaiah?: The Abolitionist-Feminist Rhetoric of Angelina Grimké." *Quarterly Journal of Speech* 93, no. 1 (February 2007): 27–57.

Jarratt, Susan C. *Rereading the Sophists: Classical Rhetoric Refigured.* Carbondale: Southern Illinois University Press, 1998.

Jarratt, Susan C. "Rhetoric and Feminism: Together Again." *College English* 62, no. 3 (January 2000): 390–93.

Jarratt, Susan C., ed. "Special Issue: Feminist Rereadings in the History of Rhetoric." *Rhetoric Society Quarterly* 22, no. 1 (Winter 1992).

Johnson, Kimberly P. *The Womanist Preacher: Proclaiming Womanist Rhetoric from the Pulpit.* Lexington: Lexington Books, 2017.

Johnson, Nan. *Gender and Rhetorical Space in American Life, 1866–1910.* Carbondale: Southern Illinois University Press, 2002.

Johnson, William H. [W. J. H.]. "Lucretia Mott." *The Lily* (February 1, 1854): 19.

Jones, Katherine Clay. *All Bound Up Together: The Woman Question in African American Public Cultures, 1830–1900.* Chapel Hill: University of North Carolina Press, 2007.

Jordan, Ryan P. *Slavery and the Meetinghouse: The Quakers and the Abolitionist Dilemma, 1820–1865.* Bloomington: Indiana University Press, 2007.

Juster, Susan. *Disorderly Women: Sexual Politics and Evangelicalism in Revolutionary New England.* Ithaca, NY: Cornell University Press, 1994.

Kaplan, Emma Nogardy, and Sidney Kaplan. *The Black Presence in the Era of the American Revolution.* Rev. ed. Amherst: University of Massachusetts Press, 1989.

Kelley, Mary. *Learning to Stand and Speak: Women, Education, and Public Life in America's Republic.* Chapel Hill: University of North Carolina Press, 2006.

Kerber, Linda K. "The Republican Mother: Women and the Enlightenment—An American Perspective." *American Quarterly* 28, no. 2 (Summer 1976): 187–205.

Kerber, Linda K. "Separate Spheres, Female Worlds, Woman's Place: The Rhetoric of Women's History." *Journal of American History* 75, no. 1 (June 1988): 9–39.

Kerber, Linda K., Nancy F. Cott, Robert Gross, Lynn Hunt, Carroll Smith-Rosenberg, and Christine M. Stansell. "Beyond Roles, Beyond Spheres: Thinking about Gender in the Early Republic." *William and Mary Quarterly* 46, no. 3 (July 1989): 565–85.

Kern, Kathi. "Re-reading Eve: Elizabeth Cady Stanton and The Woman's Bible, 1885–1896." *Women's Studies* 19, no. 3–4 (1991): 371–83.

Kimball, James. "Frances Willard as Protector of the Home: The Progressive, Divinely Inspired Woman." In *Lives of Their Own: Rhetorical Dimensions in Autobiographies of Women Activists,* edited by Martha Watson, 47–62. Columbia: University of South Carolina Press, 1999.

Knight, Frederick Knight. "The Many Names for Jarena Lee." *The Pennsylvania Magazine of History and Biography* 141, no. 1 (January 2017): 59–68.

Kraditor, Aileen. *The Ideas of the Woman Suffrage Movement, 1890–1920.* New York: Norton, 1981.

Kraemer, Ross Shepard, and Mary Rose D'Angelo. *Women & Christian Origins.* New York: Oxford University Press, 2010.

Kruczek-Aaron, Hadley. *Everyday Religion: An Archaeology of Protestant Belief and Practice in the Nineteenth Century.* Gainesville: University of Florida Press, 2015.

Kunze, Bonnelyn Young. *Margaret Fell and the Rise of Quakerism.* Stanford: Stanford University Press, 1994.

Lapsansky, Emma Jones. "Feminism, Freedom, and Community: Charlotte Forten and Women Activists in Nineteenth-Century Philadelphia." *The Pennsylvania Magazine of History and Biography* 113, no. 1 (January 1989): 3–19.

Lee, Jarena. *Religious Experience and Journal of Mrs. Jarena Lee: Giving an Account of Her Call to Preach the Gospel.* Philadelphia: Author, 1849. https://www.google.com/books/edition/.

Lei, Elizabeth Vander, and Keith D. Miller. "Martin Luther King, Jr.'s 'I Have a Dream' in Context: Ceremonial Protest and African American Jeremiad." *College English* 62, no. 1 (September 1999): 83–99.

Lerner, Gerda. *The Creation of a Feminist Consciousness from the Middle Ages to Eighteen-Seventy.* New York: Oxford University Press, 1993.

Lerner, Gerda. *The Feminist Thought of Sarah Grimké.* New York: Oxford University Press, 1998.

Lerner, Gerda. *The Grimké Sisters from South Carolina: Pioneers for Women's Rights and Abolition.* Chapel Hill: University of North Carolina Press, 2004.

Lewis, Carolyn Herbst. "Republican Motherhood." In *Encyclopedia of Motherhood,* edited by Andrea O'Reilly. Thousand Oaks: Sage, 2010. https://dx.doi.org/10.4135/9781412979276.

Lewis, Tiffany. *Uprising: How Women Used the West to Win the Right to Vote.* East Lansing: Michigan State University Press, 2001.

Lindley, Susan Hill. *"You Have Stept Out of Your Place": A History of Women and Religion in America.* Louisville: Westminster John Knox Press, 1996.

Linkugel, Wil A., R. R. Allen, and Richard L. Johannesen, eds. *Contemporary American Speeches.* 5th ed. Dubuque: Kendall/Hunt, 1982.

Logan, Shirley Wilson. *Sites of Rhetorical Education in Nineteenth-Century Black America.* Carbondale: Southern Illinois University Press, 2008.

Logan, Shirley Wilson. *"We Are Coming": The Persuasive Discourse of Nineteenth-Century Black Women.* Carbondale: Southern Illinois Press, 1999.

Logan, Shirley Wilson, ed. *With Pen and Voice: A Critical Anthology of Nineteenth-Century African-American Women.* Carbondale: Southern Illinois University Press, 1995.

Long, Kathryn. "Consecrated Respectability: Phoebe Palmer and the Refinement of American Methodism." In *Methodism and the Shaping of American Culture,* edited by Nathan O. Hatch and John H. Wigger, 281–308. Nashville: Kingswood Books, 2001.

Lucaites, John Louis, and Celeste Michelle Condit. "Reconstructing *Equality:* Culturetypal and Counter-Cultural Rhetorics in the Martyred Black Vision." *Communication Monographs* 57, no. 1 (March 1990): 5–24.

Lundy, Benjamin, ed. *Genius of Universal Emancipation.* 1821-1839.

Lumpkin, Katharine Du Pre. *The Emancipation of Angelina Grimké.* Chapel Hill: University of North Carolina Press, 1974.

Lunsford, Andrea A., ed. *Reclaiming Rhetorica: Women in the Rhetorical Tradition.* Pittsburgh: University of Pittsburgh Press, 1995.

Luther, Martin. *To the Christian Nobility of the German Nation Respecting the Reformation of the Christian Estate, in First Principles of the Reformation of the Ninety-Five Theses and the Three Primary Works of Dr. Martin Luther.* Translated by Henry Wace and C. A. Buchheim. London: John Murray, 1883.

Mace, Emily R. "Feminist Forerunners and a Usable Past." *Journal of Feminist Studies in Religion* 25, no. 2 (2009): 5–23.

Mack, Phyllis. *Visionary Women: Ecstatic Prophesy in Seventeenth-Century England.* Berkeley: University of California Press, 1992.

Mackay, Nellie Y. "Nineteenth-Century Black Women's Spiritual Autobiographies: Religious Faith and Self-Empowerment." In *Interpreting Women's Lives: Feminist Theory and Personal Narratives,* edited by Personal Narratives Group, 143–47. Bloomington: Indiana University Press, 1989.

Marilley, Suzanne. "Frances Willard and the Feminism of Fear." *Feminist Studies* 19, no. 1 (Spring 1993): 123–46.

Marshall, Peter. *The Reformation: A Very Short Introduction.* Oxford: Oxford University Press, 2009.

Mathieson, Peter, ed. *A Woman's Voice in the Reformation.* Edinburgh: T&T Clark, 1995.

Mathews, Donald G. "The Second Great Awakening as an Organizing Process, 1780-1830: An Hypothesis." *American Quarterly* 21, no. 1 (Spring, 1969): 23-43

Matthews, Glenna. *The Rise of the Public Woman: Woman's Power and Woman's Place in the United States, 1630–1970.* New York: Oxford University Press, 1992.

Mattingly, Carol. *Appropriate[ing] Dress: Women's Rhetorical Style in Nineteenth-Century America.* Carbondale: Southern Illinois University Press, 2002.

Mattingly, Carol. "Telling Evidence: Rethinking What Counts in Rhetoric." *Rhetoric Society Quarterly* 32, no. 1 (Winter, 2002): 99–108.

Mattingly, Carol. *Well-Tempered Women: Nineteenth-Century Temperance Rhetoric.* Carbondale: Southern Illinois University Press, 1998.

Maxwell, Milton A. "The Washingtonian Society." *Quarterly Journal of Studies on Alcohol* 11, no. 3 (September 1950): 410–51.

McCook, Matt. "The Second Great Awakening." In *American Religious History: Belief and Society Through Time.* Vol. 1, edited by Gary Scott Smith, 252–53. Santa Barbara: ABC-CLIO, LLC, 2021.

McGrath, Alister. *Christianity's Dangerous Idea: The Protestant Revolution, A History from the Sixteenth Century to the Twenty-First.* New York: Harper/Collins, 2007.

McGrath, Alister. *The Intellectual Origins of the European Reformation.* London: Blackwell, 1987.

Melder, Keith. *The Beginnings of Sisterhood: The American Woman's Rights Movement, 1800–1850.* New York: Schocken Books, 1977.

Melton, Gordon J. *A Will to Choose: The Origins of African American Methodism.* New York: Rowman & Littlefield, 2007.

Metzger, Bruce M. *The Bible in Translation: Ancient and English Versions.* Grand Rapids: Baker Academic, 2001.

Meyer, Michaela D. E. "Women Speak(ing): Forty Years of Feminist Contributions to Rhetoric and an Agenda for Feminist Rhetorical Studies." *Communication Quarterly,* 55, no. 1 (February 2007): 1–17.

Miller, Hilda, and Lillian Bridwell-Bowles, eds. *Rhetorical Women: Roles and Represen-tations.* Tuscaloosa: University of Alabama Press, 2005.

Minifee, Paul. "'I Took Up the Hymn-Book': Rhetoric of Hymnody in Jarena Lee's Call to Preach." *Advances in the History of Rhetoric* 18, no. 1 (2015): 1–18.

Mott, James. *Hints to Young People on the Duties of Civil Life.* New York: Mahlon Day, 1826.

Mott, Lucretia Coffin. "Discourse on Woman." In *Man Cannot Speak for Her: Key Texts of the Early Feminists,* compiled by Karlyn Kohrs Campbell, 71–97. New York: Greenwood Press, 1989.

Mott, Lucretia Coffin. *Lucretia Mott's Diary of Her Visit to Great Britain to Attend the World's Anti-Slavery Convention of 1840,* edited by Frederick B. Tolles. Supplement No. 23 to the *Journal of the Friends' Historical Society.* Haverford, PA and London: Friends' Historical Association and Friends Historical Society, 1952.

Mountford, Roxanne. *The Gendered Pulpit: Preaching in American Protestant Places.* Carbondale: Southern Illinois University Press, 2005.

Mountford, Roxanne. "On Gender and Rhetorical Space." *Rhetoric Society Quarterly* 31, no. 1 (Winter 2001): 41–71.

Neuman, Johanna. *And Yet They Persisted: How American Women Won the Right to Vote.* New York: Wiley/Blackwell, 2020.

New England Spectator. 1834–1838. https://www.loc.gov/item/sn85038225/.

Newman, Richard S. *Freedom's Prophet: Bishop Richard Allen, the AME Church and the Black Founding Fathers.* New York: New York University Press, 2008.

Newsom, Carol A. "Introduction to the Prophetic Books." In *The New Oxford An-notated Bible,* 3rd ed., edited by Michael D. Coogan, 969–73. Oxford: Oxford University Press, 2001.

Newsom, Carol A., and Sharon H. Ringe, eds. *Women's Bible Commentary expanded edition.* Louisville: Westminster John Knox Press, 1998.

Noll, Mark A. *America's God: From Jonathan Edwards to Abraham Lincoln.* New York: Oxford University Press, 2002.

Noll, William T. "Women as Clergy and Laity in the 19th Century Methodist Protes-tant Church." *Methodist History* 15, no. 2 (January 1977): 107–21.

"On Her Own Wings: Oregon Women and the Struggle for Suffrage." *Oregon Secre-tary of State.* https://sos.oregon.gov/archives/exhibits/suffrage/Pages/organizations/menu.aspx

On the Same Terms: An Exhibition. Deering Library, October 2019–June 2020. https://www.northwestern.edu/150-years-of-women/learn/library-exhibit/.

"Our History." *African Episcopal Methodist Church.* https://www.ame-church.com/our-church/our-history/

Outler, Albert C. "The Wesleyan Quadrilateral." *Wesleyan Theological Journal* 20, no. 1 (Spring 1985): 7–18.

Pagels, Elaine. *Adam, Eve and the Serpent.* London: Weidenfeld and Nicolson, 1988.

Painter, Nell Irvin. "Representing Truth: Sojourner Truth's Knowing and Becoming Known." *Journal of American History* 81, no. 2 (September 1994): 482–88.

Painter, Nell Irvin. *Sojourner Truth: A Life, A Symbol.* New York: Norton, 1996.

Painter, Nell Irvin. "Voices of Suffrage: Sojourner Truth, Frances Watkins Harper, and the Struggles for Woman Suffrage." In *Votes for Women: The Struggle for Suffrage Revisited,* edited by Jean H. Baker, 42–55. New York: Oxford, 2002.

Palmer, Beverly Wilson, ed. *Selected Letters of Lucretia Coffin Mott.* Urbana: University of Illinois Press, 2002.

Bibliography : 211

Parker, Alison. "The Case for Reform Antecedents for the Woman's Rights Movement." In *Votes for Women: The Struggle for Suffrage Revisited,* edited by Jean H. Baker, 21–41. New York: Oxford University Press, 2002.

Parker, Alison. "'Hearts Uplifted and Minds Refreshed'": The Woman's Christian Temperance Union and the Production of Pure Culture in the United States, 1880–1930." *Journal of Women's History* 11, no. 2 (Summer 1999): 135–58.

Parker, Meaghan. "Desiring Citizenship: A Rhetorical Analysis of the Wells/Willard Controversy." *Women's Studies in Communication* 31, no. 1 (Spring 2008): 56–78.

"Pastoral Letter of the Generational Association of [Congregational Ministers of] Massachusetts." *American Rhetorical Discourse.* 2nd ed., edited by Ronald F. Reid and James F. Klumpp. Long Grove: Waveland Press, 1995.

Payne, Daniel A. *History of the African Methodist Episcopal Church.* Nashville: Publishing House of the AME Sunday-School Union, 1891.

Pellauer, Mary B. *Toward a Tradition of Feminist Theology: The Religious Social Thought of Elizabeth Cady Stanton, Susan B. Anthony, and Anna Howard Shaw.* New York: Carlson, 1991.

Perkins, Linda M. "The Impact of the 'Cult of True Womanhood' on the Education of Black Women." *Journal of Social Issues* 39, no. 3 (Fall 1983): 17–28.

Perry, Mark. *Lift Up Thy Voice: The Sarah and Angelina Grimké Family's Journey from Slaveholders to Civil Rights Leaders.* New York: Penguin Books, 2001.

Peterson, Carla L. "Secular and Sacred Space in the Spiritual Autobiographies of Jarena Lee." In *Reconfigured Spheres: Feminist Explorations of Literary Space,* edited by Margaret R. Higonnet and Joan Templeton, 37–59. Amherst: University of Massachusetts Press, 1994.

Peterson, David L. "Prophecy." In *The New Interpreter's Dictionary of the Bible, Me-R,* Vol. 4, edited by Katherine Doob Sakenfeld, 622–48. Nashville: Abingdon Press, 2009.

Phillips, Kendall R. "The Event of Dissension: Reconsidering the Possibilities of Dissent." *Quarterly Journal of Speech* 101, no. 1 (February 2015): 60–71.

Phillips, Kendall R. "Spaces of Invention: Dissension, Freedom, and Thought in Foucault." *Philosophy and Rhetoric* 35, no. 4 (2002): 328–44.

Portnoy, Alisse Theodore, ed. "Defining, Using, and Challenging the Rhetorical Tradition." *Philosophy and Rhetoric* 36, no. 2 (2003): 103–108.

Portnoy, Alisse Theodore. "'Female Petitioners Can be Lawfully Heard': Negotiating Female Decorum, United States Politics, and Political Agency, 1829–1831." *Journal of the Early Republic* 23, no. 4 (Winter 2003): 573–610.

Portnoy, Alisse Theodore. *Their Right to Speak: Women's Activism in the Indian and Slave Debates.* Cambridge: Harvard University Press, 2009.

Prescott, Jeryl J. "Imagining 'Sweet Fellowship': Resisting Prejudice with Spiritual Transcendence in Jarena Lee's Imagined Community." *Prose Studies* 26, no. 1–2 (2003): 79–95.

Pushon, John. *Portrait in Grey: A Short History of the Quakers.* London: Quaker Home Services, 1984.

"The Race Problem: Miss Willard on the Political Puzzle of the South," *The New York Voice,* October 23, 1890.

Ramsey, Michael. *The Anglican Spirit.* Edited by Dale Coleman. London: SPCK, 1991.

Ratcliffe, Krista. *Anglo-American Feminist Challenges to the Rhetorical Traditions: Virginia Woolf, Mary Daly, Adrienne Rich.* Carbondale: Southern Illinois University Press, 1996.

Ray, Angela. *The Lyceum and Public Culture in the Nineteenth-Century United States.* East Lansing: University of Michigan Press, 2005.

Ray, Angela. "What Hath She Wrought? Woman's Rights and the Nineteenth-Century Lyceum." *Rhetoric and Public Affairs* 9, no. 2 (Summer 2002): 183–214.

Ray, Angela, and Paul Stob, eds. *Thinking Together: Lecturing, Learning, and Difference in the Long Nineteenth Century.* University Park: University of Pennsylvania Press, 2018.

Reardon, Bernard M. G. *Religious Thought in the Reformation.* London: Longman, 1981.

Reid, Henry. *Reformation: The Dangerous Birth of the Modern World.* Edinburgh: Saint Andrew Press, 2009.

Riches, Suzanne V., and Malcolm O. Sillars. "The Status of Movement Criticism." *The Western Journal of Speech Communication* 44, no. 4 (Fall 1980): 275–87.

Richey, Russell E. *Methodism in the American Forest.* Oxford: Oxford University Press, 2015.

Richey, Russell E., Kenneth E. Rowe, and Jean Miller Schmidt, eds. *The Methodist Experience in America.* Vol. 1. Nashville: Abingdon, 2010.

Richey, Russell E., Kenneth E. Rowe, Jean Miller Schmidt, eds. *Perspectives on American Methodism: Interpretive Essays.* Nashville: Kingswood Books, 1993.

Ritchie, Joy, and Kate Ronald, eds. *Available Means: An Anthology of Women's Rhetoric(s).* Pittsburgh: University of Pittsburgh Press, 2001.

Roberts, Mary Louise. "True Womanhood Revisited." *Journal of Women's History* 14, no. 1 (Spring 2002): 150–55.

Rossel, Garth M., and Richard A. J. Dupuis, eds. *The Memoirs of Charles G. Finney: The Complete Restored Text.* Grand Rapids: Zondervan, 1989.

Rowe, Kenneth E., ed. "The Ordination of Women: Round One; Anna Oliver and the General Conference of 1880." In *Perspectives on American Methodism: Interpretive Essays,* edited by Russell E. Richey, Kenneth E. Rowe, and Jean Miller Schmidt, 293–308. Nashville: Kingswood Books, 1993.

Royster, Jacqueline Jones, ed. *Southern Horror and Other Writings: The Anti-Lynching Campaign of Ida. B. Wells, 1892–1900.* Boston: Bedford Books, 1997.

Royster, Jacqueline Jones. *Traces of a Stream: Literacy and Social Change Among African American Women.* Pittsburgh: University of Pittsburgh Press, 2000.

Royster, Jacqueline Jones, and Gesa E. Kirsch, eds. *Feminist Rhetorical Practices: New Horizons for Rhetoric, Composition and Literacy Studies.* Carbondale: Southern Illinois University Press, 2012.

Ruether, Rosemary Radford. *Introducing Redemption in Christian Feminism.* Cleveland: Pilgrim Press, 2000.

Ruether, Rosemary Radford. "The Subordination and Liberation of Women in Christian Theology: St. Paul and Sarah Grimké." *Soundings: An Interdisciplinary Journal* 61, no. 2 (Summer 1978): 168–81.

Ryan, Mary. *Women in Public: Between Banners and Ballots, 1825–1880.* Baltimore: John Hopkins University Press, 1990.

Schell, Eileen, and K. J. Rawson, eds. *Rhetorica in Motion: Feminist Rhetorical Methods and Methodologies.* Pittsburgh: University of Pittsburgh Press, 2010.

Schmidt, Jean Miller. *Grace Sufficient: A History of Women in American Methodism, 1760–1939.* Nashville: Abingdon Press, 1999.

Schmidt, Jean Miller. "Reexamining the Public/Private Split: Reforming the Continent and Spreading Scriptural Holiness." In *Perspectives on American Methodism:*

Interpretive Essays, edited by Russell E. Richey, Kenneth E. Rowe, and Jean Miller Schmidt, 228–47. Nashville: Kingswood Books, 1993.

Schuessler, Jennifer. "The Complex History of the Women's Suffrage Movement." *New York Times,* August 15, 2019. https://www.nytimes.com/2019/08/15/arts/design/womens-suffrage-movement.html.

Self, Lois. "What Distinguishes/Ought to Distinguish Feminist Scholarship in Communication Studies?: Progress Toward Engendering a Feminist Academic Practice." *Women's Studies in Communication* 11, no. 1 (Spring 1988): 1–3.

Shaver, Lisa. "'Serpents,' 'Fiends,' and 'Libertines': Inscribing an Evangelical Rhetoric of Rage in the Advocate of Moral Reform." *Rhetoric Review* 30, no.1 (2011): 1–18.

Sillars, Malcolm O. "Romantic Idealism to Romantic Rationalism: Lucretia Coffin Mott Responds to Henry Dana, Sr." *Rhetoric Society Quarterly* 25 (1995): 1–4.

Slagell, Amy. "'Making the World More Homelike': The Reform Rhetoric of Frances E. Willard." In *The Rhetoric of Nineteenth-Century Reform: A Rhetorical History of the United States,* Vol 5, edited by Martha S. Watson and Thomas R. Burkholder, 159–94. East Lansing: Michigan State University Press, 2009.

Slagell, Amy. "The Rhetorical Structure of Frances E. Willard's Campaign for Woman Suffrage, 1876–1896." *Rhetoric and Public Affairs* 4, no. 1 (Spring 2001): 1–23.

Smith, Ralph, and Russell R. Windes. "The Innovational Movement: A Rhetorical Theory." *Quarterly Journal of Speech* 61, no. 2 (April 1975): 140–53.

Smith, Ralph, and Russell R. Windes. "The Rhetoric of Mobilization: Implications for the Study of Movements." *Southern Speech Communication Journal* 42 (1976): 1–19.

Smith-Rosenberg, Carroll. "The Female World of Love and Ritual: Relations between Women in Nineteenth-Century America." *Signs: Journal of Women in Culture and Society* 1, no.1 (Autumn 1975): 1–29.

Soderlund, Jean R. *Quakers and Slavery: A Divided Spirit.* Princeton: Princeton University Press, 1985.

Solomon, Barbara Miller. *In the Company of Educated Women: A History of Women and Higher Education in America.* New Haven: Yale University Press, 1985.

Solomon, Martha M. "The Role of the Suffrage Press in the Woman's Rights Movement." In *A Voice of Their Own: The Woman Suffrage Press, 1840–1910,* edited by Martha M. Solomon, 1–16. Tuscaloosa: University of Alabama Press, 1991.

Solomon, Martha M., ed. *A Voice of Their Own: The Woman Suffrage Press, 1840–1910.* Tuscaloosa: University of Alabama Press, 1991.

Speicher, Anna M. *The Religious World of Antislavery Women: Spirituality in the Lives of Five Abolitionist Lecturers.* New York: Syracuse University Press, 2000.

Spitzack, Carole, and Kathryn Carter, "Women in Communication Studies: A Typology for Revision." *Quarterly Journal of Speech* 73, no. 4 (November 1987): 401–23.

Spruill, Marjorie Julian. "Race, Reform, and Reaction at the Turn of the Century: Southern Suffragists, the NAWSA, and the 'Southern Strategy' in Context." In *Votes for Women: The Struggle for Suffrage Revisited,* edited by Jean H. Baker, 102–17. New York: Oxford University Press, 2002.

Stanley, Susie C. *Holy Boldness: Women Preachers' Autobiographies and the Sanctified Self.* Knoxville: University of Tennessee Press, 2004.

Stanton, Elizabeth Cady, Susan B. Anthony, and Matilda Joslyn Gage, eds. *History of Woman Suffrage.* 6 Vol. Rochester: Susan B. Anthony and Charles Mann Press, 1881–1922.

Steiner, Linda, Carolyn Kitch, and Brooke Kroeger. *Front Pages, Front Lines: Media and the Fight for Women's Suffrage.* Chicago: University of Illinois Press, 2020.

214 : Bibliography

Stewart, Charles J. "Championing the Rights of Others and Challenging Evil: The Ego Function in the Rhetoric of Other-directed Social Movements." *Southern Journal of Communication* 64, no. 2 (Winter 1999): 91–105.

Stewart, Charles J. "Evolution of a Revolution: Stokely Carmichael and the Rhetoric of Black Power." *Quarterly Journal of Speech* 83, no. 4 (November 1997): 429–46.

Stewart, Charles J. "A Functional Approach to the Rhetoric of Social Movements." *Central States Speech Journal* 31, no. 4 (Winter 1983): 298–305.

Stewart, Charles J., Craig Allen Smith, and Robert E. Denton, Jr. *Persuasion and Social Movements*. 6th ed. Long Grove: Waveland Press, 2012.

Strong, James. *Strong's New Exhaustive Concordance of the Bible*. Iowa Falls: World Bible Publishers, 1986.

Sutherland, Christine Mason. "Feminist Historiography: Research Methods in Rhetoric." *Rhetoric Society Quarterly* 32, no. 1 (Winter 2002): 109–22.

Sutherland, Christine Mason. "Mary Astell: Reclaiming Rhetorica in the Seventeenth Century." In *Reclaiming Rhetorica: Women in the Rhetorical Tradition*, edited by Andrea A. Lunsford, 93–116. Pittsburgh: University of Pittsburgh Press, 1995.

Sutherland, Christine Mason and Rebecca Sutcliffe. *The Changing Tradition: Women in the History Rhetoric*. Calgary: University of Calgary, 1999.

Sutton, Jane S. *The House of My Sojourn: Rhetoric, Women, and the Question of Authority*. Tuscaloosa: University of Alabama Press, 2010.

Tabraham, Barrie. *The Making of Methodism*. Liverpool, England: Epworth Press, 1995.

Taves, Ann. *Fits, Trances, & Visions: Experiencing Religion and Explaining Experience from Wesley to James*. Princeton, NJ: Princeton University Press, 1999.

Tetrault, Lisa M. *The Myth of Seneca Falls: Memory and the Women's Suffrage Movement 1848–1898*. Chapel Hill: University of North Carolina Press, 2014.

Thomas, Benjamin Platt. *Theodore Weld: Crusader for Freedom*. New Brunswick: Rutgers University Press, 1950.

Thompson, Margaret Susan. "The 'Cult of True Womanhood' and American Catholic Sisters: An Example of Creative Subversion." *Encounters in Theory and History of Education* 22 (2021): 268–85.

"Timeline of Women in Methodism." *United Methodist Church*. https://www.umc.org/en/content/timeline-of-women-in-methodism.

Tinkler, John F. "Renaissance Humanism and the Genera Eloquentiae." *Rhetorica: A Journal of the History of Rhetoric* 5, no. 3 (Summer 1987): 279–309.

Tolles, Frederick B., ed. *Lucretia Mott's Diary of Her Visit to Great Britain to Attend the World's Anti-Slavery Convention of 1840*. Supplement No. 23 to the *Journal of the Friends' Historical Society*. Haverford, PA and London: Friends' Historical Association and Friends Historical Society, 1952.

Trible, Phyllis. "Five Loaves and Two Fishes: Feminist Hermeneutics and Biblical Theology." *Theological Studies* 50, no. 2 (June 1989): 289–95.

Unger, Nancy. "Mott, Lucretia Coffin." *American National Biography*. http://www.anb.org/articles/15/15–00494.html.

Vonnegut, Kristin S. "Poison or Panacea?: Sarah Moore Grimké's Use of the Public Letter. " *Communication Studies* 46, no. 1–2 (Spring–Summer 1995): 73–78.

Wakefield, Priscilla. *The Beauties and Wonders in Nature and Art Conveyed in a Series of Instructive Conversations*. Vol. 1. London: Darton and Harvey, 1794.

Wasco, Jean. "The Angel in the Envelope: The Letters of Jane Welsh Carlyle." *Modern Language Studies* 27, no. 3–4 (Autumn-Winter 1997): 3–18.

Washington, Margaret. *Sojourner Truth's America.* Urbana: University of Illinois Press, 2009.

Watson, Martha. "The Dynamics of Intertextuality: Re-Reading the Declaration of Independence." In *Rhetoric and Political Culture in 19th Century America,* edited by Thomas W. Benson, 91–111. East Lansing: Michigan State University Press, 1997.

Watson, Martha. *Lives of Their Own: Rhetorical Dimensions in Autobiographies of Women Activists.* Columbia: University of South Carolina Press, 1999.

Waugh, Barry. "Henry Kollock, 1778–1819." *Presbyterians of the Past.* https://www.presbyteriansofthepast.com/2016/01/22/henry-kollock-1778-1819/.

Welter, Barbara. "The Cult of True Womanhood: 1820–1860." *The American Quarterly* 18, no. 2, Part 1 (Summer 1966): 151–74.

Wertheimer, Molly Meijer, ed. *Listening to Their Voices: The Rhetorical Activities of Historical Women.* Columbia: University of South Carolina Press, 1997.

Wesley, John. "June 13 1771, Letter to Sarah Crosby." In *John Wesley and the Women Preachers of Early Methodism,* edited by Paul Wesley Chilcote, 143–44. Metuchen: American Theological Library Association, 1991.

Wesley, John. *The Letters of John Wesley: A Selection of Important and New Letters,* edited by George Eayrs. New York: Hodder and Stoughton, 1915.

Wesley, John. "Sermon 98 on Visiting the Sick." [Text of the 1872 Ed.] https://bibles net.com/john-wesley-on-visiting-the-sick.pdf.

Wesley, John. *The Works of John Wesley.* Vol. 2. Edited by Albert C. Outler. Nashville: Abingdon Press, 1984.

Westerkamp, Marilyn J. *Women and Religion in Early America 1600–1850: The Puritan and Evangelical Traditions.* London: Routledge, 1999.

Wideman, John Edgar. *My Soul Has Grown Deep: Classics of Early African American Literature.* Philadelphia: Running Press, 2001.

Wigger, John H. *American Saint: Francis Asbury and the Methodists.* New York: Oxford University Press, 2009.

Wigger, John H. "Francis Asbury and American Methodism." In *The Oxford Handbook of Methodist Studies,* edited by J. Abraham and James E. Kirby. 51–66. Oxford: Oxford University Press, 2009.

Wigger, John H. *Taking Heaven by Storm: Methodism and the Rise of Popular Christianity in America.* London: Oxford University Press, 1998.

Wilkinson, Charles A. "A Rhetorical Definition of Movements." *Central States Speech Journal* 27, no. 2 (1976): 88–94.

Willard, Frances E. "23 July 1859." In *Writing Out My Heart: Selections from the Journal of Frances E. Willard, 1855–96,* edited by Carolyn De Swarte Gifford. Chicago: University of Illinois Press, 1995.

Willard, Frances E. "President's Annual Address." Minutes of the National Woman's Christian Temperance Union, at the Fourteenth Annual Meeting, in Nashville, Tenn., November 16–21, 1887, President's Annual Address (Chicago, Illinois), 94–95. Chicago: Woman's Temperance Publication Association, 1888.

Willard, Frances E. *Do Everything: A Handbook for the World's White Ribboners.* Chicago, IL: The Woman's Temperance Publishing Association,1895. Northwestern Digital Copy available at https://digital.lib.niu.edu/islandora/object/niu-gildedage%3A23717 or https://babel.hathitrust.org/.

Willard, Frances E. *Glimpses of Fifty: The Autobiography of an American Woman.* Chicago: Woman's Temperance Publication Association, 1889.

Willard, Frances E. *How to Win: A Book for Girls*. New York: Funk & Wagnalls, 1887.

Willard, Frances E. "Journal 18." Frances Willard Journal Transcripts. https://willard.historyit.com/items/view/transcripts/3781

Willard, Frances E. "A White Life for Two." In *Man Cannot Speak for Her*, Vol. 2, *Key Texts of the Early Feminists*, edited by Karlyn Kohrs Campbell, 317–38. New York: Praeger, 1989.

Willard, Frances E. *Woman in the Pulpit*. Boston: D. Lothrop, 1888.

Willard, Frances E., and Mary A. Lathbury. *The Work and Workers of The Woman's Christian Temperance Union*. Hartford: Park Publishing, 1883. https://archive.org/details/womantemperanceooowilla/page/n11/mode/2up.

Willis, Nathaniel Parker. *Dashes at Life with a Free Pencil Part I: High Life in Europe, and American Life*. New York: Garret Press, 1969. (Original work published 1845)

Wills, David W. "Women and Domesticity in the AME Tradition: The Influence of Daniel Alexander Payne." In *Black Apostles at Home and Abroad: Afro-Americans and the Christian Mission from the Revolution to Reconstruction*, edited by David W. Wills and Richard Newman, 133–46. Boston: G. K. Hall, 1982.

Wilson, Derek. "The Luther Legacy." *History Today* 57, no. 2 (May 2007): 34–39.

Wilson, Derek. *Out of the Storm: The Life and Legacy of Martin Luther*. London: Hutchinson, 2007.

Wilson, Kirt H. "Rhetoric and Race in American Experience: The Promises and Perils of Sentimental Memory." In *Sizing Up Rhetoric*, edited by David Zarefsky and Elizabeth Benacka, 20–39. Long Grove: Waveland Press. 2008.

Wollstonecraft, Mary. *A Vindication of the Rights of Woman: with Strictures on Political and Moral Subjects*. London: Printed for J. Johnson, 1792.

Women in Ministry. *Celebrating the Reverend Jarena Lee and 200 Years of Women Answering the Call to Preach in the African Methodist Episcopal Church*. A pamphlet printed by the AME Women in Ministry. https://amewim.org/our-herstory

Women in Ministry. "The Herstory of AMEWIM." *AMEWIM*. https://amewim.org/our-herstory

Wood, Julia T. "Women and Communication: An Introduction to the Issues." *Communication Quarterly* 31, no. 2 (Spring 1983): 99–100.

Wright, Tom F., ed. *The Cosmopolitan Lyceum: Lecture Culture in Nineteenth-Century America*. Boston: University of Amherst Press, 2013.

Yancey, Kathleen Blake, ed. Special issue: Indigenous and Ethnic Rhetoric. *College Composition and Communication* 63, no. 1 (September 2011).

Yellin, Jean Fagan, and John C. Van Horne, eds. *The Abolitionist Sisterhood: Women's Political Culture in Antebellum America*. Ithaca: Cornell University Press, 1994.

Zaeske, Susan. "The 'Promiscuous Audience' Controversy and the Emergence of the Early Woman's Rights Movement." *Quarterly Journal of Speech* 81, no. 2 (May 1995): 191–207.

Zaeske, Susan. *Signatures of Citizenship: Petitioning, Anti-slavery, and Women's Political Identity*. Chapel Hill: University of North Carolina Press, 2003.

Zaeske, Susan. "Unveiling Esther as a Pragmatic Radical Rhetoric." *Philosophy and Rhetoric* 33, no. 3 (2000): 193–220.

Zboray, Ronald J. and Mary Saracino Zboray. *Voices without Votes: Women and Politics in Antebellum New England*. Durham: University of New Hampshire Press, 2010.

Zboray, Ronald J. and Mary Saracino Zboray. "Women Thinking: The International Popular Lecture and Its Audience in Antebellum New England." In *The*

Bibliography : 217

Cosmopolitan Lyceum: Lecture Culture in Nineteenth-Century America, edited by Tom F. Wright, 42–66. Boston: University of Amherst Press, 2013.

Zikmund, Barbara Brown. "The Struggle for the Right to Preach." In *Women and Religion in America,* edited by Rosemary Radford Ruether and Rosemary Skinner Keller, 193–241. San Francisco: Harper Row, 1981.

Zimmerelli, Lisa. "'The Stereoscopic View of Truth': The Feminist Theological Rhetoric of Frances Willard's Woman in the Pulpit." *Rhetoric Society Quarterly* 42, no. 4 (2012): 353–74.

Zulick, Margaret D. "The Agon of Jeremiah: On the Dialogic Invention of Prophetic Ethos." *Quarterly Journal of Speech* 78, no 2 (May 1992): 125–48.

Zulick, Margaret D. "Prophecy and Providence: The Anxiety over Prophetic Authority." *Journal of Communication and Religion* 26, no. 2 (September 2003): 195–207.

Zulick, Margaret D., and Michael Leff. "Time and the 'True Light' in Lucretia Coffin Mott's 'Discourse on Woman.'" *Rhetoric Society Quarterly* 25 (1995): 20–31.

INDEX

abolitionism: xiii, xvi, 8, 10, 143, 174n9, 175n41, 176n44,64, 176–77n65; *see also* Grimké, Sarah Moore: abolitionism; Lee, Jarena: abolitionism; Mott, Lucretia Coffin: abolitionism; woman's rights movement: abolitionism

African Methodist Episcopal Church (AME): 22, 36; development of, 26, 27; ministry standards, 30, 40; prophetic voice, 35–36; relationship with Jarena Lee, 19, 20–21, 27, 31, 38, 45–46, 173n132; women's church roles, 24, 173n132; women's preaching ban, 27, 39–40, 41, 43, 46–47, 150

Allen, Richard: 26, 171n68; African Methodist Episcopal Church (AME) founding, 26, 27, 169n12; relationship with Jarena Lee, 20, 21, 27, 33, 34, 35, 37, 170n41; preaching, 20, 26, 31, 34; stance on women's preaching, 27, 35, 169n13

Allen, Sarah, 21

American Anti–Slavery Society/Convention: 22, 88; *see also* Declaration of Sentiments (1833); Garrison, William Lloyd; Grimké, Angelina: American Anti-Slavery Society/Convention; Grimké, Sarah: American Anti-Slavery Society/Convention; Mott, Lucretia Coffin: American Anti-Slavery Society/Convention; Truth, Sojourner

Andrews, Edward, 119

Andrews, William L., 23, 40, 169n7,10,13

Angell, Stephen, 46

Anglican Church (Church of England), 23–25, 26, 78, 118, 170n30, 171n57

Anthony, Susan B., 137, 192n187

"Appeal to the Christian Women of the South," (Angelina Grimké), 55

Aristotle, 80, 123

Articles of Religion (Church of England & Episcopal Church), 58

Asbury, Francis (Methodist bishop), 26, 27, 169n15, 171n57

Bacon, Margaret Hope, 81, 84, 85, 86, 182n26

Bannister, Mary, 112

Bartlett, Elizabeth Ann, 64, 177n66

Bassard, Katherine Clay, 21, 36, 37, 169n1

Beecher, Catharine: 11, 56–57, 101, 112; *see also* "Circular Addressed to the Benevolent Ladies of the United States"

Bercovitch, Sacvan, 16, 168n88

Berg, Barbara J., 8, 158

Berry, Amanda, 46

Bible, as revolutionary document, 141, 153

Birney, Catharine H., 52–54, 174n1, 175n19,38, 176n53

Bizzell, Patricia, 157, 188n81

Black women: 38–40, 171n68; activism, 174n161, 192–93n201; preaching, 25, 41; racial uplift, xiii, 163n7; racist stereotypes, 43; religious faith, 19, 26–27, 38; True Womanhood, xiii, 43, 163n7; *see also* African American Methodist Episcopal Church (AME); Lee, Jarena

Black, Edwin: 17, 147; *see also* second persona

Blackstone, William, 69

Blackwell, Antoinette Brown, 8, 166n45

Bloomer, Amelia Jenks, 8, 166n45, 174n7, 181n4

Booth, Catherine, 126

Bordin, Ruth, 110, 112, 136, 137, 186n12, 187n29,43, 187–88n46, 188n81, 189n93, 97, 190n104

Brekus, Catherine, xii, 38, 41, 44, 118

Brown, John Mifflin, 46

: 219 :

Brueggemann, Walter, 153, 154
Buchanan, Lindal, 158
Buckley, James M., 120
Burke, Kenneth, 16, 42, 153

Campbell, Karlyn Kohrs: 104, 146, 157, 159, 167n53, 168n72, 181n1, 184n88, 194n18; affirmation of femininity/gender roles, 75, 133; formative experiences, 9–10, 146
Camper, Martin: conflicting passages argument strategy, 67–68, 126–27, 165n20; letter versus spirit" argument strategy, 131, 132; stasis of jurisdiction argument strategy, 144, 145
Cardman, Francine, 2
Carter, Kathryn, xv
Cartwright, William, 91
Casey, Michael W., xii, 152, 166n27, 168n84, 171n75
Cathcart, Robert S., 11–12
Channing, William Emery, 102
Charland, Maurice: 17, 147, 168n97; see also interpellation; constitutive rhetoric
Chaves, Mark, 119
Chilcote, Paul Wesley, 23–24, 119, 170n30
Child, Lydia Maria, 68, 174n161, 179n133
Chittester, Joan, 15
"Circular Addressed to the Benevolent Ladies of the United States" (Catharine Beecher), 11, 167n58
Clarkson, Thomas, 84, 85
Colaiaco, James, A., 151
Collins, Vicki Tolar, 21, 170n45
Condit, Celeste, 149
conflicting passages (rhetorical strategy): 68, 126–27, 129, 144, 165n20l; see also Camper, Martin: conflicting passages argument strategy
consciousness–raising, 138, 146, 147, 166n45
constitutive rhetoric, 17, 147, 155–56
Cook, Joseph, 124, 125
Cowper, William, 86, 182n26
Critchlow, Donald T., 152
Cult of True Womanhood: xii, xiii, 10, 39, 90, 147, 163n7,9, 163–64n13,

167n53; see also Black women: Cult of True Womanhood; Methodism: Cult of True Womanhood; Willard, Frances: Cult of True Womanhood
culturetypal rhetoric, 149

Dana, Richard Henry, Sr.: Mott's critiques of, 84, 90, 93–98, 100, 102–5, 107, 150, 154; views on domestic roles for women, 83, 86, 90–93, 94, 96–97, 100, 107; views on women's political rights, 91–92, 98, 100–101
Dandelion, Ben Pink, 58
Darling, Grace, 101, 106
Darsey, James, 155
Dayton, Amy E., 157
Deborah (judge & prophet; Judges 4 & 5), 81, 97–98, 130–31, 139, 144, 162, 184n101, 185n103
Declaration of Independence, 7, 13, 88, 89, 104–5, 142, 180n141
Declaration of Sentiments (Seneca Falls, 1848), xvi, 88, 104–5, 108, 145
Denton, Robert E., 16, 145, 147, 148, 149, 155
Dickerson, Dennis C., 25
Dickinson, John, 150
discursive practices/rules, xiii, xviii, 4, 6, 11–12, 141–42, 145, 148, 153
dissent (as rhetorical strategy): xiv–xv, xvii, 12, 16–17, 142, 148–49, 151, 155: definition, 14–15, 164n20; Lee use of, 42, 44, 45; Mott use of, 87, 105, 106, 108; Sarah Grimké use of, 61, 64, 73, 74, 76, 77, 80; Willard use of, 135, 137
Dix, Dorothea Lynde, 101, 102, 106
Dodson, Jualynne E., 41, 169n13
Donawerth, Jane, xiv, 123, 159, 164n1, 168n69
Duerden, Richard, 6, 165n24
Duty, Jennie, 120

Ehrman, Bart D., 29
Elaw, Zilpha, 41, 46
Emerson, Ralph Waldo, 104
Ephesians 5:23 (submissiveness of women), 161, 164–65n5
Episcopal Church, 53, 54, 57–58

Index : 221

"Epistle to the Clergy of the Southern States," (Sarah Grimké), 55, 75, 82, 176n50

Equal Rights Amendment, 151

ethos (rhetorical proof), xvi, 16, 17, 32, 42, 80, 108, 110–11, 125, 148, 152, 155

evangelicalism/evangelical zeal: xii, xiii, 7, 8, 53, 54, 58–59, 60, 126, 142–43, 144, 151, 152, 188n83; *see also* Methodism: evangelism

Evans, Christopher, 110, 114, 115, 121, 138, 187n29, 189n97

Evans, Jonathan, 55, 88

Evans, Rachel, 41

Evanston Ladies College, 112, 114–15

expediency, argument from: 12–13, 135, 140; *see also* moral agency, argument from; natural rights, argument from

Fall (Genesis 2:15–3:24), 60, 66, 73

Faulkner, Carol, 87, 174n7, 182n21,26, 183n48, 184n88

Fell, Margaret, 5–6, 59–60, 64, 83, 99, 166n26, 178n103, 185n112

feminist consciousness, 80, 158

feminist hermeneutic (as rhetorical strategy): xiv, xvi, xvii, 142, 143–45; Lee use of, 28, 30, 45; Mott use of, 93, 95–100, 104–5; Sarah Grimké use of, 63, 66, 81, 132; Willard use of, xvii, 122, 123, 127–33

First Great Awakening, xii

Flexner, Eleanor, 9

Florence, Anna Carter, 19, 172n106

Follen, Charles Theodore Christian, 69

Foote, Julia A. J., 39, 41, 46, 173n132, 174n161

Foss, Karen, 158, 159

Foss, Sonja, 158, 159

Foucault, Michel, 3–4, 6, 142, 143, 144–45

Fowler, Charles (relationship with Willard), 114, 116, 120, 187n38

Fox, George, 59, 122

Fox, Margaret Fell. *See* Fell, Margaret

Fry, Elizabeth Gurney, 101–2, 106

Gage, Matilda Joslyn, 154

Galatians 3:28 (no gender differences in Christ), 123, 130, 162

Gale, Xin Liu, 157

Garrison, William Lloyd: 81, 174n161, 176n64, 176–77n65; American Anti-Slavery Society/Convention, 46, 88; *Liberator* editorship, 55, 57, 88; publication of Angelina & Sarah Grimké letters, 57, 61, 82

Genesis 1:27–28 (both sexes in God's image), 59, 64, 161

Genesis 3:16 (submissiveness of women), xi, 65, 66, 161, 164–65n5, 177n95

Gifford, Carolyn De Swarte, 120, 192–93n201

Giver–Johnston, Donna, 28, 39, 42

Glenn, Cheryl, 157, 159

Glimpses of Fifty Years (Willard), 109, 187n29, 187–88n46

Griffin, Cindy, 159

Grimké, Angelina: 13, 52, 164n23, 174n161, 181n200; abolitionism, 51, 54, 57, 61, 81–82, 175n19; American Anti-Slavery Society/Convention, 46, 55, 56, 176n64; lecture tour, 45, 46; letter writing, 55, 61, 81–82, 176n53; oratory skill, 53, 89; speaking to promiscuous audiences, 10, 56, 81, 89, 90; women's rights support, 61, 82; *see also* "An Appeal to the Christian Women of the South"

Grimké, John, 51

Grimké, Mary, 51

Grimké, Sarah Moore: 45, 53, 90, 174n161, 176–77n65, 177n96, 179n133, 180n179; abolitionism, 46, 61–62, 82, 177n91; agent for American Anti-Slavery Society, 46, 55, 56; defense of women's preaching, 71–72, 77, 78, 113, 131, 144, 180n148; evangelicalism, 53, 54, 58, 59, 60, 175n35; influence on Mott, xvi, 82; influence on Stanton, xvi, 50, 78, 82, 175n35, 178n101; influence on Stone, xvi, 50; influence on Willard, 78, 175n35; lecture tour, 45, 46; letter writing, 57, 60, 62–64, 66, 75–76, 78–79, 80–81, 150, 154, 176n60; *Letters on the Equality of the Sexes,* xv, xvi, xvii, 50–51, 63–66, 75, 80–81, 84, 150, 154, 178n99, 180n141,148; Quakerism, 49, 57–58, 174n9, 176n48,

177n66; speaking to promiscuous audiences, 10, 56, 81, 89, 90; support for woman's rights, 50, 63–69, 71, 73–74, 78, 105, 122, 135, 178n101; *see also* "Appeal to the Christian Women of the South"; dissent (as rhetorical strategy); "Epistle to the Clergy of the Southern States"; feminist hermeneutic (as rhetorical strategy); *Letters to Catherine E. Beecher;* moral agency (as rhetorical strategy); Morris, Israel (relationship with Grimké); prophetic voice (as rhetorical strategy); scriptural exegesis (as rhetorical strategy); Woolman, John (influence on Grimké)
Gurevitch, Michael, 155

Hardesty, Nancy A., 137, 187n38
Hatch, Nathan O., 7–8, 25, 164n18
Haven, Erastus O. (relationship with Willard), 115, 116
Hawthorne, Nathaniel, 123, 127, 190n126
Heilbrun, Carolyn G., 156
Hempton, David, 122, 127, 135, 175n35
Hershberger, Nancy, 61
Hicks, Elias, 85, 86, 88
Hicksite Quakers, 88, 174n9, 176n48
Hogan, Lisa Shawn, 94
Hooker, Isabella Beecher, 8
How to Win: A Book for Girls (Willard), 130
Hughes, Sarah Ann, 46
Hulda (prophet; 2 Kings 22:14–20; 2 Chronicles 34:22–28), 72, 81, 97, 98, 144, 154, 162, 184n101, 185n105)

I Corinthians 11:3 (submissiveness of women),
I Corinthians 14:34–35 (submissiveness of women), xii, 99, 130, 161, 164–65n5
I Timothy 2:11–14 (submissiveness of women), xii, 130, 161, 165–65n5
Indian removal, xiii, 10, 11, 60–61, 62, 76, 143, 147, 152, 177n91
inner light (Quakerism), 22, 54, 86
interpellation (Charland), 17, 147
inward witness (Methodism), 22
Ivie, Robert L., 14, 76, 148–49, 164n20

Jael, 97
Jarratt, Susan C., 157
Jerry, E. Claire, 75, 143
Joan of Arc, 70, 102
Joel 2:28 (both men and women as prophets), 28, 30, 99, 130, 161–62, 169n6
Johnson, Nan, 10, 167n53
Johnson, William H., 83
Jones, Absalom (Episcopal priest), 26, 27
Jones, Martha S., 19
journal writing (as rhetorical strategy): 21, 54, 146; Lee use of, 41, 169n10; Willard use of, 111, 112, 114
Junia (coworker with Paul; Romans 16:7), 161

Kelley, Abby, 13, 50
King James Bible, 98, 161, 163n2, 164n3, 164–65n5, 169n6, 180n179, 185n108
King, Martin Luther, Jr., 151
Knight, Frederick, 45
Kollock, Henry (Presbyterian minister), 53, 58, 175n34
Kraditor, Aileen, 12–13, 92, 140

Lee, Jarena: 173n160, 174n161; abolitionism, 22, 45–46, 135; African Methodist Episcopal Church (AME), xvi, 20, 41, 44–45, 46–47,144, 154, 173n130; call to preach, 28, 29, 30; evangelism, 21, 22, 30, 34, 36, 37, 39, 40, 42–43; femininity, 43, 44; inward witness (Wesley), 22, 23; Order of Salvation, 22, 23, 28, 30–31, 32, 42; *Religious Experience and Journal,* xv, xvi, xvii, 19–21, 24, 28, 30, 33–34, 36, 39–46, 146, 150, 169n1,9,10; religious hymns, 37–38; Richard Allen relationship, 26, 27, 172n106; spiritual calling, 20, 21, 22, 28, 30–31, 32–34, 36, 43, 114, 131; Wesleyanism influences, 24, 42, 43; women's preaching defense, 1–2, 28, 29, 33–36, 38–39, 43–44, 131, 144, 169n13, 171n75; see also dissent (as rhetorical strategy); evangelism (as rhetorical strategy); feminist hermeneutic (as rhetorical strategy); *Life and Religious Experience of Jarena Lee;* moral agency (as rhetorical strategy); prophetic voice (as rhetorical strategy); scriptural exegesis (as rhetorical strategy)

Lerner, Gerda, 49–50, 52–53, 81, 82, 166n45, 175n28, 181n200

letter writing (as rhetorical strategy): 9, 40, 50, 75, 150, 159, 166n45; Sarah Grimké use of, 57, 60, 62–64, 66, 75–76, 78–79, 80–81, 150, 154, 176n60; Willard use of, 123, 124, 125, 126; *see also* Grimké, Sarah: Epistle to the Clergy of the Southern States; *Letters on the Equality of the Sexes*

Letters to Catherine E. Beecher (Grimké), 57

Lewis, Diocletian, 117

Life and Religious Experience of Jarena Lee, 21

Linkugel, Wil A., 145

Logan, Shirley Wilson, 157, 168n69

logos (rhetorical proof), 80

Lucaites, John, 149

Lumpkin, Katharine Du Pre, 52, 53

Lundy, Benjamin, 88

Lunsford, Andrea A., 158

Luther, Martin: challenges to Catholic Church, 3, 4–5, 141; hermeneutic space, 3, 4, 141; priesthood of all believers, xv, 4, 5, 141; women's empowerment, 1, 6, 121, 128, 141, 144

lyceums, 10

male privilege, 110, 111

Mann, Horace, 102

Marshall, Peter, 3

Martineau, Harriet, 106

Mary Magdalene (prophet & preacher; particularly John 20:17–18), 2, 29–30, 43, 100, 132, 144, 162, 185n118

Matthews, Donald G., 7

Mattingly, Carol, 44, 75, 106, 158

McCook, Matt, 7

McGrath, Alister, 3, 5

Melder, Keith, 9

Merrill, Stephen, 41, 188–89n83

Methodism: 22, 25–26, 113, 169n17, 170n30, 188–89n83, 189n87; Cult

of True Womanhood, 39, 44, 119; evangelism, 23, 24, 25, 26, 34, 118; exhorting, 20, 21, 180n148; four pillars of religious authority, 22; holiness movement, 21, 24, 118–19, 133; journal writings/spiritual autobiographies, 21, 38–39, 41, 42, 150; role of experience in religious authority, 22, 123, 128, 129, 132; scriptural exegesis, 128, 136; women's roles, 118, 120, 133, 180n148; women's preaching, xvi–xvii, 20, 22, 42, 44, 46, 71, 118–23, 126, 135, 170n45, 180n148, 186n14; *see also* African Methodist Episcopal Church (AME); Grimké, Sarah; Lee, Jarena; Wesley, John; Willard, Frances

Miller, Hilda, 159

Minifee, Paul, 37, 38

Miriam (sister of Moses & biblical prophet; Exodus 15:20), 72, 81, 97, 131, 184n102, 184–85n103

Mitchell, Maria, 106

Moody, Dwight, 118

moral agency, argument from (as rhetorical strategy): xiv, xvii, xviii, 12, 13–14, 16–17, 142–43, 146, 148–49, 151; Lee use of, xvii, 13, 17, 42; Mott use of, 17, 90, 100–103, 107; Sarah Grimké use of, 13, 17, 53, 64, 66, 69, 77, 79, 81, 89, 101, 107, 146; Willard use of, 17, 115, 133, 135, 137–38, 140; *see also* expediency, argument from

moral horticulture (Willard), 115

Morris, Catherine, 49, 50

Morris, Israel (relationship with Grimké), 49, 50, 54, 174n1

Mott, Abigail, 182n21

Mott, James, Jr., 89, 182n21

Mott, James, Sr., 86

Mott, Lucretia Coffin: 174n161, 174n7, 182n26, 184n88, 185n108; abolitionism, xvi, 46, 55, 82, 83, 84, 85, 88–89, 98, 103, 104–7, 150, 183n48; American Anti-Slavery Society/Convention, 104–5, 183n48; "Discourse on Woman," xv, xvii, 93–108, 154, 184n96, 184–85n102, 185n118; embrace of femininity, 93, 94, 101, 104–6, 147; Nantucket

Index

Mott, Lucretia Coffin *(continued)*
background, 84, 85; Nine Partners, 85–86, 88; Philadelphia Female Anti–Slavery Society, 89, 183n48; as Quaker minister, xvi, 83, 84, 86–88, 95–96, 106–7, 150, 183n76; Sarah Grimké inspiration, 49–50, 60; Twelfth Street Monthly Meeting, 87, 88; women's preaching defense, 1–2, 78, 98, 99–100, 144; women's rights movement, 82, 84, 94, 104, 122, 146, 181n1; *see also* dissent (as rhetorical strategy); feminist hermeneutic (as rhetorical strategy); moral agency (as rhetorical strategy); prophetic voice (as rhetorical strategy); scriptural exegesis (as rhetorical strategy)
Mott, Thomas, 87

National American Woman Suffrage Association, 145
natural rights, argument from: 13; *see also* expediency, argument from; moral agency, argument from
new/alternative media, 149
Newman, Richard S., 26, 39
Nineteenth Amendment, xi, 1
North Western Female College (NWFC). *See* Evanston Ladies College

Oliver, Mary, 119, 188–89n83
Olivers, Thomas, 38
Order of Salvation (Wesley): 7, 42, 71, 79, 142; conversion, 20–21, 31, 53, 58, 113, 169n7; God's grace, 22, 25, 68, 113, 128, 131; justification, 22, 31, 36–37; sanctification, 22–23, 28, 31–32, 39, 42, 119

Paine, Thomas, 150
Painter, Nell Irvin, 43, 173n156
Palmer, Phoebe, 118, 119, 126, 188n81
Parker, Joseph, 125
Parker, Mary S., 46, 56, 57, 75
Parker, Nathaniel, 103
pathos (rhetorical proof), 38, 80, 124, 134
Payne, David, 39–40, 170n41
Penn, William, 87

Perkins, Linda M., xii, xiii, 163n7
Peterson, Carla, 21, 33
petitioning drives: 70, 75, 102, 136, 143, 146; abolitionism, 10, 11, 61, 62, 76, 89, 147; Indian removal opposition, 10, 11, 61, 62, 76, 147; for women preaching, 39, 40, 41
Phelps, Amos, 81
Phillips, Kendall R., 4, 152
Phillips, Wendell, 155
Phoebe/Phebe (coworker with Paul & minister; Romans 16:1–2), 2, 78, 81, 98, 162, 180n158, 185n108
Portnoy, Alisse, 11, 61, 76, 147
Presbyterianism, 31, 53, 54, 57, 58, 121, 139, 189n93
Presidents Annual Address at the National Woman's Christian Temperance Union (Willard), 121, 138–39
Priscilla (coworker with Paul; Romans 16:3–4), 72, 130, 162, 180n158
prophetic voice (as rhetorical strategy): xiv, xvii, 12, 14, 80, 155, 156; Lee use of, 44, 45, 152; Mott use of, 93, 94–95, 99, 107, 108; Sarah Grimké use of, 70, 72, 76–77, 80, 102; Willard use of, 123, 125, 135, 138–40
Protestant Reformation: believer empowerment, xv, 3, 6, 128; opening of discursive space, xiii, 1–6; empowerment women, xii–xiv, 2, 164n1

Quakerism: 58, 177n66; abolitionism, 54, 55, 56, 59, 84, 90, 174n9, 175n41, 176n44,48; direct relationship with God tenet, 58, 59; "priesthood of all believers," 5, 58, 100; racism/slavery, 54, 55, 56, 85; salvific arc, 95, 96, 100, 107, 152, 184n93; women's roles, xii, xvi, 59–60, 71, 81, 106–7, 126, 176n48; *see also* Grimké, Sarah Moore: Quakerism; Hicksite Quakers; inner light (Quakerism); Mott, Lucretia Coffin: Quakerism

Ratliff, Krista, 158
Ray, Angela, 10
Republican Party, 152
Ritchie, Joy, 157, 159

Roberts, Mary Louise, xiii
Rogers, Deborah, 86
Ronald, Kate, 157, 159
Rose, Ernestine Potowski, 8
Royster, Jacqueline Jones, 158
Ruether, Rosemary Radford, 16, 60, 66

Sand, George, 156
Sankey, Ira, 118
Sayers, Dorothy, 156
Schlafly, Phyllis, 151, 152
Schmidt, Jean Miller, 39, 112, 188–89n83
Schuessler, Jennifer, xi
Scott, Thomas, 78
Scott, William, 31
scriptural exegesis (as rhetorical strategy): Lee use of, 20, 28–30, 32–33, 34, 37, 42–43, 99, 144, 164n2, 172n88; Mott use of, 20, 78, 90, 96–99, 103–4, 144, 154, 185n103; Sarah Grimké use of, 63, 64–66, 77, 128, 130, 144, 164n3, 178n104,111,114, 179n130, 180n158, 184n97; Willard use of, 1–2, 20, 78, 123–24, 126, 127–33, 191n149,152
second coming theology, 95, 96
Second Great Awakening, xiii, 7, 9, 10, 22, 23, 25, 58, 60, 118, 142
second persona (Charland), 17, 147
segregation (in churches), 26–27, 54
Seneca Falls Convention: xi, xvi, 50, 80, 87, 89, 104, 108, 157; *see also* Declaration of Sentiments (Seneca Falls, 1848)
Shaw, Anna Howard, 119, 188–89n83
Sillars, Malcolm O., 104, 184n92
Slagell, Amy R., 137, 138, 186n12, 191n179, 192n187,190, 192–93n201
Smith, Craig Allen, 16, 145, 147, 148, 149, 155
social movements: xvii, 1, 7, 107, 143; attracting membership, 16–17, 18, 138, 147, 155; contributions to theory of, 16, 145, 147–48; need for legitimacy, 16, 39, 142, 144, 145, 148, 149, 155; reform movements, 142, 145, 149, 156; *see also* Protestant Reformation; Second Great Awakening; woman's rights movement
Solomon, Barbara Miller, 94, 115
Spitzack, Carole, xv

Stanley, Susie C., 33, 34
Stanton, Elizabeth Cady, xii, xvi, 10, 50, 78, 82, 89, 106, 137, 140, 164n22, 175n35, 178n101, 192n187
Stanton, Henry, 89
Stewart, Charles, 16, 145, 147, 148, 149, 155
Stone, Lucy, xvi, 9, 50, 166n45
Strong, James, 99
Sutcliffe, Rebecca, 9
Sutherland, Christine Mason, 9, 159

Talmadge, Thomas De Witt, 124, 134
Tappan, Arthur, 88
Taves, Ann, 23
Tetrault, Lisa M., xi, 157
Thayer, Lorenzo, 119
Thompson, Eliza Jane, 117
Tinkler, John F., 9
Townsend, L. T., 126, 127
True Womanhood. *See* Cult of True Womanhood
Truth, Sojourner, 22, 43, 46, 173n156
Tryphaena (coworker with Paul; Romans 16:12), 162
Tryphosa (coworker with Paul; Romans 16:12), 162
Tychicus (minister; Colossians 4: 7–8), 78

Van Dyke, Henry J., Jr., 126, 127
Vaughn, Jennie, 157
Vindication of the Rights of Women (Wollstonecraft), 83, 84
Vonnegut, Kristin S., 75

Washington, George, 128
Washington, Martha, 122
Weld, Theodore, 55, 57, 61, 81, 164n23, 176n50, 176n64, 179n133
Welter, Barbara, xii, 10, 74, 163n9
Wertheimer, Molly Meijer, 158
Wesley, John: 22–25, 128, 170n45; American Methodism, 25, 26, 171n57; extraordinary calling, 24, 42, 118, 125; journals/narratives, 21, 23, 42; privileging of experience (inner witness), 22, 128, 170n30; women's ecclesiastical roles, 118, 125; women's preaching ambivalence, 24, 25–26, 27, 43; *see also* Order of Salvation

Wesleyanism, 24, 25, 26
Wheeler, Edward J., 110
"White Life for Two" (Willard), 130, 131
Whittier, John Greenleaf, 57, 81, 176n64
Wigger, John H., 20, 169n17
Willard, Frances: 110, 130, 146, 154, 175n35, 187n29, 187–88n46, 189n93, 189n97, 192n190; Black civil rights, 192–93n201; childhood desire to escape gender roles, 111, 112; Cult of True Womanhood, 119, 133, 136, 147; early life, 111, 112; education innovations, 109, 110, 114–15, 122; education career, 114, 115, 116; embrace of femininity, 101, 105, 111, 133–34, 136–37, 191n176, 192n187; evangelism, 109, 113–14, 118; "home protection" argument, 136, 191n179; Methodism, 110, 113, 118, 120–21, 188–89n83, 190n104; *Woman in the Pulpit,* xv, xvii, 109–10, 122–36, 140, 150, 190n126; woman suffrage, xvi, 110, 122, 136, 138, 191n164; Women's Christian Temperance Union (WTCU), 111, 116–18, 120–21, 138–39, 150, 187n38, 192–93n201; women's preaching defense, 109–11, 113–14, 118–36, 140, 144, 188–89n83, 190n126, 191n164; see also dissent (as rhetorical strategy); Evanston Ladies College; feminist hermeneutic (as rhetorical strategy); *Glimpses of Fifty Years;* Haven, Erastus O. (relationship with Willard); *How to Win: A Book for Girls;* Moody, Dwight; Presidents Annual Address at the National Woman's Christian Temperance Union; prophetic voice (as rhetorical strategy); "White Life for Two"
Willard, Mary, 111, 112, 114
Willard, Oliver, 111, 112, 124
Williams, Richard, 34
Wilson, Amanda, 46
Wilson, Derek, 4, 5, 141

Wilson, Woodrow, 126
Wolff, Virginia, 156
Wollstonecraft, Mary: 50, 83–84; see also *Vindication of the Rights of Women*
Woman's Journal, 140, 167n64
woman's rights movement: xvi, xvii, 84, 122, 135, 150, 164n22, 179n133; abolitionism, 81–82, 176n64, 177n91; Christianity, 12, 80, 81, 87, 103, 120, 135, 141; discourse/rhetorical representations, xvi, 12, 69, 150; leadership, 10, 13, 84; property ownership, xvi, 27, 69, 122; scriptural injunction to submissiveness, xi–xii, xiii–xiv, xviii, 141; voting rights, xii, xvi, xvii, 7, 8, 12, 14, 18, 122, 124, 136, 138, 156, 164n22, 167n64, 181n1, 188–89n83
Women's Christian Temperance Union (WCTU): membership, 116, 138, 192–93n201; the "Woman Question," 120, 121, 150–51, 186n12; *see also* Willard, Frances: Women's Christian Temperance Union (WCTU)
women's rhetoric, 13, 157–59, 167–68n68
women's speaking (justification of), 10, 11, 77
women's suffrage press: 11, 167n64; see also *Woman's Journal*
Wood, Gordon S., 7
Woolman, John (influence on Grimké), 54, 59
World Anti–Slavery Society & Conference, 82, 89
Wright, Frances, 159
Wright, Henry Clarke, 57, 176n64, 176–77n65

Yancey, Kathleen Blake, 158

Zaeske, Susan, 11, 13, 61, 76, 143, 147
Zboray, Mary & Ronald, 9, 166n45
Zimmerelli, Lisa, 129, 133